Canada and the Ukrainian Question, 1939–1945

The start of the Second World War placed Canadian officials in the difficult position of trying to maintain their stated position of respect for national self-determination while refusing to further Ukrainian Canadian requests that Canada support the principle of Ukrainian independence. Bohdan Kordan shows that Canadian officials, claiming that Ukrainian independence was not in the interest of the Canadian state, used measures such as close surveillance of the community and intervention in community affairs in the attempt to manage the so-called Ukrainian problem.

Focusing on the difficulties the government faced in trying to reconcile moral imperatives and political interest, Kordan provides an innovative interpretation of government policy toward Ukrainian Canadians. Drawing extensively on Canadian, British, American, and Soviet archival material, he highlights the connection between the government's foreign and domestic concerns and the implications of each for Canadian nation building.

Meticulously researched and richly detailed, *Canada and the Ukrainian Question, 1939–1945* offers a clear but critical statement about Canada's uneven approach to ethnic integration and policy making.

BOHDAN S. KORDAN is professor of international relations in the Department of Political Studies and the director of the Prairie Centre for the Study of Ukrainian Heritage, St Thomas More College, University of Saskatchewan.

MCGILL-QUEEN'S STUDIES IN ETHNIC HISTORY
DONALD HARMAN AKENSON, EDITOR

MCGILL-QUEEN'S STUDIES IN ETHNIC HISTORY
SERIES TWO: JOHN ZUCCHI, EDITOR

Canada and the Ukrainian Question, 1939–1945

A Study in Statecraft

BOHDAN S. KORDAN

McGill-Queen's University Press
Montreal & Kingston · London · Ithaca

© McGill-Queen's University Press 2001
ISBN 0-7735-2230-1 (cloth)
ISBN 0-7735-2308-1 (paper)

Legal deposit fourth quarter 2001
Bibliothèque nationale du Québec

Printed in Canada on acid-free paper

This book has been published with the help of a grant
from the Humanities and Social Sciences Federation of
Canada, using funds provided by the Social Sciences
and Humanities Research Council of Canada. Funding
has also been provided by the President's Publication
Fund at the University of Saskatchewan and the
Publications Fund, St Thomas More College.

McGill-Queen's University Press acknowledges the
financial support of the Government of Canada
through the Book Publishing Industry Development
Program (BPIDP) for its activities. It also acknowledges
the support of the Canada Council for the Arts for its
publishing program.

National Library of Canada Cataloguing
in Publication Data

Kordan, Bohdan S.
   Canada and the Ukrainian question, 1939–45 :
   a study in statecraft
   Includes bibliographical references and index.
   ISBN 0-7735-2230-1 (bnd)
   ISBN 0-7735-2308-1 (pbk)
   1. Ukrainian Canadians – Government policy – History.
   2. Canada – Politics and government – 1935–1948.
   3. Ukraine – History – Autonomy and independence
   movements. 4. Self-determination, National – Ukraine.
   1. Title.
   FC580.K67 2001   971.063'2   C2001-900061-8
   F1034.K67 2001

Typeset in Sabon 10/12
by Caractéra inc., Quebec City

For Olga, my sister
Always there

Contents

Acknowledgments

At the end of a long and eventful journey, perhaps the greatest satisfaction for the traveller is to recall fondly both the company and the treasured moments when an assisting hand, encouraging voice, and sympathetic nod helped along the way. In this journey, I happily benefited from the good cheer and wise counsel of several individuals: Richard Hubert, the late Bohdan Bociurkiw, John MacDonald, Abraham Fox, Margaret Ovendun, Pat McGowan, Don Wolf, Michael Esler, Peter Melnycky, Lubomyr Luciuk, Bohdan Krawchenko, Nestor Makuch, Sonia Maryn, Hans Michelmann, David Smith and Don Story. Words fail to express my sincere and profound thanks for their generosity of spirit and kindness of heart.

I have relied over the years on the service and assistance of several archivists who are much appreciated, in particular Myron Momryk of the National Archives of Canada (Manuscript Division), John E. Taylor of the U.S. National Archives and Records Service (Military Archives Division), and Dacre Cole of the Historical Division of the former Department of External Affairs. In Moscow, during the first few months that followed the Soviet collapse, when everything seemed possible, I not only enjoyed the amiable company of Viktor Kravchenko (Russian Diplomatic Academy) but was ably guided by him in negotiations with several bewildered and only partially "reconstructed" post-Soviet archivists associated with the state archives of the USSR. His assistance, for which I am truly grateful, proved invaluable.

It is an honour to be associated with a fine publisher such as McGill-Queen's University Press. Any organisation, however, is only as good as its people. In this regard, I would like to acknowledge the encouragement, effort, and skill of the ever-capable editorial staff at McGill-Queen's: Peter Goheen, Philip Cercone, Roger Martin, and Joan McGilvray. It has been a pleasure and a privilege to work with them. I am especially indebted to Ron Curtis, whose keen eye and precise editorial hand has added much polish to the final text.

The Aid to Scholarly Publications Programme of the Humanities and Social Sciences Federation of Canada has helped offset the costs associated with the production of this book, and it is recognised here for its generous support. The author also wishes to acknowledge a similar grant from the President's Publications Fund at the University of Saskatchewan and the Publications Fund, St Thomas More College.

Finally, it is with much love and respect that I recognise the kind support of Danya, whose gentle soul has guided me throughout, and Christian, whose light step and smiling eyes have reacquainted me with the sweet joy of a life yet unburdened. I owe them everything.

Saskatoon, Saskatchewan, August 2000

A modified Library of Congress system of transliteration has been used throughout this book.

Abbreviations

BSC   British Security Co-ordination
CARF   Canadian Aid to Russia Fund
CPC   Communist Party of Canada
DEA   Department of External Affairs
OSS   Overseas Strategic Services
RCMP   Royal Canadian Mounted Police
UCC   Ukrainian Canadian Committee
UHO   United Hetman Organisation
ULFTA   Ukrainian Labour Farmer Temple Association
UNF   Ukrainian National Federation
USRL   Ukrainian Self Reliance League
WIB   Wartime Information Board

Canada and the Ukrainian Question, 1939–1945

1 Realism and Canadian Statecraft

On 7 September 1939, a special session of the Canadian Parliament was called. Canada's prime minister, W.L. Mackenzie King, rose in the House of Commons to address the assembled body on the prospects of war. He spoke plainly, yet forcefully, of the impending struggle and of the challenge that confronted the Canadian people, emphasising throughout that Hitler's ambitions did not stop with Poland. He called for unity and resolve in facing the evil that had been unleashed upon the world and asked his colleagues not to shrink from their responsibility, however difficult it might seem. Using his best powers of persuasion, King concluded his address with a simple, yet rhetorical, question. "I want to ask honourable members and the people of Canada: In what spirit are you going to face this crisis? Are you going to face it believing in the rights of individuals, believing in the sacredness of human personality, believing in the freedom of nations, believing in all the sanctities of human life? I believe you are. I believe that through their representatives in this Parliament the Canadian people will so indicate in no uncertain way."[1] A few days later Canada was at war.

King's words were clear and to the point. The struggle over principles was described as no less than a struggle for the very preservation of Western civilisation. It was portrayed in terms of a great moral divide – between those who were for and those who were against moral right – and hundreds of thousands in Canada rallied to the cause, persuaded that justice would be served when the enemy that would deny life and liberty to others was vanquished. In a war that would be waged in distant lands and on unknown seas, justice, then, became the watchword for Canadians.

Some six years after King's statement to Parliament, the Ukrainian Canadian Committee (UCC) presented a memorandum to the Canadian delegation attending the inaugural United Nations conference on international security, held in San Francisco. Their hope was that the rights of the Ukrainian nation, now firmly in the grip of Soviet power, might yet be protected. Noting in the memorandum that it was the unjust treatment of minorities and the violation of basic human rights that had historically threatened world peace, the UCC proposed that Canada sponsor an amendment before the conference to adopt an international bill of rights. Only through a universally binding bill of rights, they argued, could genuine international security and justice be obtained.[2] That there was good reason and some urgency for such a suggestion could be seen in the disturbing news of the imminent repatriation to the USSR of all Ukrainian refugees from the Allied occupation zones in Europe. In a separate telegram to Mackenzie King, the UCC urged the prime minister to intervene on their behalf.[3]

Upon receipt of copies of both the UCC submission and the telegram, Dana Wilgress, Canada's ambassador to the USSR and a member of the Canadian delegation at San Francisco, noted that Canada's interest in the fate of Ukrainian refugees "would be understood as an unfriendly act towards the Soviet Union." He recommended that it would be inadvisable to intervene, claiming the matter was "no business of ours ... although this could not be very well used in reply to representations submitted to us by the Ukrainian Canadian Committee."[4] John Read, assistant under-secretary of state for external affairs and the department's legal counsel, also noted in a secret memorandum to the prime minister that "It is certain that the Soviet authorities will consider any assistance to these persons [Ukrainian nationalists] as an attempt to shield them from punishment for their anti-Soviet activities."[5] Stating that the recent petitions had been "acknowledged briefly and non-committally," he proposed that "Under the circumstances ... no further action be taken in connection with the representations of the Ukrainian Canadian Committee." The prime minister penned his approval in the margin of the memorandum with an antiseptic "OK."

The question of Ukrainian refugees, however, persisted. When a further appeal was received by External Affairs, J. Riddell, a senior department officer, commented that it was "nothing more than a repetition of the earlier messages" and suggested it be filed without acknowledgment, citing King's earlier approval of such an approach.[6] The recommendation proved noteworthy. Months later, when King received a telegram signed by twenty-five members of Parliament stressing the need for intervention, Norman Robertson, the under-secretary of state, recommended that the recent policy of not replying be followed with respect to both the parliamentarians and the UCC, which continued to press its views. In a memorandum dated 12 December 1945, Robertson would counsel the prime minister that nothing should be done since "The whole question of displaced persons is one of great difficulty at the moment."[7] With a faint pencil mark in the margin of the memorandum King approved once again, the echo of a speech delivered some six years ago now nothing more than a distant memory.

Startled by reports of Ukrainian refugees being herded onto cattle cars bound for the Soviet Union and by information that panic-stricken thousands were threatening to take their own lives, the UCC, which had received no reply to its earlier petition, made one last desperate appeal. The committee members pinned their hopes on several arguments, most notably the arguments that forced repatriation was contrary to both humanitarian norms and accepted principles of international law and that Soviet authorities had no right to repatriate refugees who came from territories that had not been ceded to Russia but had been acquired by force. The UCC requested that the principle of asylum be extended to the refugees, declaring that there was a political as well as a moral responsibility in this regard. "We cannot exchange uncertain political advantages for the very fundamentals of our way of life by sacrificing these refugees to the pressure of power politics."[8] Claiming the decision to repatriate was a "verdict of death" imposed upon the refugees, the UCC asked whether this price was necessary to appease Soviet Russia. They hoped that it was not. "Surely we cannot sacrifice our elementary rights, the fundamentals of our Western civilisation, for such appeasement. To sacrifice these, we would destroy the fundamentals of the principles of democracy for which our boys fought and died in the battlefields against the barbaric warfare of Hitlerism – that is why we are pleading with you now." The UCC received no reply.

The contrast between what was said and what was done is striking. The obvious disjuncture between the objective of justice, couched in liberal-democratic terms, and the manifest interest in maintaining solidarity in allied relations points to one of the painful truths about politics. Politics is about choices. When the decision was made to ignore the appeals of the UCC, that choice, the result of an unspoken but calculated process of political distillation, would serve as a statement about what were thought to be interests that had priority. Considered vital, these interests would trump all others, including what the UCC believed to be central to the conflict – defending and preserving the fundamental principles associated with liberal justice.

The question posed by the leadership of the Ukrainian Canadian Committee – whether betraying the principle of freedom was the necessary price for Soviet appeasement – may have been unnecessarily harsh, if not simplistic. And yet behind the query was a much more profound question: wherein lay justice if not in the defence of the very ideals the government itself had persuaded young men to go overseas to fight and die for? Sacrifices had been made. Would the government now deny the importance of those principles upon which the conflict had been waged? The government's failure to respond provided an unwelcome answer. As for the source of the government's silence, it was not to be found in political cynicism, to which it was attributed by some observers. Rather, there was no reply simply because there could be no reply. A calculation had been made that certain interests superseded others, including an interest in the very ideals that had appeared to animate the recent struggle. The obvious question, of course, is, what was the rationale for placing the alliance and diplomatic relations with the Soviet Union ahead of both fundamental principles of democracy and beliefs in elementary rights?

Theda Skocpol, a historian at Harvard, has remarked that social structure conditions not only the organisation of states but also "the external ordering of states – their position relative to each other, and their overall position in the world."[9] States exist and interact in determinant geopolitical environments, and their involvement in the network of states is the basis for what Skocpol describes as their "potential autonomy of action over and against groups and economic arrangements within [their] jurisdiction." Indeed, in responding to international pressures and opportunities, the political leadership of any state may attempt policies that contradict the interests not only of the dominant class but of society as a whole. External priorities, in essence, outweigh all other considerations.

Skcopol identifies this perspective on the state as a "realist" perspective, one that is part of a long tradition in political thought.[10] It centres on the idea that states are organisations that exercise political authority over both territory and people, and it acknowledges that the legitimacy of a state is predicated on its ability to act as sovereign. Hence, sovereignty has become the chief organising principle of the international order, and it is a political value in its own right. At its core, political realism also holds that no legitimate mechanism exists whereby power, values, and resources can be distributed or redistributed in the global system. Anarchy, consequently, remains a natural condition of the global political environment. Moreover, since only a secure state can be assured survival in an anarchic world, the security of the state becomes an overriding interest and the essential political maxim to which everything else is subordinate. Policies and strategies are tailored accordingly, and due care is exercised to ensure that this most basic of all state interests – the "national interest" – is met and, concomitantly, never imperilled.

Government officials, as de facto trustees of the state, are necessarily obliged to seek and guarantee its security. They can do so because the existence of the bureaucracy is contingent on the very survival of the state. Deprived of independent interests, the bureaucracy has a vested interest in the preservation of the state, making it especially suited to implementing state imperatives. But this vested interest does not entirely explain the compatibility of the role of the official with political realism. Rather the inherent conservatism of realism requires those involved in the decision- and policy-making process to have a clear and precise understanding of state objectives and to be discriminating in the selection of political means and disciplined in their approach to politics. The goal-oriented, rational, and impersonal character of the bureaucracy complements the demands imposed by the realist framework and makes the official a natural agent for furthering state objectives.[11] To the degree that the bureaucracy enjoys a monopoly on information – a result of the increasing rationalisation of the social and economic life of the modern state – officials who are members of the bureaucracy are in a legitimate, if not privileged, position to declare what constitutes the national interest.[12]

For the official, however, political choice in such matters is moot.[13] There is only the national interest and, more particularly, national security to consider. In this sense, the logic of realism, as a primary determinant of statecraft, lays bare the argument that the official, when dealing with the "higher" affairs of state, is able to exercise free will in the decision making process and is faced with multiple choices. Bound by both duty and logic to carry out the prerogatives and needs of the state, officials methodically and rationally perform their political tasks, with full knowledge that, as a last resort, they can rely on the inherent powers of the state.

In a liberal-democratic context, however, the use of unbridled state power is potentially counterproductive. Officials, instead, seek to reinforce public acceptance in order to prevent the emergence of preferences that may diverge from the interest of the state by relying on what has been described by Eric Nordlinger as the state's "autonomy-enhancing capacities and opportunities."[14] The strategies used include playing upon the shared interests and values of state and society and minimising the perception of divergence between the two, or even changing the perception that divergent interests exist at all. Nordlinger argues that when officials fail to change perceptions, other political options are employed, such as mitigating the extent to which the rival interests can marshal resources at their disposal, diminishing their influence, or dissuading them from deploying the resources they may have. The prevailing political interest, nevertheless, remains – preserving and promoting the security of the state within the wider global context.

Significantly, during the Second World War officials sought to bring about a convergence of views that would see Canada's security interest and its interest in doing justice as complementary. They attempted at the outset of the war, for example, to reconcile the two interests by claiming that international justice would be achieved by restoring the status quo ante, the pre-1939 political order. After 1943, however, the changing nature of the global power structure demanded a different response, resulting in an interpretation linking international justice to the future of the United Nations. In promoting both, Canada – a cautious middle power anxious to shed its colonial past – had been motivated by the need to secure an image of itself as a valued ally and postwar partner. Canada's future would depend on its willingness to support and accept the political power framework in which it would have to operate, whether it was the restored prewar legal order or the new order of the United Nations. The difficulty with both scenarios, however, was that they were perceived as denying justice for Ukraine and Ukrainians. For Ukrainian Canadians, hoping that the Ukrainian independence claim might finally be recognised, the liberal-democratic notion of self-determination applied universally and without exception. Within the context of either a restored prewar or a new postwar order, it was apparent there would be no place for an independent Ukraine.

Yet, throughout the war the moral arguments made by Ukrainian Canadians on behalf of Ukraine's right to self-determination persisted. Their persistence not only proved awkward and embarrassing but it was also viewed as a threat to Canada's political prospects and future security. The clash of interests between the government and this strategically important community highlighted official inability to reconcile successfully the contradiction between the publicly embraced goals informing the struggle in the West and Canada's own security needs. To contain the problem and potential consequences, Canadian officials would engage the community, employing a range of security options, including surveillance, penetration, and control of the community. State power, however, was tempered in this instance, since a more aggressive strategy, although contemplated and well within the capacity of the state, was not applied. Such a policy, as one senior official admitted, would have been difficult to defend, if only because, paradoxically, those targeted were arguing from a position of liberal justice, in whose defence Canada had committed its best sons.

The question of Ukrainian independence made for a complex and delicate situation, highlighting during the course of the war various subtle dimensions of state behaviour. During the initial war years, political change had favoured Ukrainian national aspirations, but the dictates of realism and, specifically, the need to return to the prewar order created at Versailles precluded much support for Ukrainian independence. Only the presence of a sizeable Ukrainian community in Canada, its concentration in key sectors of the war economy, and, more importantly, the strength of the moral arguments kept their appeals from being entirely ignored. As for the perceived confluence of interests between the Canadian state and the Ukrainian Canadian community, it provided for a fortuitous, if uneasy, relationship, conditioning within the context of the emerging political contradiction the cautious nature of government policy toward this group at the time.

This policy, however, was to change with the Nazi invasion of the Soviet Union in 1941 and as the contradiction between the publicly embraced war aims and Canada's security needs became full blown. Indeed, the USSR was not only a vital ally but also a potentially important postwar partner. Since an independent Ukraine could only be carved out of the Soviet Union, the continuing calls to recognise Ukraine's right to self-determination, although set within the parameters of Allied war aims, forced Canadian authorities to intervene in the affairs of the community. They did so in order to prevent and dissuade the advocates of independence from engaging in activity deemed harmful to the national interest. As a result certain officials were prompted to reassess Allied war aims and peace policy, suggesting that the rhetoric of liberal goals be set aside by Canada in favour of statements that were more circumspect. As for those few in government who persisted in their support of Ukrainian independence – arguing the legitimacy of the claim and possible implications for nation building in Canada – they were in time dismissed from public service. Only when the geopolitical situation had changed in Europe in 1944 and victory appeared imminent were officials able to ignore the appeals altogether. But they were also convinced the "problem" would disappear of its own accord. The community, it was thought, was quickly assimilating. Prudence, therefore, dictated that the best policy was to avoid controversy. Everything else would take care of itself.

Throughout, realism provided the framework in which officials operated. But critically, their actions and decisions were influenced by a profound contradiction in the government's position on war and peace. The state could have adopted a more hostile approach in its dealings with the Ukrainian Canadian minority, as in fact it was prepared to do at several points during the war. Yet it did not. Rather, Canadian officials used other strategies in the pursuit of security. In the end, however, as they would ironically discover in their own introduction to the great-power contest that would eventually shape the postwar world, security was an elusive goal that was not easily reached.

2 The Ukrainian Question and the Politics of the Status Quo Ante, 1939–1941

For Western analysts following developments in Eastern Europe, the year 1938 ended on an inauspicious note. In December, Ukrainian deputies elected to the Polish *Sejm* (Parliament) presented a formal demand for Ukrainian territorial autonomy within the framework of the Polish state. The speaker of the *Sejm* had refused to receive the petition, stating at the time that he would deliver a pronouncement on the subject in the following parliamentary session. Most Western observers, however, believed that this refusal was a delaying tactic and that Polish authorities would try to find some legal technicalities on which to reject the demand in the form it was submitted. More importantly, it was felt that Polish reluctance to entertain even the idea of negotiations would exacerbate Polish-Ukrainian tensions and make the issue of Ukrainian autonomy an even more serious question for Poland.[1] Indeed, intelligence and press reports indicated that rioting among the Ukrainian population in East Galicia, which had at first been sporadic, had now become more commonplace and that retributive police action there served only to make matters worse.

Reports of the police measures taken against Ukrainians in Poland filtered back to the Ukrainian Canadian community, giving rise to demonstrations in Windsor and other Canadian centres. News of the demonstrations did not come as a surprise to the Department of External Affairs, and in fact the recrudescence of Ukrainian Canadian agitation had been fully expected, since, months before, the Ukrainian question had come to the foreground of European politics. According to officials in External Affairs, there was evidence to suggest that

Germany was taking a proprietary interest in Ukrainian nationalism, "[having used] the Autonomous Carpatho-Ruthene salient of Czechoslovakia as a base for Ukrainian irredentist propaganda in the USSR and Poland." This propaganda had served to excite European Ukrainians about the prospect of independence. Canadian authorities were concerned, however, that "[this] shifting [in the] political moods and objectives of the Ukrainians in Europe [was being] reflected all too faithfully in the Ukrainian population of Canada."[2] In fact, the implications of the Ukrainian question in Canada, until that moment, had not extended much beyond their effect on Canada's diplomatic relations with Poland, "which complained from time to time about Ukrainian separatist activity in Canada." The suspected German interest in the Ukrainian question, however, was for Canadian officials most disconcerting in view of the acute nature of the crisis in Europe.

The under-secretary of state for external affairs, Dr O.D. Skelton, communicated his concerns to Commissioner Stuart Wood of the RCMP, indicating that the agency would be of great assistance if intelligence officers compiled as full and accurate an account as possible of "the organisation, activities, foreign connections and relative strengths of the various Ukrainian political associations that [worked] in Canada."[3] Wood replied that such information was already on hand but that time was needed to analyse it. As for Skelton's specific inquiry about the nature of the Ukrainian Canadian disturbance in Windsor, the commissioner could only offer that it had been caused by a desire to see the liberation of Western Ukraine, an objective shared both by Ukrainian Canadian nationalists and by communists. Speculating, he added that more of the same kind of activity could be expected from one or the other group, including the canvassing of funds to finance a liberation movement in Western Ukraine.[4] Skelton was not surprised and communicated to Wood that he would inform the RCMP of any further developments that he might be apprised of and that he would share any correspondence he might receive that could be of interest or use to the agency.

Accordingly, in January 1939 Skelton brought to the attention of the commissioner an appeal from Ukrainian Canadians in the form of a letter received by Prime Minister Mackenzie King, a letter that Skelton considered particularly interesting because of the persuasive manner in which the nationalist argument was presented.[5] The author argued that the lesson of Munich was that the unresolved issues and dangers created by the Treaty of Versailles could now no longer be ignored and that what needed to be addressed above all, in view of recent European events, was the issue of self-determination for the peoples of Europe. Of all the actors, Germany exclusively recognised the importance of the principle and, despite its antidemocratic character, had assumed the role of champion of oppressed nations. This role stood in contrast with the behaviour of other European powers, which "preached" democracy but at the same time either "opposed" or "remained neutral" to the question of self-determination. The correspondent concluded that although there were certain political commitments and constraints that obviously could not be entirely ignored, the Ukrainian question would be resolved with or without British participation and that what would count for most in the end was the British Empire's "moral" position on the question. In this regard, it was stressed that no fundamental conflict existed between British and Ukrainian interests and "that a favourable stand of responsible people within the British Empire ... [would have been] a very hopeful investment for her own good and the maintenance of peace in Europe."

Skelton was impressed with the forcefulness of the argument. But what prompted him to bring the letter to the attention of the RCMP commissioner was not the argument per se. Rather, what concerned him was a passing, albeit troubling, reference to a major declaration on the Ukrainian question being prepared by an ad hoc committee of influential citizens within the nationalist segment of the Ukrainian Canadian community.[6] The committee, called the Representative Committee of Ukrainian Canadians, reportedly had broad community support.[7] For Skelton, who had suspected as much, it was confirmation that moderate opinion was shifting and that it was being pulled by the tide of events in Europe.

Developments in Europe were, indeed, moving quickly. Despite Czech concessions to Poland and Hungary, as well as diplomatic attempts to secure a guarantee of the frontiers of Czechoslovakia from the four signatory powers of the Munich Accord, it was evident that both Germany and Italy were unwilling to follow the provisions of the agreement. Nothing short of a breakup of the Czechoslovak Republic was being sought. In February 1939 Germany rejected the arrangement proposed by the Prague government to guarantee the neutrality of Czechoslovakia, and in March the movement of German troops on the Czech frontier was stepped up. Among Ukrainian nationalists there was much uncertainty about the future of the autonomous Ruthenian region within the Czechoslovak federation, but there was still hope that the Ukrainian interest there could be preserved.

However, the prospect of a future independent Carpatho-Ukrainian republic under the aegis of Germany placed Ukrainian Canadians in a precarious position. Understandably, to lessen the effects of what would amount to a compromising situation, they sought to influence government opinion to favour their side of the Ukrainian question.

This shift among the moderates toward a more proactive stand – correctly identified earlier by the under-secretary of state for external affairs – was a function of the need both to keep pace with European developments and to push Canada and Britain into adopting a more sympathetic attitude toward the Ukrainian claim for independence.

March 1939 proved to be a decisive month as German forces invaded Bohemia and Moravia. In the tumult of the invasion, a provisional Ukrainian government was established in the provincial town of Khust in the subcarpathian region of the Czechoslovak federation and an independent republic declared. The Carpatho-Ukrainian Republic, however, was short-lived, as Hungarian troops quickly overran its makeshift defences. In two short weeks all resistance was eliminated and the region annexed by Hungary, Hitler's ally.[8] In Canada the collapse of Carpatho-Ukraine evoked mixed feelings among Ukrainian nationalists, their relief only thinly masking a more profound disappointment. The belief was that an opportunity had been lost. But Germany's willingness to look askance while Hungary seized the region also confirmed their initial suspicions. Immediately after the German invasion of Czechoslovakia, a loose coalition of prominent Ukrainian Canadians published a declaration – the same ad hoc committee that had earlier given Skelton cause for apprehension – indicating that their position had not changed: if there was to be peace in Europe, the Ukrainian question had to be addressed.[9] But more importantly, they indicated also that only Britain, which alone had moral weight in the matter, could provide the necessary leadership in resolving the question of Ukrainian self-determination. The Department of External Affairs answered the declaration with a standard acknowledgment – the views expressed would "receive careful consideration."[10]

In keeping with the notion that a change in policy on the future of Ukraine would have to be supported by Britain, the declaration was sent to the London-based Ukrainian Press Bureau, with whom the ad hoc committee was in contact. The Ukrainian Canadians expected that as British subjects their views would receive a hearing and requested that the Ukrainian Press Bureau bring the appeal to the attention of the British government through their office. The bureau, however, expressed reservations about doing so because, even though there was no dispute that the eventual goal was Ukrainian independence, "the line taken [was] not likely to impress the British government, which, at the moment, desire[d] to maintain the European *status quo*." A more realistic approach to the question had to be adopted. The bureau's own considered policy, for example, was to press for autonomy rather than outright independence. Two factors, in particular, recommended that approach. First, it reflected the situation in East

Galicia, where the local Ukrainian political parties had agreed to support Poland on the basis of future political concessions. Second, and perhaps more importantly, the bureau noted that the British had repeated on a number of occasions that the conditions in East Galicia necessitated autonomy for the Ukrainian minority in Poland. The predicament in which Poland found itself, therefore, offered a rare, if unusual, opportunity to press British officials on precisely this point.[11] The Ukrainian Canadians, however, would not be deterred. Consequently, the Ukrainian Press Bureau decided, notwithstanding its reservations, that it would submit the declaration to the Foreign Office – but without comment.

The confederates who had authored the document and still others within the Ukrainian Canadian community who had played a leadership role were anxious about the German invasion of Czechoslovakia and what implications it would have for British policy in Eastern Europe. Indeed, closer collaboration between Poland, the Soviet Union, and Britain was expected. It was felt that additional lobbying would be required to ensure that British and Canadian policymakers did not lose sight of the importance of the Ukrainian factor in Europe. With this in mind, a decision was made to send an authorised delegation to discuss with Ottawa plans that would assist Ukrainians in Europe. W.A. Tucker, the elected member of Parliament for Rosthern, Saskatchewan, a riding with a large number of ethnic Ukrainian constituents with whom he was in close contact, was approached specifically to help facilitate a meeting with Prime Minister King.[12]

Tucker, a politician with keen electoral instincts, was sympathetic to the idea that a Ukrainian Canadian delegation should meet with Ottawa officials and broached the subject with the under-secretary of state for external affairs. He felt that the Ukrainian Canadians would value a meeting with the prime minister and that a meeting would do much to increase the prestige of the government within the community. Skelton's objection, communicated to Mr Tucker, was that with Britain looking to Poland and the Soviet Union as allies, neither the British nor the Canadian government could be expected to encourage a separatist movement that had as its goal the breakup of both countries. Tucker replied that Ukrainian Canadians understood the delicacy of the situation and that they were simply anxious to put their case on record before the Canadian government. If nothing else, they "would be merely pleased to have an interview [with the prime minister], without any commitments to support their aims." The under-secretary, however, was sceptical, commenting in a memo to King that, despite the political setback in Europe, Ukrainians "[were] still hoping that out of the flux something [could] be done."[13] Believing this to be the beginning of a campaign, he cautioned the prime minister that "it would be in the national interest to try to keep this large group from making trouble either abroad or at home." King concurred, noting that a meeting, whether it was with a delegation or a representative, would generate publicity, division of opinion, and a desire for counter-representations from other groups, notably the Poles.

The prime minister's decision was communicated to Tucker. Tucker persisted, however, sensitive to how news of the decision would play among the many Ukrainian Canadians in his riding. Indeed, appreciating that there could be no turning back since the group had now chosen a delegate to represent them, Tucker again attempted to persuade Skelton, claiming that the delegate in question, W. Burianyk, represented the moderate element in the community. In the hope of allaying any fear that the under-secretary might have, he communicated his confidence that the group would be satisfied if their views were simply presented and would not seek any commitment on the government's part. But he also predicted that if a simple audience – which "would hold them fast and steady" – was not granted, the matter would be "very serious" for both the national and the party interest.

Tucker's remarks were not to be taken lightly. As Skelton pointed out to King, Tucker was one of a good number of western Canadian members of Parliament who were upset over the agricultural and monetary policies of the government. If the Ukrainian "difficulty" were added to the other grievances, King was told he could expect dissension within his own party and perhaps a public backlash in the Canadian West.[14] Careful to insulate the prime minister from possible controversy, the under-secretary proposed that a short audience be scheduled in Ottawa with the Ukrainian Canadian representative. King agreed.

Burianyk was an official with the Ukrainian Self Reliance League (USRL), a lay organisation of the Ukrainian Orthodox Church, and Skelton knew him through indirect correspondence.[15] He considered him well informed, with an uncanny ability to predict the course of European events. But he was more impressed by Burianyk's penchant for free and uninhibited discussion, in some measure a factor in the final decision to grant Burianyk an audience.[16]

Skelton was not to be disappointed.[17] During the course of the meeting, where it was made clear to the Ukrainian Canadian representative that it was "inappropriate" for the Canadian government to champion Ukrainian independence, Burianyk revealed an extraordinary plan to create a Ukrainian Army of Canada that could be used to instigate a popular revolt in Ukraine. This and other intriguing topics suggested that Norman Robertson, the department's liaison with the RCMP on enemy alien and security matters, might find it useful to meet with

Burianyk. An evening repast, therefore, followed by after-dinner conversation, was arranged. Revelling in the opportunity, Burianyk, who in his own words "let it all hang out," was immensely satisfied with the results. Moreover, he was pleased with the level of knowledge demonstrated by Robertson, "who was well informed about all the convoluted politics which divided the Ukrainian community." In fact, Burianyk concluded from Robertson's specific comments and pointed questions "that someone in Ottawa was following very carefully what appeared in the Ukrainian press," interpreting it as a sign of government interest in the Ukrainian question.[18]

Encouraged by the discussions, the resourceful Burianyk took the initiative on his last day in Ottawa to introduce himself to the United Kingdom's high commissioner to Canada, Stephen Holmes. Astonished to discover that Burianyk had managed to secure meetings with the prime minster and other officials, the high commissioner invited the Ukrainian Canadian for a private talk, ostensibly to elicit from the unsuspecting representative information on Canada's position. Holmes was to learn that nothing untoward had transpired, and he conveyed to London the impression that "the Prime Minister's observations as reported seem to be entirely characteristic, including his fear of getting mixed up in a European controversy."[19] As for Burianyk's views on Eastern Europe, particularly Britain's need to support the Ukrainian independence claim, they were ignored on the grounds that "the position and complaints of the Ukrainian minority in Poland were not of course a new topic [being] ventilated in the past with frequency and at length." They were ignored also because news being received in London from the region, although sparse and at times contradictory, was nevertheless encouraging from the British perspective and suggested that nothing be done to complicate the situation.

The British consul general in Warsaw, for instance, had reported that Count Los of Lvov (Lviv) had enlisted the support of the Uniate Archbishop, Andrii Sheptytsky, in an attempt to bring about a rapprochement between Ukrainians and Poles. Count Los, however, was only mildly optimistic, because he believed the feeling was widespread among Ukrainians that Germany would get the better of Poland and that Poland's necessity was their opportunity. On the other hand, it was reported that the populist Ukrainian National Democratic Union had recently indicated it would support the government of Poland, albeit on the basis of limited territorial autonomy and future parity rights for Poland's Ukrainian minority. The consul general believed that in the context of the current crisis, the Ukrainian position – which appeared to be more flexible than it had been in the past – would lead to a normalisation of relations between the two peoples. But this remained to be seen. Meanwhile, "Polish authorities [were] continu[ing] their policy of dealing firmly with any tendency by Ukrainian organisations to conduct illicit activities [and] unless Germany or some other outside Power decide[d] to make a major question of the racial issue there, the Polish government [would] have no difficulty in maintaining tranquillity."[20]

The March declaration of Ukrainian Canadian citizens, which had been submitted to the Foreign Office by the Ukrainian Press Bureau, had by this time circulated among elected British representatives and reportedly was favourably received in some quarters. The sentiment in Canada was to follow up and consolidate this opinion by sending someone in authority to London to speak to these and other sympathetic officials, making "it possible for [British officials] to obtain ... direct information regarding the reaction of [a] British subject of Ukrainian descent in Canada towards the existing conditions in Ukrainian territories under different occupations and particularly [his] viewpoint regarding the possible solution of the Ukrainian problem in Europe."[21] It was thought prudent that before proceeding to London, the delegate should acquaint the under-secretary of state for external affairs with the aim of the visit. Through the office of the premier of Saskatchewan, an interview was secured for the delegate, W. Kossar, with the under-secretary, O.D. Skelton, who as a courtesy to the premier agreed to the meeting. Skelton, who had recently met with Burianyk, however, also thought that it would be useful to meet and gauge other corners of opinion among the community leadership.

Skelton listened with interest to Kossar, who was a member of the executive of the Ukrainian National Federation and by profession an agronomist at the University of Saskatchewan. Kossar spoke briefly and to the point.[22] Outlining the fortunes of the Ukrainian national movement, Kossar insisted that the principle of self-determination alone would determine the peaceful course of events in Europe, whose history was in the process of being remade, but with an uncertain outcome. Only those states whose internal affairs were in order would be able to stand and resist German encroachments. Pointing to the nationality question as the source of the current weakness of both Poland and the USSR, Kossar indicated that, in the event of war, it would be, in his opinion, the eventual cause of their demise. Consequently, to avert a total political catastrophe in Europe, it was imperative that Britain convince both the Polish and Soviet governments to grant a measure of autonomy to the Ukrainians. In the final instance, however, as Kossar was quick to point out, this was a decision for Britain alone to make. Ukrainian Canadians did not pretend to have influence over British foreign policy and, indeed, as devoted British subjects, he claimed, they would support whatever policy was adopted. However, to the degree that the Canadian government recognised the political merits and moral arguments underlying the Ukrainian claim, Kossar hoped that it would react positively and assist him in a presentation before officials of His Majesty's government in London to consider Ukraine's right to self-determination.

Skelton listened patiently, explaining that, although he could appreciate the strength of Kossar's personal convictions, "as a Canadian he [Skelton] was primarily concerned with the interests of Canada, not of any part of the European Continent."[23] Skelton also wished him to understand that both the British and French had made or were in the process of making overtures to Poland and the Soviet Union and that the alliances would not be conditional on the treatment of minorities or, for that matter, on other issues of an internal nature. Under the circumstances, the government, he claimed, could not undertake to present either his views or the views of any other Ukrainian Canadian representative. Nor would it ask the British government to receive him, since this would be to give an indirect endorsement of those views, which was impossible at the time. The meeting ended on a cordial note, neither one having convinced the other.

Skelton's intent, of course, was to discourage Kossar from undertaking his mission. But sensing that he was nevertheless inclined to go, Skelton thought it advisable to alert London to Kossar's pending visit. Describing him and other Ukrainian Canadians with whom he had contact as individuals who were sincere in their desire to put Canada first, Skelton nevertheless cautioned that they were equally strong in their belief that an independent Ukraine would be in the interests of Britain and, indirectly, of other members of the Commonwealth. Since he understood that this was not the position of His Majesty's government, he asked the Canadian high commissioner in London to reassure British officials that Canada had no intention of endorsing Ukrainian claims, especially since the representations were being made by "a group which, so far at least as many of its members [were] concerned, [was] more European than Canadian in its interests."[24] He concluded his communication to the high commissioner on a cautionary note, advising that the whole situation had to be considered with care, since "Ukrainian national aspirations are undoubtedly an important factor and may become a more important factor in the Eastern situation, which has become of special interest to the United Kingdom since the Vistula became one of its boundaries."[25]

The growing agitation among the "foreign-born" groups in Canada paralleled the increased tension in Europe and prompted a response by the government. In May of 1939, only months before the outbreak of war, a statement was read in the House of Commons that served as both a condemnation and a warning to those groups, who were engaged in activity characterised as disruptive.[26] Attributing the uneasiness among Canada's ethnic minorities to the work of agitators, the government strongly reproached those who were working actively or indirectly toward dividing the Canadian public. Declaring that it would not tolerate the propaganda, which had become much more active and truculent as of late, it gave a warning to those "who, with loose thinking and muddled emotions, allowed themselves to believe that they can be both bond [bound] and free, lightly accepting the privilege of citizenship in this country while retaining other loyalties which are incompatible with it." The authorities said that they were prepared to take appropriate "measures" if circumstances warranted and had "powers to deal effectively with individuals whose activities along these lines exceed the bounds of public tolerance: not the least among these powers is the capacity to revoke certificates of naturalisation." As for those ethnic organisations that were susceptible to such propaganda and that were being used as agencies for the promotion of foreign political interests, it was incumbent upon them to recognise the importance of the obligations of citizenship:

Is it too much to ask of our newer Canadians to bear in mind that Canada is the freely chosen country of their adoption, in which their children are going to live? For their sake they must realise that full loyalty to our country and its institutions is not compatible with continuing participation in the tribal feuds and rivalries with which Europe is beset. Whether their racial origin be Polish or Ukrainian, German or Jewish, Italian or Czech, Canadian citizens living and earning their living in Canada owe their single and unqualified allegiance to this country and its institutions. The job of welding this vast half-continent and those peoples of every race and tongue and cultural tradition into a new Canadian nationality is big enough in all conscience without having it made more difficult for us by political, racial, and class propaganda originating beyond our frontiers.[27]

The government's public admonition and perturbation over the "un-Canadian" attitude of elements within the "foreign-born" population did not dissuade Ukrainian Canadians from further petitioning officials. Government representatives received appeals throughout the summer of 1939. The left-wing Democratic Alliance for the Defence of the Ukrainian People, for instance, stressed in a memorandum to the prime minister the need to strengthen the relationship between both the Ukrainian and Polish peoples against the threat of fascist aggression. But it also urged the Canadian prime minister to impress upon the Polish government the necessity of fulfilling all treaty obligations with respect to the Ukrainian people, noting that "As Canadian citizens we take the liberty to remind the Government of the Dominion of Canada that as one of the signatories of the treaties referred to in the memorandum, it guaranteed its due performance by the contracting parties."[28] The alliance was confident that the Dominion government, in its role as one of the guarantors, would, minimally, render assistance and cooperation in securing just treatment for the Ukrainian minority in Poland.

Similarly, petitions from the nationalist community implored Mackenzie King to raise the case of Ukrainian self-determination before the British, who, it was believed, were alone in a position to effect a just political solution in Eastern Europe. Although recognising that existing political commitments currently prevailed against an immediate solution to the Ukrainian problem, the hope was expressed that, in the event of the breakup of the Soviet Union into its constituent parts, Britain would adopt a sympathetic attitude to the national aspirations of the Ukrainian people.[29]

O.D. Skelton brought these and other appeals to the attention of the RCMP.[30] Recent information regarding Ukrainian Canadian organisations had convinced him of the necessity of doing so. Skelton, in fact, had obtained, through Tucker, correspondence from Burianyk, who had begun to assume a more surreptitious role after meeting with Skelton and the prime minister in his capacity as a delegate representing the Ukrainian Self Reliance League (USRL). The immediate context was a trip that Kossar had made to Europe.[31] The larger context, however, was the intense rivalry for community leadership between the USRL and the Ukrainian National Federation (UNF).

Upon learning of Kossar's trip to Europe, Burianyk quickly wrote to Canadian authorities. Since Kossar was known to be a proscribed man in Poland, Burianyk concluded, "he could only have visited Germany or some other German-controlled country, which did not speak well of his mission." It was also rumoured that while in London Kossar had had a meeting with Chamberlain and that in New York, on his return, he had supposedly conferred with the European Ukrainian leader, Andrii Melnyk, and other high-ranking members of the suspect underground Organisation of Ukrainian Nationalists. Burianyk recommended that External Affairs check up on the Kossar trip "and his talk with Chamberlain, whom he may have approached under false colours." As Burianyk remarked, "it would do no harm to keep our eyes peeled to the things that go on around us."[32]

Skelton was aware that Burianyk's accusations were motivated by strong personal antipathy to the rival UNF, but he could not afford to overlook what Burianyk had to say on this and other occasions.[33] Nor could the RCMP. Nothing, for that matter, could be assumed or ignored in view of the looming crisis in Europe.

On 26 August 1939 the RCMP commissioner submitted to the minister of justice recommendations to be adopted in case of war. The strength of the RCMP force, then pegged at 2,541, was to be increased by 700 men, to deal with "specialised" work, while an additional 1,100 men were to be engaged as special constables to guard eighty-five points across the country. It was also decided that all potentially hostile enemy aliens throughout the country, principally members of organisations believed to be controlled by Rome or Berlin, would be arrested and interned. In this regard, a recommendation was made to ban, by order-in-council under the War Measures Act, not only the German Bund but also Ukrainian nationalist organisations, including the UNF.[34] The ban, however, would not be confined to the political right, the RCMP having further proposed that the Communist Party of Canada (CPC) and its auxiliary organisations be banned and their property confiscated.

The proposal to ban the CPC was influenced by events that had transpired only days before the commissioner submitted his package of recommendations. On 23 August 1939 a nonaggression pact had been signed between Germany and the Soviet Union. Soon after, political and military developments took on a momentum of their own. Germany attacked Poland on 1 September and three days later – in keeping with its treaty obligations – Britain issued a declaration of war against Germany, as did France. On 9 September a formal submission regarding Canada's intention to declare war was dispatched by cable to His Majesty the King, in London, and that submission was approved. Canada was officially at war the following day.

On 17 September, in a stunning turn of events, Soviet troops crossed Poland's eastern frontier under the pretext of extending "fraternal aid" to Ukrainians and Belorussians. Within one week only sporadic resistance remained, and with the signing of an agreement in Moscow on 28 September the Polish Republic formally ceased to exist. The Nazi-Soviet agreement established new frontiers so that 72,806,000 square miles of Polish territory, inhabited by twenty-two million Polish citizens, came under German rule, while the remaining 77,720,000 square miles inhabited by thirteen million Polish citizens was assumed by the Soviet Union. Virtually all the historic western Ukrainian and Belorussian lands formerly under Polish rule were now incorporated into the Soviet Union.

The Soviet-German Pact had come as a surprise to Canadian communists. Even more unexpected was the Soviet attack on Poland, whose struggle with Germany was supported by the Communist Party of Canada. The Soviet move resulted in a major policy reversal, the Comintern now condemning the "warmongers" in London and Paris. The new orientation was quickly adopted by the CPC, which called for Canada's withdrawal from the "imperialist war," a line that was immediately taken up by the pro-Soviet Ukrainian press in Canada. The war was described as being against the wishes of the Canadian people and as conducted at the expense of the working class, while the government's policies were characterised as "criminal."[35]

Not surprisingly, Ukrainian Canadian nationalists welcomed the war, although objecting to the occupation of Ukrainian territories by Russia, Germany, and the other Axis powers.[36] It was a unique opportunity, the Soviet-German agreement and the subsequent partition of Poland having cleared away the political obstacles that had previously so hobbled the Ukrainian national movement. The way to independence appeared open, and it was in this unprecedented situation that the UNF, hoping to capitalise on events of the moment, boldly submitted a plan to the prime minister for his consideration, a plan proposing the organisation of ethnic Ukrainian military units within the Canadian army.

The proposal argued that the "minority" question, which had been so effectively used by both Germany and the Soviet Union in advancing their geopolitical interests, still remained, and had, in fact, been aggravated by the expansions of the two states. The problem, however, of minorities, which had so beset the Western democracies in recent years, had now become the problem of both Germany and the Soviet Union, placing the Western democracies in a position to avail themselves of a new opportunity:

Superficially, [the recent territorial conquest] constitutes a strengthening of the two totalitarian States; in reality, however, it presents the most serious danger to their existence. We feel that recognition of this situation by the Western Powers may introduce a new element into their practical policy against Germany and Russia during the present war. So far Hitler and Stalin were using the grievances of submerged Nations to their own advantage. Now it seems time is ripe for the Western Powers to exploit the same weapon against them.

It seems to us that the day of a complete victory of the British Empire and France over Germany would come much sooner and with much less sacrifice on the Western front if they took full account and availed themselves of the dynamic strength not only of the Czech, Slovak and Polish "minorities" now under Germany, but also the Ukrainian, White Russian, Georgian and other "minorities" now under Russia. We stress that the "minorities" in both these states should be considered at the same time. The victory over Germany alone will not provide a sufficient basis for a lasting peace. A conquered Germany, with Russia left in her present boundaries, will always use these unsolved problems in her efforts to inaugurate a new wave of aggression.[37]

In the light of recent developments it was suggested that in addition to the creation of free Polish and Czech military contingents within the Allied force, similar Ukrainian units in the Canadian army, perhaps patterned after the Canadian Highlanders and given the title of the Canadian Ukrainian Fusiliers, could be formed. This would assist in local recruitment, especially on the Prairies. But it was also felt that, from a propaganda perspective, these units could help encourage the organisation of sympathetic forces for the Allies in the Soviet Union and in Germany proper. The proposal concluded by declaring that should their suggestion be considered impractical and the formation of distinct Ukrainian units in any form regarded as undesirable, the UNF would nevertheless induce their members and other Ukrainian Canadians to enlist privately as individuals in the Canadian armed forces.[38]

The submission alarmed Canadian officials, for although the government had been made aware of the idea before, there was now anecdotal evidence to suggest that the matter was being taken seriously and that preparations were being made.[39] Skelton, upon seeing the proposal, wrote a hurried memo to ensure that no action would be taken by the Department of National Defence or some other quarter to encourage the formation of ethnic Ukrainian units within the Canadian forces. The only exception to this policy was that "if the Polish government were permitted to seek recruits among its own nationals in Canada, it would be free to induce Poles of Ukrainian ancestry to enlist – if it could."[40]

Significantly, in London the prospect of a dialogue between recent Polish and Ukrainian émigrés was made possible because of the circumstances that each group found themselves in. Indeed, the German-Soviet occupation presented the possibility of a natural, if uneasy, alliance. Discussions, consequently, were occurring for the first time in as many years, centred around the belief that it was only now possible to work out a common course of action that would benefit both peoples. It was clear, however, that émigré Ukrainians were lacking in their ability to present a coordinated front before either the Poles or the British. In view of their unique position as British subjects and as a factor in the British war effort, it was felt by certain elements within the Ukrainian diaspora that Ukrainian Canadians could potentially play a leading role. A recommendation consequently was made by the London-based Ukrainian Press Bureau urging Ukrainian Canadian community leaders to create an "external affairs" committee that would not only monitor political developments but also liase between the various Ukrainian centres, on one side, and between Ottawa and London, on the other.[41] It was also recommended that a united, representative committee be formed, to give greater legitimacy and weight to Ukrainian objectives. From the point of view of expediency, it was suggested that the director of the bureau, Dr Kaye-Kisilevsky, a Ukrainian Canadian residing in Britain, be empowered to act on behalf of the committee there.[42]

Time was of the essence. Kaye, writing from London, sought to impress upon the disparate Ukrainian Canadian nationalist organisations that party and personal interests, which to date had been so harmful to the general Ukrainian interest, had to be set aside if the objective of Ukrainian independence was to be realised.[43] The USRL, to which some of Kaye's communications had been directed, replied that distrust and political divisions within the Ukrainian Canadian community ran deep and that the prospect of creating a united council seemed remote at best.[44] The only point to which the USRL was prepared or willing to concede was the need for a London correspondent of the Ukrainian Canadian press, who, they thought, could be attached to the press division of Britain's Ministry of Information.

The idea that a Ukrainian could be placed on staff with the British Ministry of Information was naive. In fact, British officials were beginning to express concern over the growing number of Ukrainian representations being made through various channels to His Majesty's government. Dr Kaye, himself a frequent visitor to the Foreign Office, often brought in exiled officials associated with the short-lived 1918 Ukrainian Republic for an exchange of views. R.A. Leeper of the Foreign Office thought that negotiations with Ukrainian politicians were unseemly in view of current relations with Poland and in any case would not amount to much because "there was no organisation and there was nothing to build on." He advised that such meetings be avoided. Leeper, however, was not without his detractors. Although not wishing to minimise his concerns, other analysts concluded that private conversations did not constitute negotiations and that there was no harm in informally receiving individual Ukrainians such as Dr Kaye if publicity was avoided. A few, in fact, believed there was much to be gained from encouraging the Ukrainian movement if that approach was handled properly through the Poles and channelled in the right direction. L.A. Collier, a senior analyst with the Central Department in the Foreign Office, went further, suggesting that the practical side of politics also dictated that "if the Poles will not play properly, and if the attitude of the Soviet government makes it desirable for us to raise up Ukrainian trouble for them, I trust that we will not be deterred by undue regard for Polish susceptibilities from dealing directly with any Ukrainian leaders one can get hold of."[45]

The opportunism that coloured official British policy allotted Kaye a certain amount of room to manœuvre, and he used it to full advantage. The British Ministry of Information proposed that Kaye, a recipient of several university degrees including a doctorate from the University of London, undertake a scheduled December broadcast on the BBC concerning the Ukrainian question. Kaye seized the moment, recognising that there might be some benefit in a public airing of the Ukrainian question. But perhaps more importantly, the broadcast was to be radioed back to Canada, allowing Kaye to speak simultaneously and directly to Ukrainian Canadians on their role, tasks, and obligations. The opportunity was not lost on Kaye, who not only pleaded passionately for the Ukrainian cause but emphasised that the best hope for the Ukrainian people lay ultimately with the liberal democracies:

The events which preceded the outbreak of hostilities between Great Britain and her allies on the one hand and the present rulers of Germany on the other hand, indicate clearly what is to be our decision.

The powers, which have made up their minds to end once and for all the rule of force in Europe, have always showed great sympathy and understanding for all that stand for a noble cause. Their interests in the problems of Eastern Europe have been and are now benevolent. The rights for which we Canadian Ukrainians have always pleaded on behalf of our racial relatives, Britons and Frenchmen are now risking their lives to defend and uphold on the continent of Europe.

Our present interest in what is going on in Europe is twofold: firstly, we are concerned as citizens of this free Commonwealth of Nations; secondly, we are concerned because it is on the soil of our forefathers that the present tragedy is being enacted. We are determined to preserve those liberties, which had been won by previous generations under the British flag, and we wish to extend those liberties to our kinsmen whose future is so dear to us. How else but through the forces of liberty and freedom can we hope to realise our aims? It is only by acting with the great democracies for which the rights of man are essential truths that we can hope to win for our noble cause.

Those who have arrayed themselves against such rights boast of a mailed fist. Our racial brothers in Ukraine are not in a position to face force with force. But the freedom loving nations of Europe have organised both physical and moral forces of all free people against that mailed fist. They are now the last resort of justice.[46]

Kaye's public passion was equalled only by his personal industry. Empowered to act as the European delegate of the USRL, Kaye took further steps to strengthen contacts with officials both in Britain and elsewhere. On 27 December, he wrote to the USRL executive, reporting that in his capacity as a representative of Ukrainian Canadians he had met with the Finnish foreign minister and discussed with him the possibility of cooperation. This and other official meetings with Finnish representatives, he argued, had had positive results, leading to a Finnish request for discussions about the possible creation of a Finnish-Ukrainian committee serving as a liaison between the two peoples.

The Finnish connection, however, according to Kaye, was important for other reasons. As he was at pains to point out, the Russo-Finnish conflict had convinced a number of policymakers that Soviet Russia, after Germany, was the most dangerous factor in Europe. It was necessary now, however, to capitalise on this current of opinion. Kaye declared that "the importance and gravity of the present day situation cannot be stressed enough. The Ukrainians will be compelled sooner or later to take active part in this European struggle, make decisions and carry them out. We already decided one major thing: we have thrown our lot with the Democratic Powers, which is the logical and only possibility for us to do."[47] He believed that personal ambitions and interests had to be set aside because Ukrainian Canadians alone were in the most favourable position to influence policy as it could affect Eastern Europe. The community leadership, therefore, had to move swiftly, as there in fact had been hints from well-placed individuals that the next peace conference would take place in London and that a national committee along the lines of the Czech Committee would serve the Ukrainians well in their bid to have standing representation with the Allied powers.[48]

Kaye's persistent entreaties were not entirely lost upon elements within the community leadership. There was growing recognition that future success depended on planning and coordination. Consequently, some initial effort was made to build a coalition. But the steps taken to bring the various Ukrainian Canadian nationalist organisations together on a representative basis could not overcome entrenched positions and the petty ambitions and suspicions.[49] The politicking and manœuvring would eventually leave the nationalist community sharply divided into two camps, with recriminations and denunciations becoming the norm in the Ukrainian Canadian press.[50]

During the winter and spring of 1940, there was little evidence of the war in Western Europe; the military situation being reduced to a stand-off on the Maginot Line. This was not so in the occupied lands in the East. German security police were fully engaged in a program of repression in the conquered Polish territory, while Soviet internal security forces were busy at work in the newly annexed Baltic states,

Western Ukraine, and Belorussia. Intelligence reports relayed news of widespread terror and mass deportations in the Soviet occupied territories.[51] It was within this setting that the Ukrainian government in exile, located in Paris after the final defeat of republican forces in 1920, assured the Allied governments that official Ukrainian policy supported the Allied position, opposing both German and Russian imperialism, which in their view threatened global stability equally. The Ukrainians, however, did not speak with one voice.

In March 1940 the press bureau of the Ukrainian government in exile, operating independently from Rome, within the Axis, released a press communiqué loudly condemning the factionalism within the Ukrainian émigré community. Denouncing as counterproductive the false pride that flowed from narrow political interests, the communiqué argued there was no "right" or "wrong" side to the war, only the goal of Ukrainian sovereignty. The only interest that should concern Ukrainians in the political power struggle between European nations, it claimed, was to secure political independence for Ukraine, irrespective of the competing claims of justice made by one or another of the belligerents:

It is understood that Ukrainians ... are in conscience bound to show their sympathies to one or the other belligerent but in their sympathies they should not go the length of the Committee in Paris or the Ukrainians in Canada and, in part, of those of the United States of America.

The Ukrainians, as all other peoples, include democrats, nationalists and monarchists. We all, however, should understand that the victory of our cause does not depend upon an ideology but upon the solidity of our nation and the wisdom and tact of its leaders.

We consider it harmful to analyse, as this is being done by Ukrainians in Canada and France, which of the belligerents fight for "justice in this world" and which for the "domination of the world."

The present-day combatants do not care for liberal justice but only for their own interests, and, as far as the Ukrainian cause is concerned, they will add it to their aims only when this will be to their own interests.

The Ukrainians in Canada and France, and to a certain extent in other countries, began to accuse Germany of "treason," accusing her of the unfortunate fate of the Western Ukraine.

These accusations are self-understood. Our "Crown prosecutors," however, forget that the Russo-German pact came as a surprise. They forget that the whole world expected something quite opposite, namely, not a Russo-German pact but a military pact between the Soviets, England and France.

How would the Ukrainians, particularly in Canada and France, have felt if Anglo-French diplomacy had shown more "cleverness" and gone hand in hand with the Bolshevik "democracy"? Would it have been right then to say that the Western democracies were fighting for "justice" and would then the Ukrainians have remained on the side of France, England and Poland?

In the seventh month of this fratricidal war we are sorry to state that we do not know the aims and plans of the belligerents with respect to the Ukrainian Question. We must however, conscientiously and seriously, and not in an operetta manner, remind everyone of the truth: the actual historical aim of the Ukrainian nation always was and will be against two imperialisms – the Russian and the Polish, but not the German or any other imperialism. We also must remember that the Ukrainians never were enemies of the Germans or the English or the French and that an artificial sowing of enmity towards one of the two belligerents is very detrimental to our cause.[52]

Embarrassed by the communiqué and fearful of being implicated by association, the nationalist leadership in Canada sought to distance itself from it by bringing it to the attention of Canadian authorities.[53] Canadian censorship officials, however, already had a copy in their possession and were not impressed. External Affairs, immediately alerted, were told that the current difficulties in Canada were the result of this sort of propaganda, which was aimed at exploiting weaknesses in the Allied camp. They were also cautioned that more of the same could be expected to come Canada's way.[54]

Representations made to the Department of External Affairs by the two principal groups within the nationalist community became standard fare throughout the spring of 1940. Wasyl Swystun, an executive officer with the UNF, for instance, was able to secure an interview with O.D. Skelton in April, the latter being very much interested in meeting him, since Swystun in some ways had gained notoriety for his outspoken views on British policy and Ukrainian independence. The purpose of Swystun's visit was to present two memoranda for government consideration. The first emphasised the need for a formal Allied statement on Ukrainian independence, while the other dealt with the mobilisation of Ukrainians in France by the Polish government in exile.

During the course of their conversation, Skelton repeated the official position of the Canadian government, informing Swystun that although Canada realised the importance of the Ukrainian question and would continue to give its solution "earnest attention," a commitment was not possible at the time. Since an independent Ukraine would have to be carved out of the territories of the USSR and Poland, "What was desirable and possible in Eastern Europe would depend very largely on the military developments of the next few months. [Canada] could not, therefore, give any undertaking as the policy that would be supported by the Canadian government."[55] Responding to Swystun's request that the memorandum on Ukrainian independence be brought to the personal attention of the prime minister, Skelton indicated that he would forward it but told Swystun that his organisation could expect only a formal acknowledgment. As to the possibility of transmitting a copy of the memorandum to authorities in Britain and France, Skelton bluntly stated that it would amount to an official endorsement, which from a Canadian perspective was unacceptable. This view also applied to the second memorandum that opposed the Polish initiative in France, proposing instead the recruitment of Ukrainian émigrés under Ukrainian colours. Skelton remarked that the government of France would not only reject but also regard receiving such a memorandum as untoward, in view of its active recognition of the Polish government in exile, recently reestablished in Paris.[56]

The meeting made an impression on the under-secretary.[57] Skelton noted that Swystun's legal training had served him well in his ardent defence of the Ukrainian claim. He was as convincing as he was articulate. To less suspecting or abler minds, the increasingly sophisticated political arguments made by Swystun and others, couched as they were in the language of the democratic struggle, appeared legitimate. As Skelton observed, there was some danger in this, in so far as the potential existed for unwitting officials to be drawn in by the arguments, and their statements could then possibly place Canada in an awkward, if not difficult, situation. Shortly thereafter, Skelton instructed that submissions from Ukrainian representatives be directed to him personally and that reports on meetings with any government official be sent to him immediately.[58]

Skelton was anxious and feared the worst. Consequently, upon learning of Swystun's proposed visit, as part of a delegation, to Washington, where he was to attend a Ukrainian American congress as an observer, he readily agreed to see Swystun after the latter offered to come to Ottawa for a further exchange of views. For Swystun it was a political opportunity to again promote the Ukrainian case. But it also enabled him to establish his personal credentials and the credibility of the UNF with External Affairs. This was a matter of some importance, since the Ukrainian Press Bureau in London, now effectively controlled by the USRL, had made certain representations to the Foreign Office to block Swystun's visa application for entry to the United Kingdom.[59]

Outlining again the Ukrainian claim, Swystun referred to several new points that caught the attention of the under-secretary. Swystun, hoping to promote the UNF at the expense of the USRL, which along with several other political associations had collectively organised under the name United Ukrainian Central Committee, stated that the opposition was "neither pure in [its] motives or tactics."[60] Swystun, for example, personally knew Theodore Datzkiw, head of the monarchist United Hetman Organisation (UHO) in Canada and editor of the Ukrainian language newspaper *Kanadiiskyi farmer* (Canadian Farmer), and suggested that his loyalty was not as it should be. Skelton was suspicious of the allegation, since it was but one of the many all too frequent charges and countercharges being made privately or publicly. What concerned him, however, was that the divisions were leading to numerous accusations and were making it impossible to distinguish truth from fact. From Skelton's perspective, objective intelligence was required both to sort out the situation and to determine to what degree there was a threat, if any.

Of more interest, however, was Swystun's comment that having briefly perused the Ukrainian-American press, he had concluded that a German orientation could now be detected among the Ukrainians in the United States.[61] If what Swystun had to say was true, then it was inevitable that opinion within the Ukrainian Canadian nationalist community would be affected, causing no end of trouble for Canadian authorities. The under-secretary was worried. He immediately wrote to Commissioner Wood of the RCMP asking, first, that the agency verify whether the situation in the United States was as Swystun had suggested and, second, whether Datzkiw was disseminating propaganda that would be harmful to Canadian interests.[62]

The RCMP commissioner read the under-secretary's letter with considerable interest because, as Wood admitted, the UNF had been the subject of police surveillance "for some time." It was therefore useful to know who was saying what about whom. Swystun's information, the commissioner reported, could not be confirmed or denied. His own view was that the Ukrainian national movement in other countries such as the United States appeared to be "apathetic" about the Allied cause or at the very least "neutral," but that the situation, overall, was much too fluid for any solid conclusions to be drawn. The only assurance that he could give was that as long as Germany maintained its ties with the Soviet Union, a more favourable attitude on the part of Ukrainian nationalists towards the Allies could be expected.[63] As for the allegation against Datzkiw, it could not be confirmed. The information, however, was significant enough to warrant investigation, providing the RCMP with a pretext to undertake a more detailed investigation of the UHO – the first in a series that were to be conducted on Ukrainian nationalist organisations and that led to several major reports.

The possibility of an internal security threat, whether from the left or the right, prompted Skelton to request the director of the Civil Service Commission, Charles H. Bland, to submit recommendations regarding possible precautionary measures to help safeguard the government.[64] Quickly responding to the request, Bland did not mince words. Giving vent to his worst fears and prejudices, he argued that the single greatest danger to Canada was the large number of "foreign-born" persons in Canada who, potentially available to foreign powers, were in a position "to create disturbances and to carry out a *coup d'état.*" There were two aspects to the question that, according to Bland, Canadian authorities needed to address immediately, one political and the other practical.

On the political side, Bland highlighted the problem that in the case of a coup, without a Canadian government to invite American troops into Canada or without the preexisting approval of Congress, the American government would be powerless to act in time. From the perspective of the United States and, by extension, Canada, the situation would be "fatal," since the United States was not in a position to equip and train a North American army quickly enough to repel the German forces that would have gained a foothold on the continent. "It seems obvious," according to Bland's own curious blend of logic, "that the Government of the United States [should] be prevailed upon to respond to a formal invitation by this country by taking in advance whatever action is required on the part of Congress to give to the President power to order troops into Canada when, in his opinion, conditions in Canada and internal disorders might endanger the Democratic nation of Canada, and in turn the United States."

As a practical matter, however, Bland also suggested that Canadian authorities had been negligent in their duty by failing to take the necessary precautions. He personally advised that a regiment of trained and reliable citizens be organised and held in reserve, to be dispatched at a moment's notice to protect not only key installations in Montreal, Toronto, and Ottawa but also the Cabinet and other officers of the government. In this regard, Bland fully stressed the need to secure the confidence of the "two principal races" in Canada and the importance of appointing a Canadian-born officer to the post of director general for internal defence, for only in this way would there be the necessary assurance that "this important function will receive the attention that is essential to our domestic order in the face of the stupefying threat which hangs over us."

Bland's wild speculations on a "foreign-born" coup were a testimony to the increasingly anxious mood within the country. Bland was not alone in his views. In addition to the overactive imaginations of many citizens, nativist resentment resulted in regular reports being received by the government detailing a host of suspicious activities purportedly carried out by "foreigners." Charges of fifth-column activity and political conspiracies all resulted in inquiries by either the RCMP or the provincial police.[65] Information pertaining to the activities of members of the Communist Party of Canada, however, attracted the special attention of the RCMP, which had a long-standing interest in the organisation.

Within the RCMP, the communist threat was considered the more serious, and under the provisions of the emergency Defence of Canada Regulations, which accorded extensive powers to the state, the activity of the CPC was targeted.[66] Censorship powers, for instance, were used to silence the CPC in the fall of 1939 when its French and English-language press organs, the *Clarté* and *Clarion,* respectively, were banned. This, however, did not put an end to the political work. Broadsheets continued to be distributed by the party not only calling for Canada's withdrawal from the war and encouraging labour protest but also encouraging desertion among armed forces personnel. In May 1940 the Canadian government, responding ostensibly to the deteriorating military situation in Europe but acting more immediately on the advice of the RCMP and the minister of justice, E. Lapointe, outlawed the CPC and a number of other closely affiliated organisations, including the Ukrainian Labour Farmer Temple Association (ULFTA). Further orders in council provided for the confiscation of the properties of the banned organisations – most notably ULFTA community halls – and the suppression of the left-wing ethnic press.[67] As instructions went out for the arrest and detention of prominent members of the CPC, the leadership, having either fled the country or gone underground, urged members and supporters alike to redouble their efforts in the campaign to stop the war and demand the release of members who had been interned.[68]

Security and political stability in Canada were of concern not only to Canadian authorities but to the British as well. The war in Europe was going badly. France had fallen, and Dunkirk demonstrated, in terms of preparation, the weakness in Allied strategy. There was every indication the Germans were planning a channel crossing and the war in the Middle East was entering a difficult stage. In view of the situation, great importance was attached to North American opinion, especially in Canada – "the arsenal of the Empire." British officials thought it advisable to consolidate opinion there, sending Ministry of Information propagandists, under the umbrella of the National Council for Education, to North America in 1940.

British preoccupation with Canadian developments centred not only on creating a sympathetic environment toward the British war effort but also on alerting Canadian officials to potential domestic security threats. The perceived security risk posed by Ukrainian Canadian nationalists was high on the list, and intelligence gathered through British consular offices was communicated to Canadian authorities.

According to the reports, at least five organisations were thought to be "reactionary," if not outright "fascist," while just as many newspapers were alleged to have "fascist leanings."[69] The Ukrainian monarchist group, the UHO, with its contacts in Berlin was considered the most menacing. Suspicious of the worst, the British cautioned External Affairs, through their Washington chancery, that members of the group who were "active in the Canadian Red Cross [had to] be watched for fifth-column activity" and advised that the use of their halls for purposes of alien registration was nothing short of dangerous.[70] The Dominion Office also made clear through Canada House that the United Kingdom government could only foresee trouble if Wasyl Swystun, of the UNF, were to arrive in England, where he was proposing to travel. On the basis of Polish intelligence and given Swystun's European political connections, Canadian authorities had to be "warned ... with a view to his being refused facilities to proceed to England."[71]

Skelton passed on this information, as well as press reports of alleged Ukrainian sabotage in the United States, to the RCMP.[72] The undersecretary, however, chose to reserve judgment, for his own impression of Swystun, for example, was quite "favourable." Indeed, although he was not prepared to say whether Swystun's first loyalty was to Canada or an independent Ukraine, neither was he willing to accept, uncritically, Polish evidence against the leaders or policies of the Ukrainian national movement, which coloured the British reports.

For a few brief months [Ukrainian nationalists] saw in the establishment of an autonomous Sub-Carpathian Ukraine the promise [of] their more ambitious program for reuniting parts of the Ukraine under Poland and under the USSR with what had been under Czechoslovakia appreciably nearer fulfilment. When Germany handed over the autonomous Ukrainian Republic to Hungary, Ukrainian nationalists all over the world suffered a great let down. They recognised that their faith in German policy had been misplaced. Swystun's speeches, made in the months after Munich, did not read very much better than most other political speeches made in that period. However, it should be remembered that when Ukrainians were rejoicing in the break up of Czechoslovakia because it led to the establishment of Ruthenia, the Poles were equally complacent and equally grateful to Germany for the opportunity it had given them to seize Teschen.[73]

Skelton felt that it was inadvisable to take any precipitous action to proscribe the activities of Ukrainian nationalist organisations "either here or in London," at the insistence of Polish authorities. Skelton's own view of British intelligence, with its unabashed pro-Polish orientation, was that it was highly speculative and unreliable. Any premature action, therefore, would have been inappropriate and potentially dangerous. Indeed, reports from the Canadian Censorship Co-ordination Committee corroborated Skelton's assessment of the situation: Canadian Censorship showed strong disagreement with the British in matters of interpretation and opinion. Inclined to accept the views of the Canadian censors, if only because they appeared "to be based both on firmer ground and a more complete understanding of the details," Skelton nevertheless remained cautious.[74] For one thing, there was disturbing confidential information coming from a source within the community.[75] More distressing, however, was an interview granted by the high-ranking American-Ukrainian Catholic heirarch, Bishop Ivan Buchko, which had appeared in the Ukrainian Canadian publication *Trident*, causing considerable excitement among the nationalist community with its discussion of Ukraine and Allied war aims and objectives.[76]

Adding to an already testy and fractious debate among the competing nationalist organisations, Buchko's statement, from the government perspective, was an unwelcome development. Professor George Simpson of the University of Saskatchewan, an adviser and specialist on Ukrainian affairs working closely with the Canadian government, wrote to the cleric with the hope of convincing him to issue a retraction and thereby stem the tide of further controversy. Indeed, Simpson, an occasional advocate of the Ukrainian cause, fully expected that, in light of his high personal esteem within the community, he would have some influence.

In his letter, the academic Simpson spoke of his concern that the bishop, to whom many of the Ukrainian Catholic faithful looked for leadership, had reduced the global conflict to simple "power politics," and he criticised him for not recognising that the matter went beyond that. In Simpson's opinion, the issue was more fundamental. Hitler was imposing a form of rule on Europe that threatened the very principles of liberal democracy as represented by the English-speaking nations. Consequently, in this desperate hour, when the Allies were defending the core values of Western civilisation, he was hard pressed to understand how the bishop could dismiss the struggle as merely "a matter of prestige." Nor could Simpson see how such views could be reconciled with the ideal of a democratic and independent Ukraine:

You state elsewhere that England has no interest in the Ukraine. If you mean by this that the freeing of the Ukraine is not among the expressed war aims of Great Britain, as is the freeing of Norway, France, Holland etc. you are correct. You should know, however, that the British and Canadian governments are very much interested in the Ukrainian Question. At any time they can make that interest a matter of active policy. Indeed, England is the only Great Power whose interest would not mean subjection, as is the policy and practice of Germany.

The views of Hitler and his party regarding the inferiority of all Slavs is well known. Hence it is our belief here in Canada, that only a victory of England over Germany, offers any prospect for a free Ukraine in Europe. The Ukrainians in Canada are constantly working for that end. One of the greatest difficulties which they experience is the fact that the freeing of the Ukraine is so commonly associated with German intrigue and German ambition. The enemies of Ukrainian freedom are, of course, constantly on the watch in the attempt to connect Ukrainian patriotism with German propaganda. It was, therefore, in my opinion, most regrettable that your views regarding England could be construed indirectly in this way, since no less a person than Hitler himself used the expression "Senseless" in referring to the continuation of the struggle.[77]

Simpson expressed regret over the bishop's insinuation that England preferred to see the Soviet Union continue to exist as a unified state. England, claimed Simpson, had always supported the principle of nationality on the continent. And while he conceded that mistakes in carrying out this policy had been made, Simpson wished to impress upon Buchko that England had historically demonstrated "goodwill" to other peoples. This principle of goodwill was evident in its relationship with many of its colonies, a principle, Simpson noted, that allowed members of the Commonwealth to unite in free association with one another in defence of freedom and peace. Moreover, "If Europe is to be stabilised in the future," Simpson added, "then there is no other principle which offers the hope of united national freedom for every people with common action to maintain security and protection."

The Catholic hierarch, however, was not easily persuaded by Simpson's arguments. Buchko apologised – albeit perfunctorily – for the distress he had caused Simpson, a recognised and respected friend of the Ukrainian people, but he emphasized that his characterisation of the war as "senseless" was motivated first and foremost by his pacifism and a duty to his God. Furthermore, opposition to the war did not necessarily mean that he neglected to take into account the effects of the German occupation in Europe. On the contrary, the bishop pointed out, he was only too aware of the nature of German policy, because he had claimed that from the standpoint of the Ukrainian people, their position had worsened, being menaced directly by the prospect of "physical extermination." He acknowledged that Ukrainians had unfortunately been convinced at one time that a new war would bring them liberty, "but today, as we see, war [has] brought them only greater subjugation." It was from this perspective, he stressed, that his statement on the detrimental character of the war had been made.

As for the "goodwill" of England and its support for the principle of national self-determination, this was a moot point. "It is true,"

Buchko maintained, "that the Germans not a few times profited by the Ukrainian problem in order that they could arouse sympathy for themselves. But it is also true that England could have done the same but neglected to do so. England's alliance with Russia in the [Great] War and her alliance with Poland in the present war have prevented the Ukrainians from expecting any aid from her in their aspirations for a rebirth of their country. Today we have learned from that experience. We [also] know well that Hitler will not give Ukraine freedom, and his propaganda, although the loudest, no longer interests Ukrainians." Buchko concluded that the present silence of Britain spoke for itself, just as it did when millions died in the grip of Stalin's famine-terror, and Ukraine – "a voice crying in the wilderness" – had been abandoned by those who were busy administering their own interests. Then as now, "We know that we have been left alone in a warring world."[78] Simpson did not reply.

Within the community the clamour for organisational unity was steadily growing. Sensing this, Kaye-Kisilevsky, who had until this time been heading up the Ukrainian Press Bureau in London, returned to Canada hoping to negotiate a settlement between the two principal nationalist factions. In correspondence with a close friend and confidant, Tracy Philipps, Kaye wrote that at the grass-roots level Ukrainian Canadians were demanding the formation of a single and authoritative representative body and that there would be much resentment if the various organisational leaders did not set aside their personal ambitions.[79] Kaye spoke of his efforts during a recent speaking tour to persuade these leaders and others that the acrimonious debates were unproductive.[80] He remained sceptical, however, about the future, given the various personalities. If the leadership failed to recognise the importance of the moment, Kaye concluded, as in the last war, "events will pass over their heads – with all of its consequences."[81]

Philipps was familiar with the Ukrainian question in Europe and with the situation among Ukrainians in Canada. He had worked in Eastern Europe and Ukraine, in particular, after the war as a relief commissioner under Fridtjof Nansen, and his acquired interest in Ukraine had resulted in a close association with Kaye, who had completed graduate work at the University of London.[82] Moreover, Philipps, who had been sent to the North American side of the Atlantic to work among labour groups for the British Ministry of Information, was kept abreast of developments in the community by Kaye. Consequently, when Sir Edward Beatty of the Canadian National Railway's Department of Colonisation, with whom Philipps had been in contact on the issue of war information, proposed at the conclusion of a speaking tour Philipps had undertaken among ethnic labour groups that he consider another tour aimed specifically at Ukrainian Canadians, Philipps accepted. The purpose was to do a more detailed study of the Ukrainian situation in Canada for the government.[83]

Philipps' quasi-private status and his personal contacts among the Ukrainian leadership, which he had cultivated through the course of his earlier speaking engagements across the Prairies, made him a perfect candidate for the undertaking. But more importantly, having learned of the proposal, Philipps was directly encouraged by both the Department of National War Services and the Department of External Affairs, each recognising it as a possible opportunity to build consensus in the group and temper some of the more "extreme" views within the community. Kaye, who was informed of the initiative, indicated to Philipps that he could count on his assistance in developing contacts and providing further information on conditions if required.

Philipps embarked on the tour in late September under the auspices of both the Ukrainian Catholic Church and the Association of Canadian Clubs. The church, knowing Philipps as an individual who in the past had expressed solidarity with the Ukrainian struggle, had invited him earlier in August to present a series of lectures on the political situation in Eastern Europe. The invitation, therefore, was fortuitous, offering the guise of a community initiative while masking government involvement. From the outset the tour was a success. The public received Philipps with enthusiasm, his lectures drawing huge crowds. Press coverage was also extensive, given the unusually large audiences that gathered wherever he went.[84] However, Philipps, who was personally satisfied with the public relations aspect of the tour, expressed disappointment with his inability to convince community leaders of the importance of community solidarity. The representatives with whom he met stressed that every effort had been made to reach an accommodation between the competing factions within the community, yet to date this goal had proved impossible to achieve. As for the future prospect of some sort of an agreement, he was told in so many words that it was unlikely.[85]

Philipps returned to Ottawa and reported his observations both to External Affairs and to the minister of national war services, the Honourable James Gardiner, who had an active interest in integrating ethnic communities into the mainstream of public opinion.[86] That Philipps was unable to bring about a settlement between the competing factions or to relay sufficiently to the leadership the importance that the government attached to the idea of bringing the divergent groups together was not unexpected, although it was disappointing.[87] Indeed, the Ukrainian issue, already an irritant on the diplomatic front, now threatened domestic war work as well, distracting wide sections of the population with its divisive discussion of European events. The agitation among Ukrainian Canadians was palpable and increasing with each passing week, leading Gardiner to conclude that the time had come "to have a Ukrainian 'on tap' as a barometer in Ottawa." It was felt that such a person would be useful if the political situation began to deteriorate completely.[88] Philipps, whose advice was sought, recommended Kaye for the position.

Unexpectedly, in mid-October, shortly after his initial tour, the Ukrainian Catholic Church offered to arrange a speaking itinerary for Philipps in the communities that had been missed in the first go-round. Norman Robertson of External Affairs and the associate deputy minister of national war services, Justice T.C. Davis, with both of whom Philipps had had long talks on the subject, saw the utility in continuing "this rather novel and favourable approach" and encouraged him to pursue the offer.[89] There was no way of knowing what the results would be. There was, however, nothing to lose and much to gain, especially if Philipps could finally convince the parties to quit their acrimonious debates and fall without condition squarely behind Canada's war effort.

The lectures were scheduled for early November, and, as was with the original tour, the public greeted Philipps warmly. The strong surge of interest, however, may have been caused by wild accounts circulating that hinted at the possibility of an announcement assuring some conditional support for the idea of limited autonomy for Ukrainians in Europe. Philipps, it was rumoured, had been designated by both the British and the Canadian governments to assess and gauge reaction at this time. In this regard, he was perceived not simply as working in a public information capacity but also as operating on behalf of the government. Among the organisations jockeying for political legitimacy, who sensed that an opportunity to be identified with the government initiative might lend prestige both to their organisations and to the policies they advocated within the community, there was a strong desire to be associated officially with the tour. Equally powerful was the fear that their rivals would outmanœuvre them to gain an advantage.[90] Every attempt, consequently, was made to curry favour with Philipps. Philipps not only rebuffed requests to appear under the sponsorship of one or the other group, on the pretext that he was not interested in further promoting sectional interests, but also upbraided them for their ambition, threatening to cancel the tour and publicise his reasons for doing so.[91]

Philipps' rejection had an extraordinary effect. Because they were under intense pressure but also because they feared political isolation, when Philipps suggested that a meeting of representatives from the various Ukrainian organisations take place for the purpose of discussing their role in how best to promote the Ukrainian interest, the proposal was accepted.[92] A closed session was scheduled for 6 November in Winnipeg. Phillips offered to address the group.

In preparation for the deliberations, Philipps, along with George Simpson, who also had been invited, spoke to the participants at a private luncheon. It was a chance opportunity. With full knowledge that a similar situation was not likely to arise, Philipps and Simpson not only spoke of "the local advantages" that unity could bring but emphasised the possibility of reinforcing those general principles and war objectives, which only unity could confer, and emphasised also that as British subjects they were in a position to exert some influence.[93] Philipps had attempted to impress upon the nationalist leadership that whether they helped or hindered the cause of Ukrainian independence would depend on their attitude to the war. By working for Canada, they would, in the end, help Ukraine.

Although they were anxious to make some progress, the two mediators had no apparent effect on the body. The discussions of 6 November had stalled, the seemingly minor differences among the parties masking the deeper divisions that had their origins in past accusations and the political uncertainty that might result from unsatisfactory negotiations.[94] The following day, deliberations proved only slightly more promising. With time running out and sensing an opportunity might be missed, Philipps, who, along with Simpson, had been called upon to arbitrate, abandoned all pretence. Hoping to break the impasse, he showed them numerous official and confidential documents from Ottawa and London with reference to his mission among Ukrainian Canadians. He made it clear that the Allied governments had more than a passing interest in Ukrainian Canadian affairs, which made unity among Ukrainian Canadians paramount.[95] Stunned by the revelations and hoping not to provoke the government unnecessarily, the parties in attendance were inclined to put aside their differences. Indeed, although Philipps' exact status remained something of a "mystery" to them, the evidence suggested there was risk in ignoring the government's interest.[96] After some difficult last-minute wrangling and negotiation over the distribution of executive posts, the parties agreed to come together under the name Ukrainian Canadian Committee (ucc). The final representation was varied and included republicans, monarchists, liberals, and socialists – all those with a perspective that at least called for an independent and sovereign Ukraine.

The creation of the ucc and public reaction to the tour, which now continued under the sponsorship of the new group, were being closely watched by both the Department of National War Services and External

Affairs.[97] Burianyk and others who were in contact with the government declared the matter an unequivocal success, the community's reaction to recent developments being characterised as enitrely positive.[98] Justice T.C. Davis, pleased with the results, indicated to Norman Robertson at External Affairs that if nothing else came of the exercise, "at least Ukrainians were now under one roof" and the "Ukrainian problem" could be dealt with more easily.[99] Indeed, it was thought that a newly proposed interdepartmental committee that was assigned the task of developing policies and initiatives aimed at the "foreign elements" – policies that would help cultivate and nurture "a proper attitude" towards Canada and the war – would have an easier time of it, at least in relation to the "Ukrainian problem," now that a united committee was in place.[100]

Officials in Ottawa roundly congratulated Philipps for his excellent work.[101] He remained, however, something of an enigma. Having come highly recommended by British authorities with seemingly impeccable credentials, he inexplicably appeared to hold some unorthodox views, especially as they pertained to the broad political objectives of British foreign policy in Eastern Europe.[102] Confidential letters concerning Philipps' views – made known during the course of his tour – were sent circuitously to senior officials in External Affairs and National War Services for their information.[103] Various officials reacted differently to the reports.

O.D. Skelton chose to disbelieve the accounts, suggesting that they treated questions of high policy rather light-heartedly and doubting very much whether Philipps would have agreed with the statements as presented.[104] Judge Davis at National War Services was more circumspect. Rumour had it that Philipps "suggested that the British government should now announce its postwar policies with respect to the Ukraine and that the Canadian government might desire to present views to the British government with respect to this policy, and ... that perhaps the Ukrainians of Canada might make representations to the Canadian government with this thing in view."[105] This was a matter not to be treated lightly. Through an intermediary, Davis instructed Philipps to make no further public or private, direct or indirect statements along these lines. "I pointed out to him the difficulty the British government was in due to the neutrality of Russia [and that] an independent Ukraine must be carved out of Russia. It is clear that nothing could advisably be said about this matter at this stage in the war."[106]

Philipps, stung by the inference that he had somehow committed a transgression, responded indirectly by stating that with regard to policy he emphasised no other except the one that encouraged Ukrainian Canadians to unite and pull alongside their fellow Canadians to win the war. Besides, the British people could ill afford, under the circumstances, to have another war on their hands, especially since the Soviet Union was, in practice, neutral. Since this argument was self-evident, he did not believe it was necessary to state it. However, since the matter had been raised, he did feel it was necessary to point out that long-term political strategizing was often ignored by policymakers and had become one of "the weakest points" of the war. British policy on the Ukrainian question was a case in point that, according to Phillips, had tremendous implications for cultivating among Ukrainian Canadians the right attitude towards the war and the war effort. Because of its wider importance, Philipps felt compelled to outline his views at length.[107]

Philipps began by indicating that whatever policy was adopted toward the Ukrainian question it had to be based on sound and logical propositions. He believed this desideratum also applied in relation to the Polish and Soviet positions, which equally impinged on British policy in Eastern Europe. Unfortunately, he claimed, sentimentality appeared to be the cornerstone in British thinking and policy in the region. As he argued, it was unfortunate, but usually the case, that the British who spoke either Polish or Russian were inclined to identify with one or the other linguistic community and that this predilection often translated into political prejudice, which often translated, in turn, into short-sightedness. It was insufficiently recognised, Philipps argued, that on the question of the status of the European nations in the Russian Empire, tsarist Russian émigrés were "solid" with the Soviet government in their opposition to Ukrainian self-determination, a perspective, he suggested, that was shared by the Poles. According to Philipps, these attitudes were misleading and therefore dangerous, in that their influence on the way policy was being formulated jeopardised genuine British interests in the region.[108]

In Philipps' opinion, one had to be clear about realities as well as possibilities. There was no escaping the fact that the peoples of Europe were being told that the Allies "were fighting against aggressive and suppressive tyranny and for the rights of nations to organise themselves as independent units." As a general principle, this presumably applied to Ukrainians as well, a strategically located population whose patriotism was reaching a level of "burning mysticism." More to the point, however, if that patriotism were properly channelled, it could work actively for the benefit of the liberal democracies. According to Philipps, the potential dividends were enormous. The alternative, on the other hand, was that Hitler could offer the Ukrainians

"a Danish-type independence" ... something far more advanced than their present political serfdom under Moscow. If he were successful, he could draw from fifty million Ukrainians labourers and soldiers both to develop and protect Ukraine. So far there has been no response. For the British peoples, the logical development would spell misfortune ... If, in Europe, Ukrainians have no hope of any other support, it is not unreasonable to suppose that the German proposition will at least receive careful consideration. It is clear that, if Moscow remains neutral in fact, Britain is in no position to offer hope for Ukraine. But this does not excuse us from planning beforehand for all eventualities.[109]

As for the argument that the Allies were fighting for the right of nations to organise themselves along national lines, Philipps considered it to be both morally wrong and politically imprudent to pretend to Ukrainians that the British peoples were in a position to implement that principle. However, since the war was being conducted on this very premise, there could be no avoiding the fact that in the end the Allies would eventually have to face up to their declarations. Indeed, political justice was one of the central themes that Ukrainian Canadians were advancing, in the hope of achieving recognition for Ukraine's claim to independence. If this was a conflict about freedom, then surely, they claimed, Ukrainians were entitled to determine their own future. He concluded that because they had no national state of their own, dependence was forced on them by other nations that, both in the past and in the present, were determined to assimilate them by discrimination and by force. This dependence, Philipps argued, explained the Ukrainian personality – the "inferiority complexes" that made for what he described as "difficult characters." The point, however, was that if they were just left alone, they would feel neglected and alienated, and they would eventually become despised. "If they feel neglected, their Old Country patriotism will tend to supply the loyalties and whatever else British Canadians may not always realise to be the things for which, with such temperaments and antecedents, the oppressed and transplanted peoples always yearn."[110]

This was an unusual statement – certainly not one that normally would have been expected from a former British public servant. But Justice Davis, who had received a copy of Philipps' remarks, was nevertheless satisfied with them.[111] Philipps' implicit recognition of the British and, more generally, the Allied position was perceived to be sufficient, enabling Davis to gloss over Philipps' other remarks and to consider them as nothing more than hypothetical musings.

The success of Philipps' tour and the positive community response prompted several individuals and groups, including the UCC, to express their appreciation to government officials. In a conversation with the under-secretary of state for external affairs, W. Swystun, the representative for the UNF on the UCC executive, indicated that the new committee was working well. When asked about the Ukrainian monarchists who were still of some concern to the RCMP, Swystun replied that although he had initially doubted the wisdom of including them, they had proven to be a loyal and positive force. He did, however, qualify that observation by stating that he was still "inclined to keep an eye on them and make sure that they lived up to their new professions."[112] As regards the policy of the UCC on the Ukrainian question, Swystun stated that all members of the executive realised that it was not "feasible" at the moment to try to influence British policy in Eastern Europe. But the idea remained, and at the appropriate time Ukrainian Canadians would press this objective with the Canadian government. For Skelton, whose expectations for the committee were high, it was not a propitious beginning. The only consolation was that an independent Ukraine appeared to be secondary to their interests as Canadians.

Meanwhile, Justice T.C. Davis had asked Philipps to prepare a report at the conclusion of the tour on the Ukrainian Canadian community. More broadly still, Philipps was asked to submit recommendations on how best to deal with the group.[113] For Philipps, the requests offered an opportunity to organise and elaborate on some of his thoughts about immigrant integration and nation building and the significance of both for national security. In his report, Philipps began with the assertion that the "Europeanism" of Ukrainian Canadians was both pervasive and persistent, the result of the pull of events in Europe. He cautioned, however, that these events were at the centre of attention of everyone, not only the Ukrainian Canadians. It was, therefore, a mistake to suggest that this problem was endemic to the group. It was equally unfair to assume that the "Europeanism" of the group could be addressed without formulating a policy that acknowledged their concerns or, at least, included an understanding of what was required to draw them into the mainstream of national opinion.

In an age of constantly shifting and uncertain allegiances, one of the central tasks confronting modern states, Philipps believed, was to make the processes of national and social integration more effective. In the case of Canada, this task would depend on the effort and sincerity of Canada's leadership in promoting the values associated with the Anglo-American liberal-democratic tradition. Philipps felt that only through a commitment to the rule of law and individual political and social rights could the underlying tensions, which were common to all the great immigrant nations, be resolved. He argued that a liberal belief system, inclusive and accepting of differences, was the only foundation, under the circumstances, upon which a new and lasting civic culture could be built. And yet Philipps understood that pluralism, which accompanied individual rights and underpinned liberal ideology, was potentially divisive. Therefore, he encouraged parallel support for a national conception of community, one that emphasised the country's unique history, distinctive traditions, and ultimately liberal ethos. Indeed, a corporate or national vision was required to strengthen those societies that had to accommodate differences. It was his view that failure to promote policies that aimed at reinforcing a corporate, but liberal, understanding of society would result in a country that was culturally separated and racially divided. Hence, among his recommendations Philipps not only proposed a program of civic education that focused on political rights and obligations, a campaign to nurture social and cultural tolerance, and legislation to combat discriminatory practices in the workplace, but he also called for increased efforts at raising historical awareness among Canadians and, through public information, providing a Canadian perspective on events and issues.

Central to this project, according to Phillips, was the need to reflect the experiences of a culturally and socially diverse people in policies that had as their goal the building of a nation. It was absurd to think, he claimed, that these policies could be ignored or dismissed or to believe that political solutions could succeed without duly acknowledging a people's expectations and desires. Indeed, the idea of a community would be accepted only when the citizens who were asked to participate saw something of themselves in the fabric of the country. If they were used in the shaping of policy, their experiences would serve as reference points in their patriotic acceptance of Canada and in their evolution as citizens.

For Philipps this approach had practical implications. He suggested, for instance, that in the case of Ukrainian Canadian labour, those on the left but not aligned with the CPC should be encouraged to fill the vacuum created by the ban placed on the Ukrainian Labour Farmer Temple Association. He pointed to the "Lobayists" – former CPC members who had broken with the leadership on the nationalities question in the USSR – as the ideal element to be cultivated, a group whose labour orientation could potentially draw Ukrainian supporters away from the Communist Party, which continued to work actively against the war.[114] In this regard, Philipps advocated the use of the sequestered halls – familiar community institutions – to enable "ethnic labour to speak to ethnic labour." Indeed, according to Philipps, now more than ever it was necessary to cultivate, not alienate, labour. Moreover, given the significant involvement of Ukrainian Canadians in war industries and food production and the obvious security implications, Canada could ill afford to ignore their contribution and needs.

From Philipps' perspective, the issue of security was also fundamentally tied to loyalty. It was often assumed that security could ultimately be achieved only through the power of the state. But as Philipps argued, if a genuine and effective security were to be realised, it had to emanate from within a community, when members of the community freely assumed responsibility for each other and sectional interests were subordinated or set aside for the good of the whole. The security of the nation, in essence, could be assured only when individuals saw the necessity of the tasks at hand and the importance of each other's contribution in the work ahead. Among labour and the foreign-born element this could occur only when working men spoke to working men, immigrants shared their experiences with other immigrants, and political interests were voluntarily put aside for the sake of the common good. Predicated on a profound sense of mutual interest – "the stuff of nations" – genuine security would be based on cooperation, tolerance, and accommodation. It would have to begin with the community but would ultimately be nurtured during this "transitional" period by an unprejudiced and broadminded government, committed to a program of citizenship through education.

It followed logically, Philipps concluded, that the government's recent indirect intervention, through his efforts, into the affairs of the loyal but obstreperous Ukrainian Canadian community was a mistake. He considered the method applied in uniting the Ukrainian organisations altogether "unsatisfactory" and believed the artificial character of the coalition would eventually be its own undoing. He was convinced that unresolved tensions would allow the situation to simmer, if only because those involved failed to appreciate the political significance of the wider conflict and the consequences of their actions. Philipps advised against further "surgical interventions" of this sort in tempering other group or interethnic rivalries. As for the future of the UCC, Philipps was not optimistic. It would have "to be brought along" and "nursed" to survive.

Alongside these domestic considerations, there was, in Philipps' opinion, a foreign-policy dimension that directly affected the process of nation building. As Philipps observed, in the current conflict there was the unfortunate tendency among the Allies to issue statements about war aims and objectives that served only to confuse and distract those who hoped for some solution to the difficulties that faced their ancestral homes. On the one hand, the struggle, it was declared, was about freedom. Yet in practice it was discovered to be about freedom that had recently been lost and not about freedom that would necessarily be extended to others. Freedom was to be restored to those who had been deprived of their liberty; others would have to demonstrate they had earned it. From Canada's perspective, it was an awkward predicament. Did Canada stand for the liberal definition of freedom with an eye to the future, or did it support the narrow definition with an emphasis on the past? In Philipps' estimation, for Canadian policymakers interested in consolidating opinion around the democratic institutions of the country, the former was the only real alternative. And the conduct and objectives of Canadian foreign policy needed to follow the logic of this orientation more closely.

To be sure there were constraints. There was, for instance, Britain's support for the restoration of Poland within its prewar frontiers. But this commitment, Philipps argued, could only be made at the expense of the Ukrainians. Hence the conundrum. Either the struggle with fascism was in support of the principle of freedom, or it was not. With its large number of citizens of Ukrainian ethnic origin, Philipps felt that Canada could ill afford to ignore entirely their concerns and desires, especially since they were set within the parameters of the publicly stated Allied objective in the struggle. The implications for Canada and its ability to promote certain values that would resonate with a people who were in many ways outside the nation were profound. In the end, Philipps argued that support, at least in principle, for Ukrainian sovereignty was both politically logical and morally right. It may even have been strategically necessary as well, since events were moving ahead of the Allies, who were without an adequate plan.

What positive and constructive plan has so far been proposed by the Allies (the British peoples, Dutch, Poles, Norwegians, Czechs, etc.) to heal the breach and to close a most disunited front in the vital area between the Russian empire and Germany? Since 1939, any pro-Ally feeling among those important intermediate peoples is being cunningly disunited or annihilated.

In 1939 the Germans seized two Ukrainian ethnic areas. The Germans' allies, the Hungarians, seized another. This million-odd of Ukrainians, now in their hands, are being actively favoured and politically exploited by the Hungarians against the Russians and by the Germans against the Poles. The promised Ukrainian State is called the "Danish pattern." This model is the least oppressive of the German protectorates. It would not touch Germany, but it would put the Poles between the pincers. Neither the Poles nor the British appear yet to have constructed any positive counter-policy.

When the Russians seized half of Poland, they also occupied eastern Galicia (Western Ukraine). Here Ukrainians are in a solid majority over the Poles. It is only incidental that this was also the old Ukrainian kingdom of Galicia-Volhynia (capital Halich).

Contingent on victory, the Allies have already guaranteed that the Poles shall be an independent nation. This can now, in any case, only be at the expense of the imperialistic aggressions of the Russians. But it will be no more at their expense than was in 1918 the freeing of the Baltics, the Ukrainian Republic and Finland. These countries were (and are) no more inhabited by Russians than France is by Germans or China by Japanese.

Uncomfortable as it may be, there are overwhelmingly more Ukrainians in Europe than Poles. If, within the existing Allied undertaking to the Poles, the Poles themselves were to guarantee the full freedom of "Western Ukraine," even on the Curzon Line, they would thus at least be showing the way for some common ground to begin to reduce the deep Ukrainian distrust of them, towards a less wholly disunited front.[115]

Philipps' report and, in particular, his views on the Ukrainian question, again, surprisingly, did not produce a reaction. Justice Davis and other officials were more impressed with his recommendations on countering the influence of the CPC, choosing to ignore and treat as benign some of his other policy prescriptions, specifically those dealing with foreign policy. Besides, he had already indicated elsewhere that, as far as Allied policy in Eastern Europe was concerned, war with the Soviet Union was out of the question.[116]

A month after his report had been submitted, Philipps repeated many of his recommendations in a follow-up memorandum to Justice Davis. He also asked at the time for some clarification of his status in light of both the government's initiative with respect to the Ukrainian Canadian community and the deputy minister's own proposal to set up a government-sponsored organisation that would liase with "foreign language" groups. Philipps expressed the view that a "technical specialist," most logically attached to the Department of External Affairs, should handle the matter.[117] Understandably, Philipps had himself in mind for the position.

Davis, who favoured the idea of creating an organisation that would deal with ethnic affairs, believed there was room to accommodate Philipps as a "technical" assistant. Discussions were therefore initiated in January to have him appointed to the RCMP as an adviser in the Department of Justice, intimating to some degree the role expected of him. Philipps, in turn, aware that he was being considered for a position with the RCMP, began to offer advice to the agency with a view to influencing policy. He reiterated the importance of constructively using the sequestered halls to draw traditional Ukrainian support away from the Communist Party. The halls, he thought, might nominally come under the jurisdiction of the recently created umbrella committee, the UCC, but they should be used by labour only to reinforce a Canadian perspective.[118] He was opposed to having them turned over to individual nationalist organisations, a counter-productive move and most certainly an invitation to trouble.[119]

Government officials initially favoured Philipps' idea of having the halls come within the scope of the UCC, but the economics of maintaining the buildings led to a decision to dispose of them through judicial sales.[120] Once up for sale, a number were immediately purchased by nationalist organisations. Philipps predicted a disaster and immediately set about trying to convince the authorities and others who could influence the government to block further sales.[121] His appeals, however, had little effect. The halls continued to be sold.

Philipps' apprehension was well founded. As soon as the Ukrainian National Federation had acquired the flagship ULFTA hall in Toronto and requested an operating license from the municipal government, the organisation was denounced before the Toronto Board of Police Commissioners as a body with fascist proclivities.[122] The UNF executive denied the charge, but the Toronto Police Commission decided in favour of a probe after the city mayor publicly declared, in response to pressure from the press, that no "subversive element" would be tolerated. The dispute had also reached the front pages of the major dailies in Toronto and later became the subject of editorials. Philipps felt inclined to intervene, since wanton and irresponsible editorialising, such as that of the *Globe and Mail*, served only "to create an atmosphere [of] mutual distrust and racial resentment between Canadians on obsolete issues."[123]

Eventually, invited to speak before the police commission, Philipps tried to diffuse the situation. Only after reviewing the politics of the community with them was he able to convince board members to wait until a federal policy was in place upon which decisions could only then reasonably be made. Philipps encouraged Justice Davis to follow up and consolidate opinion on the commission by impressing upon them that policy coordination at the provincial, municipal, and federal levels was essential in such matters. Philipps also stated his concern to Davis that under the threat of these attacks the UCC would disintegrate if "no signs of satisfaction or guidance" were given. Philipps felt that he was not in a position to offer specific advice about what government measures should be taken to settle some of the immediate problems. But he did state that the difficulties that faced authorities would have to be addressed by a comprehensive policy and that any further delay in this regard would mean that the work completed to date would come undone.[124]

Privately, Philipps was concerned and increasingly frustrated with the lack of an adequate response.[125] This was not, however, due to a lack of political desire. Justice Davis recognised the importance of keeping the UCC afloat, but for the moment he could only authorise a telegram to be sent to the executive of the UCC stating that "its continued functioning [was] very much in the national interest."[126] Developments in Toronto, nevertheless, were significant enough to convince him of the need to bring Philipps on line as an adviser. When he was formally approached to work for the government on contract, Philipps accepted and was immediately attached to the RCMP, as a European specialist in the Department of Justice, and directed to work with the objectives of the agency in mind.[127]

Despite his connection with the RCMP, an agency with its own particular orientation and objectives, Philipps did not retreat from his original ideas, emphasising that the questions of security, whether national or hemispheric, had to be addressed globally. That the interests of the Department of Justice, with its emphasis on public security, had to be taken into consideration was obvious. But as Philipps would repeat, it was equally clear that External Affairs alone was in a position to provide advice and direction. For instance, the leadership within the Ukrainian Canadian community, Philipps claimed, was already looking to the department for guidance. And although the natural tendency was simply to ignore them, he cautioned against doing so, given the contribution of ethnic labour to the war effort and the potential effect of German propaganda on Canada's ethnic groups. Equally important, there was also the need to consider the wider consequences of how German propaganda would affect the promotion of those values needed to acculturate the many diverse groups and bring them into the mainstream of Canadian national life.[128] In Philipps' opinion, this issue was important, since "the march of events on the continent of Europe" threatened to bring the situation to a head, and in the confusion to follow – when old allegiances would be competing with new loyalties – only a Canada secure in its identity and in its knowledge of its purpose could prevail.

[The situation] arises from the inevitable rekindling in Canada of European nationalisms. Under the threat of calamity to their Old Countries and to their brethren in it, old Anglo-Canadians as well as new Ukrainian Canadians are more than ever before looking anxiously over their shoulders towards the lands where their race was bred. These are among the oldest and deepest of human emotions. Any counter-mysticism has also to be partly in the realm of the emotions, for Canada.[129]

Information from the continent was contradictory and unreliable. In view of the reports that Germany was preparing an invasion of the

Soviet Union, British officials, wary of the aspirations of Ukrainian nationalists, nevertheless felt compelled to monitor the opinion and the activity of Ukrainian émigré groups. Indeed, the belief was that Germany was not above using the Ukrainian factor as a way to advance its interests, and it was thought that the activity of Ukrainian nationalists overseas might offer some evidence about whether this was in fact the case. British diplomats in North America and elsewhere were consequently instructed to gather information. Reports were subsequently compiled and sent back to London, with British consular officials in the United States providing the most critical assessments. Believing this intelligence might be of use to Canadian authorities, the reports were passed on for their information.

Several of the reports were scrutinised by Philipps, who, in a detailed analysis, demonstrated the shortcomings of the interpretations provided by Britain's diplomats.[130] For Philipps the more critical question, which he posed rather rhetorically, was why now the sudden interest in Ukrainians? He explained, "Owing to the fight for existence, the English-speaking peoples are discovering in a key position an unknown nation in which they refused to be interested, and which they still refuse to interest in our cause. What we need to know is what in practice, is being done about it, if anything." The guiding war aims of the Allies, according to Philipps, were fundamentally conditioned by the principle of political self-determination. That principle, he pointed out, was precisely what Ukrainians were seeking to achieve. He argued:

We cannot now honestly (or safely) pretend that our declarations mean that we are out to help only our nearest and strategically useful neighbours, and … God help the rest.

From the day of the British guarantee to Poland, it has been clear that the Ukrainians are the main key to the relations between the Russians' and the Prussians' empires who are allied against us. The reality of these relations is vital to us. If our declarations are true, then no new promise is necessary for Ukrainians. If we have the courage to be clear and to dissipate doubts of the clarity and sincerity of our declarations, which in the last war did our reputation so much deadly damage among the peoples of the Near East, such as the Jews and Arabs, Bulgars (Neuilly) and Turks (Sevres), we shall not have to make voluminous reports about Ukrainians as potential enemies or at least as doubtful friends. It is in light of this background that such reports as this now have to be read.

The point is that, within the last few years, disillusion and repression and suffering have fired a people of nearly fifty millions with a militant mysticism of nationhood such as united the divided peoples of Italy and Germany in the last generation. It may be inconvenient, but merely to deplore it is futile. For us, at war for our life, that is not even the question. The point is as to how, in practice, to prevent this new and burning nationalism from being a danger to us. Much more than that, how can we harmonise their Cause with ours and canalise it to help generate more power for the Cause of the English-speaking peoples, of whom a million and a half Ukrainians of North America are now a part.

Norman Robertson, who replaced O.D. Skelton as under-secretary of state for external affairs following the latter's sudden and untimely death on 28 January 1941, approached the same British reports with an equal amount of distrust and scepticism as Philipps, but only with regard to the quality of the intelligence. Having perused the reports, he explained to Commissioner Wood of the RCMP, "I suspect that most of the United Kingdom information about Ukrainian movements and personalities comes, naturally enough, from quasi-Polish sources. This origin does not discredit it but does suggest the need for a close countercheck to balance the inescapable political bias which I have always found in any Polish appreciation of the Ukrainian Question."[131] In the same letter to the commissioner, however, Robertson also commented on Philipps' "weakness for mystification," which he believed served only to create "difficulties" for himself.

That Robertson would consider Philipps' views bewildering was no surprise. In view of the worsening European situation, constancy would be the watchword for the future and political determinacy the principle that, it was to be hoped, would see Canada through the difficult times ahead. Philipps, on the other hand, was suggesting and offering something entirely different, a strategy to cope with a world that was changing daily – and dramatically.

AN ASSESSMENT

When the political events surrounding the collapse of Czechoslovakia in 1939 had run their course, Western diplomats and analysts were not especially surprised by the outcome. There was, however, one unexpected twist, and that was Germany's unwillingness to offer the same guarantee of independence to the Carpatho-Ukrainian Republic that it had given to Slovakia on the dissolution of the Czechoslovak federation. That Germany would approve of the Hungarian annexation of the Carpatho-Ukraine was also somewhat puzzling, since among Western observers the Carpatho-Ukraine had long been interpreted as Germany's vantage point in its predicted drive to the East. Indeed, German intrigue was considered all along to be the invisible, yet guiding, hand behind the resurgence in Ukrainian political activity in Europe during the 1930s. Therefore, Germany's abandonment of the Carpatho-Ukrainian Republic left some observers who were concerned with such matters wondering about the future of German-Ukrainian relations. Those Ukrainians who had initially been hopeful were now persuaded that the professed German aim of a new European order based on the principle of national self-determination was false and that its intentions in the East could not be trusted.

Significantly, the disillusionment with Germany would lead various Ukrainians in the Western liberal democracies to declare later that the young defenders of the Carpatho-Ukrainian Republic were the first to die in the fight against fascism. Yet they were mistaken, because the sacrifices were not the result of a struggle *against* fascism but a result of the struggle *for* Ukrainian independence. It was a subtle yet important distinction, often obscured at the time by both the debate over political right and the need for legitimacy.

In some respects, the need to identify the Ukrainian independence struggle with the cause of the democratic nations was the result of a genuine reassessment of the perceived identity of interests existing between German revanchism and Ukrainian irredentism. However, for those Ukrainians in states that were quickly aligning themselves against Germany – including Canada – the "choice" was already predetermined by their civic responsibility and duty; the Carpatho-Ukrainian affair simply confirmed for them that the only prospect for an independent Ukraine was for Britain and its allies to emerge victorious. But neither was the choice onerous. The principles associated with liberal political democracy would ensure at the very least that Ukrainian claims to self-determination would be heard, while the sacrifices of the Carpathian defenders could be pointed to as the "first instalment" paid in the fight for liberty.[132] In any case, it was vitally important for Ukrainians in North America to create sympathy for the Ukrainian cause by equating in the public mind the Ukrainian independence struggle with that of the democratic nations against fascism. In due course, much energy would be expended in advancing this argument, a task made easier when, in August 1939, the Soviet Union aligned itself alongside Nazi Germany. The stage was set and the prospects for an independent Ukraine never seemed better.

Among those who had been caught off guard by what appeared to be a change in German policy on the Ukrainian question was O.D. Skelton. Skelton had long thought, as had other Western analysts, that the Ukrainian factor, the unknown variable in the Eastern European political equation, was something to be watched. For Canada, however, it had additional significance. The large Ukrainian Canadian population meant that an internal security dimension had to be considered. It was therefore something of a relief when the political drama unfolded as it did. In a memo to the prime minister dated April 1939 Skelton indicated that Germany's action in permitting Hungary to seize the Carpatho-Ukrainian Republic had had a sobering effect on Ukrainian attitudes toward German policy. Nevertheless, he cautioned that Ukrainian Canadians were "still hoping that out of the flux something [could] be done." Skelton's comment revealed his unease. For even though, as he himself noted, Ukrainian Canadian nationalists had lost "faith" in Hitler, he strongly believed that "it would be in the national interest to try to keep this large group from making trouble either abroad or at home."[133]

What concerned Skelton were not the political inclinations of the nationalists in Canada – Hitler had cured them of any illusions – but rather their persistence in putting forward the Ukrainian claim to national self-determination, hoping in the uncertainty of the moment to seize an opportunity to secure that claim. The problem, as Skelton and others pointed out, was that as long as the British looked toward Poland and the Soviet Union as allies, neither Britain nor Canada could be expected to encourage the Ukrainian separatist movement.[134]

Critically, the issue was not the prospect of future alliances, at least in the traditional sense of the word, as much as it was maintaining the status quo ante. The principal revisionist power in Europe was Nazi Germany, and since any change to the existing balance of European power relations would necessarily work to the detriment of both France and Britain, the race was on to contain Germany's efforts at restructuring the political map. Both powers, therefore, would look to the Soviet Union not as an ally with a common political vocabulary but as a state that in the 1930s had shown a keen interest in preserving the geopolitical balance. The irony, of course, was that once the Soviet Union participated in the partition of Poland, it would be seen to be part of the problem as much as part of the solution. Yet the hope was that the Soviet Union would come around to the side of the Allies. Consequently, it was felt that nothing overt should be done that might jeopardise the prospects of a future alliance.

As for Poland, by late September 1939 it no longer effectively existed as a European state. Therefore, the rationale behind Britain's continued support for the principle of Polish territorial sovereignty was not located in a need for a military or political alliance. Rather, the idea that underpinned Britain's support was the notion of reestablishing Europe's prewar geopolitical structure. And yet, paradoxically, British insistence on a return to prewar boundaries threatened the very relationship it sought to cultivate with the Soviet Union. The Soviet Union was by no means perceived to be a revisionist power, but its territorial aggrandisement, primarily at the expense of Poland, could not be accepted. To be sure, within British foreign policy circles there were those who agreed that the Soviet Union had a justifiable claim in wishing to see the reunification of the historic Ukrainian and Belorussian lands. But it was also acknowledged that a territorially reduced Poland would undercut the regional balance of power and ultimately undermine the Anglo-French position vis-à-vis their traditional European rival, Germany. The Polish position would have to be defended.

For Canada, the worsening climate of 1938–39 underscored the precarious, if not ambiguous, nature of its international role. Although the Imperial Conference of 1926 had effectively changed the character of the Anglo-Canadian relationship, especially in the conduct of foreign affairs, this change was more than balanced by Canada's cautious desire to retain the advantages of a British connection. Trade, commerce, and security were dividends that flowed from the historical association. But with dividends also came obligations, and with war on the horizon the price associated with the relationship would have to be paid. Still further yet, in the shadow of European uncertainty Canada also needed to pursue a line of policy not dissimilar to that of the other great English-speaking power, the United States; in moments of global distemper, strong friends were always useful and sometimes necessary. In short, the circumstances highlighted Canada's predicament and ultimately its role as a minor and marginal player in international politics. With war all but assured, Canada would necessarily look to Britain and America for the lead in foreign affairs.

And yet Canada was not convinced of the necessity of war. Indeed, in the context of the events of 1938–39, Canadian officials were placed in what one observer described as the unenviable role "of a spectator making pointed comments on a game in which his favourite team was losing, and into which he was apprehensive of being drawn in the clothes he wore."[135] Canada, like the United States, belonged to a group of nations who had little vested interest in the political developments that threatened to embroil Europe in another conflict. Canada wanted peace. But in its support for peace, it accepted the ideology of the status quo ante and perforce supported the position of the status quo powers.[136] In doing so, Canada would also accept the contradictions that accompanied the role.

That there were contradictions in the Allied position was more than evident, and these contradictions were pointed out on various occasions by Tracy Philipps (the European adviser to the Department of National War Services). Philipps argued that since Poland no longer existed as a European state, by necessity a resurrected Poland would have to be "carved" out of the Soviet Union. Moreover, the premise upon which such an action would have to be based was the principle of the sovereign rights of nations. But the dilemma was that the same principle had equal moral weight in the case of other nations not considered candidates for independence. If Poland was to be "carved" out of the Soviet Union on the basis of prewar boundaries, then this would necessarily have to be done at the expense of the Ukrainians. The problem, of course, as Philipps pointed out, was that it was false to assume that the peoples fighting for liberty would not expect to hold the Allied democracies to their publicly declared war aims.[137]

The contradiction, in the end, would have little bearing on the politics of the status quo. In part, the Ukrainians in North America understood this, conditioning their need to couch the issue of Ukrainian independence in terms that not only made it palatable to officials and the broader public but would also provide the high ground from which to argue, at a minimum, the case for Ukraine's self-determination. Others would even appeal to the political sensibilities of policy-makers, indicating that practical and geostrategic considerations recommended support for Ukrainian claims. These considerations, however, would not be heard. Moreover, as long as Ukrainian Canadians continued to put forward the Ukrainian claim to self-determination, they had to be considered a threat.

It is for this reason that at the same time that the Ukrainian Canadian nationalists were expressing loyalty to Canada and the Allied cause, the RCMP – Canada's security agency – was recommending a ban on one of their organisations and internment.[138] In the final analysis, no action was taken in Canada against domestic advocates of Ukrainian independence. The contradiction stemming from the government's public pronouncements on the political objectives of the war would, by its own admission, have made any such action difficult to defend. Where it did not matter, as in the case of the ULFTA and the Ukrainian Canadian communists, the state acted forcefully, decisively and with little compunction about the violation of political rights. As for the nationalists, nothing could be done except to keep watch over the community and the activities of its leadership.

Senior officials, of course, welcomed information from individuals within the community who often liberally and candidly provided information on rival organisations and personalities. Although the authorities were judicious in their assessment of the intelligence acquired – attributing accusations of fascism and fifth-column activity to personal rivalries and historical antagonisms within the community the information simply demonstrated a need to bring the various organisational groups in line with mainstream public opinion. It was also evident that monitoring the situation was not an altogether adequate response to the problem; the option of shaping, or at the very minimum neutralising, preferences within the community had to be considered. The formation of a central and authoritative committee was thought to be the best means of consolidating the government position, providing a mechanism with which the government could discretely penetrate the nationalist community.[139] With official encouragement, the creation of the Ukrainian Canadian Committee was the result of this line of thinking. Indeed, as Justice Davis would comment immediately after its formation, since it was now "under one roof," the problem could be more easily handled.

The state's ability to shape the outcome was facilitated by at least two factors. The first was the internal momentum towards unity within the nationalist community, which was based on a desire to assist their ethnic kindred in the homeland; and the second was the need among Ukrainian Canadians to legitimise the Ukrainian claim to self-determination. The legitimacy so desperately sought by the Ukrainian Canadian nationalists and the seeming legitimacy granted the nationalist community through the semiofficial sanctioning of the UCC guaranteed, in part, that throughout the rest of the war the nationalist leadership would attempt to accommodate the government's views and wishes. There was, however, an added advantage in encouraging the community leaders to come together. Mutual suspicions would ensure that each would guard against the other jeopardising the "good standing" and "credibility" of their respective organisations with the government. The authorities would maximise this opportunity, tapping the fractious and often quarrelling nationalist leadership for a better sense of where it stood.

The formation of the UCC was not the result of a policy formulation as such. It was an ad hoc measure that nevertheless reflected the basic thrust of the government's orientation. Typically, that orientation would interpret Ukrainian Canadian nationalist claims as a threat to state interests, a threat that would foster excessive suspicion in some official quarters. For instance, the proposal submitted by the Civil Service Commission to organise a defence force in Canada against the "foreign-born" element, which it feared could potentially carry out a coup, although extreme, was to a certain extent indicative of the suspicion among officials at the time.[140] Ironically, it was Philipps who, concerned with the issue of Canadianization as a factor in public security, would urge Canadian officials to take bold, new, constructive steps, whether in foreign or domestic policy, to secure the allegiance of the various ethnic communities and integrate them into the body politic on a lasting basis. In his opinion, it was to the government of Canada that these people looked for their lead, and it was only the government of Canada that could provide the context in which to shape the Canadian nation.[141] The Canadian state, however, had its own agenda, dictated by what were perceived to be more pressing concerns.

3 Realism, Canada, and the Grand Alliance: Political Obligations, Contradictions, and Costs

Within days of Germany's invasion of the Soviet Union it was clear to Soviet authorities that radical steps would have to be taken to stem the tide of the Nazi juggernaught. Ignoring its own role in the partition of Poland in 1939, the Soviet Union appealed to Polish nationals, urging them to assist the Soviet Red Army in turning back and defeating the Nazi invader. The Polish government in exile proposed to the Soviet government that the appeal would be officially endorsed if Poland's pre-1939 frontiers were again recognised.[1] The Polish proposal elicited a strong and quick reaction from Canada's Ukrainian minority. The Ukrainian Canadian Committee (UCC) pointed out that the proposal's flagrant disregard for the political rights of Ukrainians illustrated Poland's continued rejection of the Supreme Council decision of 1919, which ordained autonomy for the Ukrainian minority in East Galicia.[2] They emphasised that war had been declared by the British Commonwealth nations "for freedom against tyranny and for the right of peoples to organise themselves as independent national units." It was for these goals, they claimed, that Ukrainian Canadians were rendering service and offering the ultimate sacrifice. Believing that the declared Allied war aims were not "false" and their objective not an "illusion," they asked for an immediate interpretation from the Canadian government of "this apparent fundamental contradiction between the war aims of Canada and the principles of Poland.[3]

The Ukrainian Canadian demand for an interpretation produced a spate of activity among those departments that concerned themselves most immediately with the Ukrainian question. The Department of

National War Services called for an urgent meeting with key government officials to adopt a strategic plan. External Affairs, on the other hand, hoping to make the best of what appeared to be a deteriorating situation, sent a dispatch to the Polish government in exile, via its high commissioner in London, asking for a Polish statement that would take into account the Ukrainian desire for autonomy.[4] In this course of action, External Affairs was apparently influenced by the counsel of the European adviser Tracy Philipps, who cautioned that "wisdom" be used in providing an interpretation. He argued that premature or adverse statements that dismissed Ukrainian claims could have a detrimental effect on Canada's war effort, especially since Germany was daily giving its own interpretation to Ukrainians over the radio.[5] That it was a delicate situation was confirmed by RCMP commissioner Wood, who was of the opinion that due to the change of events in Eastern Europe "a certain section of the Ukrainian nationalist element [would] turn pro-Nazi in the hope that Hitler [would] eventually establish an independent Ukraine."[6]

The appeal from Canada was not entirely ignored. The official Polish response, however, was somewhat unexpected. Instead of a conciliatory statement, a plan was proposed to facilitate the passage to Canada of several prominent Ukrainians from continental Europe. The belief among Polish officials was that these individuals would be able to put forward a strong argument in support of the Allied position and favourably channel opinion within the Ukrainian nationalist community in Canada.[7] The Central Department of the British Foreign Office, however, on whose goodwill the plan ultimately depended, rejected the proposal, the danger of arousing Soviet suspicions being considered too great. Nothing, it was felt, should be done "for these, or other Ukrainians, roughly on the ground that the Ukrainian Question (like the Irish Question previously) was an internal Soviet one."[8]

It was left to the Department of National War Services in Canada to deal with the problem. On 27 June 1941, Justice T.C. Davis (the associate deputy minister for war services) proposed to the newly appointed minister, the Honourable J.T. Thorson, that a "foreign languages section" be created immediately that would be in contact with the immigrant groups in Canada.[9] The duties of the section, as initially conceived by the deputy minister, were to carry out plans and propaganda among the groups, with a view to integrating them into the national fabric, while providing direction and leadership, especially in their attitude to the war. The unusual situation that resulted from the new trends in the war made the recommendation all the more pressing. As Davis remarked, "We went into the War with France as an ally and

Russia as an enemy. Now Russia is an ally and France is an enemy. It is no wonder there is confusion."[10]

The importance and urgency of providing direction where the ethnic, and especially Ukrainian Canadian, press was concerned was brought home by an editorial published in the nationalist newspaper *Novyi shliakh* (New Pathway) that censorship authorities considered particularly injurious to Canadian interests.[11] Justice Davis' own assessment, after he had considered the censorship reports, was that he did not think that Ukrainian Canadians would pursue a policy in Canadian affairs that was actuated by developments in Eastern Europe. Uncertainty, however, dictated caution. An adviser who was often consulted by the government on matters concerning Central and Eastern Europe, Professor Simpson of the University of Saskatchewan, was asked to comment on the editorial and, more generally, to give his opinion on the Ukrainian position in the war between the Soviet Union and Germany.[12]

Simpson obliged. Replying to Davis' enquiries, he noted that censorship officials selectively used excerpts from the editorial, while critical passages were ignored altogether, resulting in a distorted text. Simpson further added that he personally knew both the editor of *Novyi shliakh* and the leader of the Ukrainian National Federation – the organisation that the newspaper represented – and that they had communicated to him on several occasions their conviction that Germany would not grant Ukraine independence, even admitting that "in Canada a German victory might lead to political repercussions in which they [the Ukrainians], as a very vulnerable group, would probably come off extremely badly."[13] Simpson claimed Ukrainian Canadians were generally sensitive to any suggestion that they were less loyal than their fellow citizens and pointed to the danger arising from inaccurate and false statements appearing in print. Notable in this regard, according to Simpson, was the article in *Saturday Night*, Canada's national magazine, published under the heading "Ukrainian-Canadians and the War's New Phase" and penned by R.A. Davies, a contributor to the *Canadian Tribune*, the Communist Party weekly that had replaced the banned *Clarion*.[14] It was precisely this sort of journalism, Simpson suggested, that needed to cease.

The article to which Simpson referred made several important allegations, claiming for instance that a quisling regime would shortly be established in Ukraine headed up by individuals who had some support within certain Ukrainian Canadian circles. Davies argued that the matter required the immediate attention of the Dominion government, given the extensive participation of Canada's Ukrainians in the vital war industries. Although Davies stressed that the majority of Ukrainian

Canadians were loyal to Canada, he urged the government to make every effort to win over Canada's Ukrainians and frustrate the attempts being made to create a "Nazi fifth column in Canada," one that would eventually be directed by a fascist puppet regime in Kyiv.

The article outraged prominent nationalists, who promptly and angrily wrote to the editor of *Saturday Night*. The editor-in-chief, B.K. Sandwell, responding to Wasyl Swystun, the respected lawyer and influential leader within the nationalist community, expressed regret that the Davies item had appeared in print, since he personally knew many of the statements to be false.[15] Sandwell, explaining that a "naive" assistant editor had approved the manuscript without his authorisation, extended his apologies and invited Swystun to pen a rebuttal. Two weeks later an article by Swystun appeared.[16] The accusations levelled against the nationalists had had their effect, however. The controversy, which was picked up by the mainstream press, gave some urgency to the RCMP in completing the intelligence reports on Ukrainian Canadian organisations and their representatives.

The RCMP reports – four in all – were varied in nature and in content. The Eucharistic Congress of Eastern Rites held in Chicago provided the setting for the first investigation, which sought to ascertain the attitude of the Ukrainian Catholic, or Uniate, Church, with its large following in Canada, toward the German invasion of Ukraine. The opinions expressed disclosed nothing of consequence, although the assessment did conclude that there was no firm guarantee the Uniate Church would not align itself with some of the more militant nationalist organisations.[17] It was an observation that was of interest if only because the subject of the second RCMP investigation, the Ukrainian National Federation of Canada (UNF), had been under surveillance for some time.

The occasion for this investigation was the Eighth National Convention of the UNF. Originally scheduled for 1942, the convention was moved up in response to criticism from within the ranks regarding the executive's relative inaction in the face of unfolding international developments. Many of the organisation's members believed that the recent Allied accord with the USSR appeared to contradict the principles of the liberal-democratic nations at war. They urged the leadership to challenge the government to provide an explanation for this apparent contradiction.

In the ensuing debate at the convention, the UNF leadership stressed that the situation was difficult. Arguing that Ukrainian independence continued to be a priority, they pointed out, however, that statements that questioned Canada's foreign policy could be misconstrued as an attack on Canada. Resolutions that lent themselves to misinterpretation had, consequently, to be avoided. This was not to imply that there would be a retreat from the goal of Ukrainian sovereignty, but the arguments had to emphasise the natural and complementary interests of an independent Ukraine and the geostrategic role it could play in the region. Moreover, this had to be done in the context of members' civic obligations and responsibility to Canada. In short, any untoward statements would be seen as a provocation, and therefore the only option available to Ukrainian Canadians was both full participation in the war effort and continued loyal support.[18]

Given the past influence of European politics and personalities on the direction of the UNF, the views expressed were remarkable. This was implicitly recognised in the RCMP report, which documented the change in attitude. And yet, without minimising the importance of the public expressions of loyalty voiced at the convention, the report speculated that "a certain section of the UNF members as well as other Ukrainians in Canada [would] likely sympathise with a 'puppet government' in the Ukraine." This opinion echoed an earlier observation made at the Eucharistic Congress, namely, that the unexpected turn in the war had presented Ukrainians with a favourable opportunity to gain independence, even though it was generally understood that Hitler and Stalin were "one and the same evil" and that Ukrainians under Hitler would have "to pay dearly" for their independence. The report, however, did not wish to overstate the case and concluded that "it is hardly possible that the UNF or any other similar group of Ukrainians in Canada, excepting the communists, [would] cause any serious trouble for the country [at this time] or at some serious critical period in the future."[19]

Of all the Ukrainian Canadian nationalist organisations, the reputed Nazi-connected, monarchist United Hetman Organisation (UHO) was of most concern to the RCMP.[20] The pretender to a Ukrainian throne – Hetman Pavlo Skoropadsky – had resided in Germany since 1918, and his presence there and possible German influence on the movement did not sit well with Canada's security officials or with External Affairs. In late 1940 an investigation of the UHO had been initiated after accusations were made against the movement's Canadian representative, Dr T. Datzkiw. Only now, under these most urgent circumstances, was the report finally completed.

Like the others, the document revealed little that was incriminating. Datzkiw reportedly believed that a puppet Ukrainian regime would not be created, if only because Nazi Germany had demonstrated little interest in solving the Ukrainian question. His own sense was that a German governor would be selected to administer Ukraine as a colony – a disaster, in his opinion, not only from the perspective of Ukrainian independence but, given the racial policies of the Nazi regime, an outcome that would also have untold consequences for the population. As for Hetman Skoropadsky, Datzkiw was appreciably aware of the unseemly appearance of his residence in Germany, which was proving disconcerting to some of the organisation's membership. But he gave his assurance that if Skoropadsky were to be installed as ruler of Ukraine and his investiture were to depend on German goodwill, then the organisation was prepared to sever all ties with the Hetman centre in Berlin. He insisted that participants in the movement were committed monarchists and that their interest derived alone from the conviction that a constitutional monarchy was the most appropriate form of government for Ukraine. As for the rumours that a German-inspired Ukrainian government, to which the name of Skoropadsky was linked, had been set up, Datzkiw offered that "not much stock should be taken in these reports as they usually emanate from sources which are hostile to Ukrainians."

The report was received by Commissioner Wood of the RCMP with a cover letter that suggested nothing untoward about the organisation. Wood, however, did not share the investigator's conclusion about the benign nature of the organisation. In an accompanying letter sent to External Affairs, Wood counselled that the UHO still had to be regarded as a "potential danger" as long as it remained in contact with the Hetman centre in Berlin.[21]

Completing the cycle of intelligence reports, finally, was a brief profiling the various personalities on the executive of the Ukrainian Canadian Committee. Submitted to both National War Services and External Affairs, it provided no new insights into the community leaders and their attitudes. What the report did show, however, was that quarrelling and friction among members of the UCC executive continued unabated. Indeed, although there appeared to be consensus on the cardinal issues facing the committee, it was reported that disagreement over "methods and other minor details" predominated.[22] This disagreement was deemed unfortunate, since the government had hoped the differences and antagonisms would slowly dissipate with the creation of the committee. The UCC, incapable of fulfilling the role Ottawa originally envisioned for it, would require some guidance.

Justice Davis' recommendation on 27 June to create a foreign languages section in the Bureau of Public Information to deal with ethnic groups was tentatively accepted on 30 October 1941 at an interdepartmental meeting. George Simpson – an individual long since considered a candidate for the position – was confirmed as director of the commission, while Tracy Philipps, then working in the Department of Justice in a technical capacity, was appointed "European Adviser."[23]

The meeting also provided for an exchange of views on the function and aims of the section. Because Philipps, who was invited to the meeting, strongly opposed the idea that the body be restricted to propaganda work, a compromise was reached whereby it was agreed the section would make suggestions and recommendations on the basis of observable trends within the various communities.[24] It was felt that the Foreign Languages Section – whose name would subsequently change to the Nationalities Branch – could in this way provide information on broad developments from which policy guidelines could be drawn. The understanding, however, was that External Affairs would reserve for itself the right to formulate policy, a particularly crucial matter from the point of view of Allied relations. Norman Robertson, the under-secretary of state representing External Affairs at the meeting, in fact indicated in this regard that there already was a full exchange of information with the governments of the United Kingdom and United States on the question of "foreign-born" communities.[25]

The increased RCMP surveillance of the Ukrainian nationalist community[26] and the general move to create a special section that would deal primarily with this and other ethnic groups arose from other, deeper considerations. In July 1941 a far-ranging discussion took place within External Affairs on the future of Canadian-Soviet relations. It was apparent to those concerned that the interests of the Allies lay in assisting the Soviet Union. If the Soviet Union could not be kept in the war, the situation for the Allies would be precarious. Canadian authorities, consequently, were giving careful thought to the idea of increased military, economic, and political assistance to the Soviet Union.[27] This idea, however, was not a simple formality. There were perceptible dangers in establishing closer relations with the USSR, and, it was explained, they could not be ignored. For one, public inertia on the question suggested that a premature policy could run against public opinion. As officials in External Affairs were deeply aware, large segments of the population were ill-disposed to the Soviet Union, an attitude born in part from the Soviet-Nazi Pact of 1939, which was seen as "one of the vital links in the chain that led to Germany's subsequent attack on Poland and Western Europe." There was also the role of the USSR in the division of Poland and the calculated political risks involved in a closer relationship, "[given] the probability that the present Holy War [could] again become an Imperialist War the moment Russia [is] knocked out."[28]

Relations with the Soviet Union, however, could not be postponed indefinitely. Huge amounts of war materiel were being expended daily on the Eastern front, forcing Canada and the other Allies to increase direct military assistance. In October the Soviet minister counsellor to the United States raised the matter of consular representation with the Canadian legation in Washington, in order to deal with problems arising out of the increased shipments of supplies from or via Canada to the USSR.[29] Since it was thought that low-level consular relations of a purely technical character would do little harm, especially if publicity were avoided, Canada tentatively agreed to the exchange. Unexpectedly, however, the Soviet Union asked in December, again through its legation in Washington, for a full exchange of diplomatic representatives with Canada beyond the consular level.

The request came as something of a surprise. Canadian officials could not reject the proposal out of hand, for fear of appearing insincere. But neither could they accept it without first determining the political costs. After much internal discussion, the Department of External Affairs concluded that on balance the grounds for establishing closer relations were more cogent at the time, and would become increasingly so in the future, than the grounds against such action. The arguments in favour included the need to maintain closer contact with Allied governments on special wartime questions, to obtain information on Soviet policies and attitudes in order to formulate Canadian policy, particularly since the USSR was expected to play a major role in the postwar peace conference, and to give further indication of Canada's genuine commitment to the Allied struggle.[30] There was, of course, the possibility of public reaction to consider, especially among the East European communities and in Catholic Quebec, where anticommunist sentiments ran deep.[31] Canadian officials, however, were confident that they could weather the storm of protest by pointing to the already "well established principle that diplomatic relations should not be governed by attitudes of approval or disapproval of the social system of such countries, but by the common interests which demand solution."[32]

On 14 December 1941, after some hesitation, Prime Minister Mackenzie King indicated that as soon as the "right persons" were secured, he would agree to full diplomatic relations. For External Affairs the question of personnel was no small matter, the department insisting that staff positions be occupied by individuals who did not hold "preconceived anti-Russian ideas."[33] An expression of the widespread apprehension regarding the possible difficulties that might be encountered as a result of the relationship, it was not an entirely groundless reaction, since the UCC, for instance, had proposed, through political channels, the unlikely scheme of placing a Canadian of Ukrainian extraction on staff in Moscow.[34]

The suspicion that closer relations with the Soviet Union would involve complications was soon borne out. At the time when the exchange of consular representation was raised, the Soviet Union requested that Canada, as an Allied partner, declare war against Germany's client states – Finland, Hungary, and Romania. The request was brought before the Cabinet War Committee. Conscious that refusal would arouse Soviet suspicions about the extent of Allied cooperation, the members of Cabinet also understood there were other aspects of the relationship that had to be taken into account. For one, it was felt that the Soviets were looking to reinforce their position in the postwar settlement with possible concessions and reparations from Germany's partners. But the difficulty with declaring war against Germany's client states was that, aside from the fact that public opinion was expected to oppose further declarations of war, "particularly at the instance of the Soviet [Union]," there was in the case of Finland a clear sense that the Canadian public was inclined to support the Finns against the Soviets, since the USSR was perceived to be the original aggressor in the conflict. More importantly, the reaction of the large numbers of Finns and Hungarians working in the vital war industries of Canada had to be considered: their "present situation ... was not, at the moment, unsatisfactory, but would be adversely affected by a declaration of war."[35] It was decided that a message should be sent advising the Soviet Union that Canada was not prepared, at least for the time being, to declare war on those states.[36]

Apart from the immediate complications that sprang from the relationship with the Soviet Union, there were, however, other more profound implications of the alliance. The United Kingdom and the British dominions had entered the war on behalf of Poland. Poland had become a benchmark in British war policy, serving as an important element in a system of European power relations that aimed in the interwar years at containing Britain's chief continental rival – Germany.[37] The problem, however, for Britain, which was now allied with the Soviet Union, was that Poland had been a victim of both Nazi and Soviet aggression. The Soviet Union was seen to be as much a threat to the reconstruction of the prewar European power structure as was Nazi Germany. In this regard, the historic Atlantic Charter, signed by both Roosevelt and Churchill off the coast of Newfoundland in August 1941, with its emphasis on political freedom, was aimed as much at the Soviet Union as it was against Nazi Germany.[38] Indeed, it was made clear by both Britain and the United States, in the context of the charter and elsewhere, that no territorial changes would be recognised, including changes to Poland's eastern borders.

Political self-determination was the Atlantic Charter's philosophical starting point, and although the declaration, it appears, was never really intended to have universal application, its ambiguity allowed for a liberal interpretation.[39] The reasons for the ambiguity are not hard to understand. Both Germany and Japan attempted to discredit Britain on the basis of its political and economic hegemony in both Europe and the Far East. For Britain, to argue openly for a return to the status quo ante, where the international system was interpreted as being structured in its favour, would, in fact, have laid the way open to the charge of British global domination. This was undesirable, since the distinction between Britain and the Axis, made from the very outset of the war, was that Britain sought the liberation of various peoples, while Germany, Italy, and Japan sought their domination. It was a distinction Britain had to maintain, but it also had certain advantages. Indeed, since the distinction involved the issue of nations stripped of their liberty, it had the beneficial effect of being seen as a democratic gesture, while nevertheless implying a return to the old, if not benevolent, order.

In the European context the distinction – and therefore the charter – had a very precise meaning, allowing British officials, for instance, to treat Ukrainian independence as a nonquestion and to view the issue of territorial disputes in Eastern Europe as a simple matter of returning to the preexisting order. Outside the European context, however, the manner in which the declaration was being interpreted would have serious ramifications. Since the restoration of the old order necessarily meant a return to colonial rule, restoration was not a real alternative for British colonies. A more robust interpretation of the Atlantic Charter, on the other hand, presented them with an opportunity to advance their political and historical claims to independence, a matter of some speculation and debate in Southeast Asia.[40] Although these claims were rejected, they were not done so summarily. This would have exposed the contradiction between the ideals articulated in the declaration and the reality of British policy. Rather, the novel, albeit ambiguous, argument was made that political maturity, demonstrated primarily by a nation's commitment to the international community, would be a necessary condition of the step toward independence.

The argument, by its very nature, reinforced the liberal interpretation of the charter and had profound implications not only for British colonial dependencies but also for those peripheral nations of Europe, such as the Ukrainians, who had historically been without a state. The "nonhistoric" peoples would first have to demonstrate their capacity for independence. It was a crucial point, the significance of which was not lost upon the Ukrainian nationalist leadership in Canada.[41] Meanwhile, security warranted caution. Downplaying the importance of the Ukrainian claim in Europe, United Kingdom authorities, taking what at first glance appears to have been an inordinate and unusual interest in the Ukrainian situation in North America, would collect intelligence through the British Security Co-ordination in New York, exchanging information and offering advice when it pertained to European affairs.[42]

Britain, politically, could afford to dismiss the Ukrainian question. Canada could not. The sizeable Ukrainian minority working in the vital war industries made it an unavoidable and immediate problem. Canada, therefore, having to follow Britain's lead in European political affairs, would have to contend not only with the particular problems that the Soviet alliance posed in Allied-Polish relations but also with the complexities arising from the introduction of the Ukrainian question into the East European equation. Ukrainian independence was unacceptable in the context of Allied relations. But to deny its legitimacy, falling as it did, logically, within the parameters of the charter, would have been seen to contradict the spirit, if not the letter, of the declaration. More importantly, it would have seriously discredited Allied credibility by disclosing that the basic thrust behind Allied policy in Europe was the restoration of the prewar status quo, in which there would be no place for an independent Ukrainian state.

There was, of course, the liberal argument that linked independence to "political maturity" and "international responsibility" and that could be used to offset the claim. But this argument was dangerous in the Canadian context. Ukrainian Canadians could point to the million plus of their armed ethnic kindred fighting and dying in the struggle against fascism on the Eastern front and tens of thousands enlisted in the Canadian armed forces as evidence of both maturity and responsibility.[43] The Atlantic Charter offered the best hope for those committed to Ukrainian independence.[44] But from the official Canadian perspective, it was not to be encouraged. Prudence dictated that, domestically, Canadian officials should simply impress upon Ukrainian Canadians their obligations as citizens of Canada, while avoiding any public discussion of charter aims, particularly with respect to postwar settlements.

In their external relations, of course, especially with the Soviet Union, Canadian authorities would attempt to present a picture of Canada as a responsible and committed ally. In time, signals would be given to the Soviet Union showing that Canadians were well intentioned. But since the problem immediately concerned British and American authorities, Canadian officials felt obliged to share information with both Allies on developments within the Ukrainian Canadian community. Indeed, it was thought that the recently produced RCMP reports on Ukrainian Canadian nationalist organisations might be of use to British authorities "who were wrestling with the problem of postwar frontiers and organisation of Eastern Europe."[45] In the meantime, however, because their ability to act was severely circumscribed, little else could be done except to monitor the situation and wait for the inevitable criticism that was expected in the wake of Canada's diplomatic recognition of the USSR.

And the inevitable was not long in coming. Fearful that closer diplomatic relations with the Soviet Union would undercut the Ukrainian sovereignty position, the nationalist press expressed regret at Canada's decision but was confident that the principles of the Atlantic Charter still applied and that the Soviet Union would respect them.[46] It was unwelcome press, but the statements made were not threatening, certainly not in the same way as was the address delivered by Anthony Hlynka in Canada's Parliament on 2 February 1942. A parliamentarian representing Alberta's heavily populated ethnic Ukrainian constituency of Vegreville and a former UNF executive officer, Hlynka, a Social Credit member, reacted to Canada's decision with the claim that on the basis of the charter the Ukrainian nation had a political and moral right to self-determination. Moreover, since the Ukrainian people were not in a position to represent themselves, being currently occupied by the Nazi invader, he called upon the Allied governments to make it possible for them to be represented internationally by inviting delegations from Canada, the United States, and elsewhere "to express the view of 50 million Ukrainian people at conferences held by the allied nations."[47] It was an extraordinary statement that caught officials in External Affairs off guard.

Asked to comment in the context of criticism from the pro-Soviet elements, George Simpson, recently appointed as director of the Department of National War Services' Nationalities Branch, remarked that Hlynka's speech resulted from the feeling among nationalist Ukrainians that if they did not make their argument now, their position would be settled in the public mind before the matter was even fairly discussed. The nationalists, he claimed, saw Canada as one of the few countries that would have a natural interest in a Ukrainian state, and it was therefore imperative from their perspective "to have the sympathetic understanding of a country which has no predatory self-interest."[48] From the perspective of Canadian-Soviet relations, the speech, Simpson conceded, was not helpful. But as he pointed out, "Mr Hlynka did not go outside the terms used by the allied statesmen in the Atlantic Charter and elsewhere in putting forward the claims of the Ukrainian people to consideration in the future settlement of Europe. Nor did he go outside the terms of the Soviet constitution itself in suggesting that eventually an independent state might arise through the voluntary secession of the Ukrainian Soviet [Republic]." As for the reaction from the pro-Soviet Ukrainians, Simpson noted it was to be anticipated. This was small comfort to the Department of External Affairs.

Pro-Soviet Ukrainian Canadians had, in fact, seized upon Hlynka's speech as being directed against an ally, and they portrayed it as inspired by fascism. Petitions were gathered condemning the statement, while letters were being addressed to members of Parliament, government officials, and the English-language press.[49] The Association to Aid the Fatherland, for example, challenged the government directly in a widely distributed circular, putting officials on notice that it would constitute an "unfriendly act" if the government of Canada were "to participate in, far less originate, proposals for the dismemberment of Britain's greatest ally and friend in the common struggle to save humanity from Nazi barbarism."[50]

As for the public and the media, the sentiment was one of impatience and disbelief that anyone, let alone a member of Parliament, would introduce such an awkward question at a critical time, when it could possibly embarrass Canada's relations with the Soviet Union. The *Toronto Star* identified Hlynka's address as a "peculiar speech," noting that under the Soviet constitution the Ukrainian republic had the right to secede and that it had not done so, no doubt, because "the people of that province had not desired it."[51] Stronger opinions were voiced elsewhere. The *Canadian Grocer*, for instance, called for a reevaluation of Canadian immigration policy, since, like the "cocky Japanese," there were many Ukrainians who "thought they owned the place."[52] Meanwhile, a particularly incredulous correspondent would write in the *Edmonton Bulletin* that

Canada's dead must groan in their graves as they consider how Anglo-Saxons have handed away our heritage, go cheerfully to fight in all the far corners of the world, while staying behind are these people who came to a ready-made British freedom which gave them legal protection to vilify and sneer at the country which gave them land, food, work, shelter, and in sickness and in unemployment – how quick they were to rush for relief – and how slow they are to rally to the colours.

It's time for the truth. We are in a fair way to losing this war ... First John Bull was going to save us; now it's Uncle Sam. Perhaps we should try to save ourselves. But we are not going to fight à la Mr Hlynka, Ukrainian-Canadian MP, Vegreville, for the dear old Ukraine: we want to see the aliens rounded up to fight for Canada. If not naturalised, their own governments are more than welcome to them.

I have said that this is an alien district; and so it is, preponderantly Ukrainian, and not one single man of that race or racial strain has volunteered for the active army from this district ...

The lines have been drawn very sharp in this war: there are only two sides – those who are for us and those who are against us.[53]

The letter published in the *Bulletin* did not pass without notice or response. The executive head of the Ukrainian Self Reliance League condemned it as racist and questioned the judgment of the editors for publishing what was described as "mindless prattle." The letter was harmful as much as an affront, and the *Bulletin's* editor-in-chief was told that it was difficult enough to convince young men to go overseas and face the prospect of death without having to contend with hostile xenophobes who questioned their loyalty on the basis of their ethnic origin.[54]

More serious, however, were the unmeasured published statements of the Ukrainian Canadian communists who played up the pro-German comments that the Ukrainian nationalists had made during the period before Munich.[55] W. Kardash's pamphlet *Hitler's Agents in Canada* was notable in this regard. Vitriolic and shrill, it portrayed the Ukrainian National Federation as a "fascist" organisation with agents in Canada working for Berlin; its anti-Soviet views were said to be a "smokescreen" that masked the organisation's support for Hitler.[56]

The pamphlet, the articles in the press, and the public agitation led some of the moderates within the nationalist community to wonder privately whether in fact it would not be more useful to come to terms with the communists in order to avoid public confusion on Ukrainian matters.[57] Others, however, hardened in their anticommunism, were only too willing to take up the debate, condemning government officials along the way both for their prevarication and for their lack of resolve.

On one hand we hear the appeals for national unity, and at the same time we see that this communist scum is being given all the latitude to besmirch, denounce and publicly cast vile aspersions against individuals and organisations which were opposed to Communism. Our people resent this very much and the committee [the UCC] gets many letters asking for some action to stop these unfair and unfounded denunciations. As you know, our press has been very lenient toward the Communists since the USSR became our war partner, and the moderate attitude was not practised for lack of ammunition against the Communists, but for sake of national unity. I am afraid that if the powers that be do not give the Communists a pertinent hint that their disruptive tactics will not be tolerated, then our press and our committee will take up the challenge, and then the fat will be in the fire properly.[58]

At the Nationalities Branch, Simpson tried to dissuade the more militant element from engaging in a polemic, claiming that it served no one's interest. He stressed that Canada was an ally of the Soviet Union and that as a partner in war, "[Canada] must not fall into the error of appearing to oppose the Russian war effort."[59] To do so would have

been disastrous from the point of view of maintaining a picture of una-
nimity in the Allied camp. His suggestion, therefore, was to issue a
simple denial. If the UCC was inclined to defend its record, then he
recommended that only a short public statement emphasising the UCC's
loyalty be made, characterising it as "unlike those Ukrainian Canadians
who spoke only in terms of 'our' Soviet Fatherland and 'our' Red Army."
His personal advice, however, was simply to leave the matter alone.

Despite lingering public suspicion of the Communist Party of Canada,
opinion favouring the Soviet Union was on the rise. In August 1942, a
Gallup poll revealed findings of a survey undertaken to gauge the public's view of Soviet postwar intentions. A full 57 percent of the sample
polled believed that the Soviet Union would work with the United States
and Britain in the postwar political reconstruction of Europe and that
the spirit in which the Atlantic Charter was conceived would be upheld
by the USSR when the time came to implement it. Sixteen percent were
undecided. As the pollsters at Gallup noted, the results marked
"another milestone in the historic shift of democratic opinion towards
Russia since the Russo-Finnish war, and the signing, three years ago
this month, of the German-Russian nonaggression pact."[60]

Public opinion was largely being shaped by developments on the
Soviet front. News of the staggering losses and the image of hardship
borne by the civilian population was leaving its mark on the public
conscience. This change was viewed with some uncertainty and mis-
giving in Washington, where it was felt that in the case of the British
public there was too much emphasis on identifying the progress of the
war with the campaign on the Eastern front. It was felt that the
consequence of this attitude was a disposition on the part of British
officials to agree to Soviet demands, including territorial guarantees.
The acceptance of those demands, it was thought, would severely
undermine both the "moral position of the United Nations" and the
Allies' strategic position in Sweden and Turkey, both of which looked
upon the Soviet Union with suspicion and hostility.[61] Norman Robertson (the under-secretary of state for external affairs), to whom this
view was communicated, was not of the same opinion. Although he
personally considered Soviet requests for territorial guarantees unnecessary at the time, Robertson felt that since they had been made, there
was no reason to reject them out of hand. In fact, the under-secretary
thought that to do so would be unwise, given that "the present mutual
lack of confidence between the Western Allies and Russia was a very
uneasy foundation for a vitally necessary military collaboration."[62]

Robertson's opinion was conditioned by information received from
the Dominion Office that British statesmen were inclined to view an
Anglo-Soviet treaty – which necessarily included territorial guarantees –

of such importance that they were prepared to negotiate unilaterally with the Soviets and hazard a political storm with the United States. The British attitude was being formed by the persistence of Stalin, who was pressing for nothing less than a guarantee of the Soviet borders of 1940. The belief that Stalin's demands were a test of British sincerity to cooperate during and after the war was also a factor. "A plain refusal," it was thought, "might bring a deterioration in Anglo-Soviet relations, and in the collaboration of Great Britain, Russia and the United States."[63]

Britain had approached the United States to see whether in fact it would agree to Soviet demands that included all territories acquired by the Soviet Union during 1939–40. Roosevelt rejected the British entreaties to participate in any negotiations, claiming American public opinion would not stand for a secret treaty or any other treaty that considered the question of territorial concessions. Despite American objections, British officials notified the United States government that a separate Anglo-Soviet treaty recognising Soviet claims to the frontier of 1940 had to be concluded, except where Poland was concerned, on the grounds that the United Kingdom "as a European Power for whom co-operation of a victorious USSR after the war will be essential, cannot afford to neglect any opportunity of establishing intimate relations with Stalin." Moreover, since the Soviet Union was carrying the lion's share of the fighting, "the limitations of British assistance make it all the more necessary not to refuse a political concession."[64]

Among Canadian officials the argument against such a treaty was that it conflicted with the spirit, if not the letter, of the Atlantic Charter and that in this regard it contradicted the general British position, which stressed no territorial commitments would be made before the peace conference. It was also suggested that commitments of this sort would "lend to the destruction or weakening of certain small nations, and perhaps later of others." Although the Canadians appreciated the advantages favouring the decision – injecting an element of confidence in Allied relations, compensating for small-scale British assistance, and laying the basis for postwar entente – they were concerned about the implications. As they noted, Canada was morally bound to the charter. In this sense, "even in the general form in which it is expressed, the second of the principles [of the Charter] may be interpreted as in opposition to such intergovernmental decisions on the transfer of territories as are envisaged under the projected treaty."[65]

The litmus test, however, was public opinion. The belief in Canada was that there would be a negative reaction to the treaty. External Affairs felt the Lithuanians, Estonians, Latvians, Finns, and Romanians in Canada would suffer disillusionment, while the Poles, and especially the Ukrainians, would vehemently oppose the extension of the principle to the contested territories. The pro-Soviet elements within these groups, it was assumed, would favour closer relations with the Soviet Union, but the general thinking was that "on the whole the effect would probably be bad."

Officials at External Affairs concluded there were only three options open to Canada: 1 to stand aside, 2 to oppose the treaty, or 3 to support and adhere to it. The second alternative was immediately ruled out. The third was a possibility, but the potential domestic consequences were deemed profound and could not easily be ignored. It remained to consider the first option. Canada's obligation under the terms of the Atlantic Charter gave sufficient grounds for its legitimate abstention. And although Canada's aloofness could be interpreted as a point of real contention between American and British policymakers, External Affairs defended the Canadian position by rhetorically asking what the American alternative was: "To liberate the Baltic states as against Russia?"[66] At a Cabinet War Committee meeting, held 29 April, it was resolved that Canada would not adhere to the treaty. The decision was transmitted to London with full knowledge that the British government was prepared to act without Dominion participation.

On 23 June, Prime Minister Mackenzie King informed Parliament that the United Kingdom had signed a treaty with the Soviet Union. King underscored the fact that Canada was neither a party to the agreement nor bound by it, reflecting Cabinet's concern with adverse public opinion and the government's "cautious preference" to avoid bringing attention to matters that could have had further important consequences.[67] Nevertheless, although Canada was not a signatory, the British move was bound to have an effect on the segment of Canada's East European population that, according to External Affairs, had retained or revived a self-conscious nationalism. An internal discussion, was initiated, therefore, and a paper drafted on what policy was to be adopted toward foreign groups, especially the "non-recognised Free movements."[68]

The question of "non-recognised Free movements" was particularly difficult for External Affairs. Although there was consensus that they were useful in their opposition to the Axis, these movements tended both to complicate policy and to weaken the cooperation among the Allies. Notable in this regard was "the policy of the groups representing the Russian borderlands." Clearly a problematic issue, it suggested to officials in External Affairs that in their effort to encourage an anti-Nazi and anti-Fascist stand, it would have been unwise "to pursue far the distinction between democracy and authoritarianism." This would require an awkward discussion of the alliance with the Soviet Union, which External Affairs was not prepared to do. The problem also suggested, however, that bolder initiatives should be taken in bringing these groups into the mainstream of public opinion.

From the point of view of officials in Ottawa, there was considerable wisdom in distancing Canada from such movements. But still, from a policy perspective, this strategy was thought to be insufficient, since only "the negative side of the question" was being covered – "omitting any means of control." The suggestion of control was not entirely new. A precedent already existed in the case of Japanese Canadians. Although there was some objection to the idea of resorting to "unnecessary suppression," it was noted there was still a significant difference between the "vigorous control" of Japanese Canadians and the "relative freedom" of other groups.[69] The implication was that firmer action at this level could not be entirely ruled out. Nor, as it was suggested, would such action have been wholly inappropriate, although it was acknowledged that "to suppress one or more of [the independence movements] would be difficult to defend, and probably do more harm than good."[70]

This conclusion did not, however, prevent the government from pursuing other options. The author of the proposed policy, George Glazebrook, a special wartime assistant to the under-secretary who would later rise through the ranks, recommended that a ruling be laid down that would prohibit the Free movements from conducting propaganda considered damaging to the Allied cause.[71] If left ambiguous, the ruling, he felt, would have placed the government in "a much stronger position" to deal with such groups. He also recommended that surveillance be maintained, but in cooperation with British and American authorities. Cooperation with the latter was especially critical because of the "particularly close relationship between the problems of foreign groups in Canada and the United States." Indeed, "a close watch on the foreign groups" had to be maintained, particularly on those communities whose interests had some bearing on relations with the Soviet Union. For as Glazebrook noted, "it is difficult enough to keep Canadian opinion on an even keel without additional interference from the trimming," that is, from those groups who would complicate and possibly jeopardize Canada's interests.

That closer cooperation was needed between Allied authorities on Ukrainian affairs – especially North American Ukrainian affairs – was not a coincidence. American intelligence agencies, including the Overseas Strategic Services (OSS), were already busily engaged in collecting information on Ukrainians in both North and South America.[72] Indeed, inasmuch as it was thought that the Ukrainian national movement in the United States did not constitute a separate phenomenon but was part of a general development, intelligence gathered from whatever source, it was felt, would be useful in appraising the Ukrainian situation in the United States. Similarly, American authorities were prepared to share their own information compiled on Ukrainians with Canadian officials. Of four copies of a report produced by the OSS entitled "Ukrainians in the United States," one was sent to the Nationalities Branch in the Department of National War Services for the information of Canadian authorities.[73] In addition, censored correspondence, transmitted telegrams, information about suspicious activities, and virtually anything thought to be of interest was shared by both parties. This was also true of the British, who passed on, received, and even requested detailed information on individual Ukrainian Canadians.

The growing interest of British intelligence in North American Ukrainian affairs was a function of what was described as an "international tie-up" between Ukrainian organisations in North America and "fascist" Ukrainian groups in Europe.[74] For the OSS, the domestic considerations were of primary importance because of the participation of a great number of Ukrainians in the heavy industries of Pennsylvania and New York:

The [Ukrainian] foreign born are definitely opposed to the Russians and Poles as they feel there is no chance of fair treatment from either the Soviet Union or the Poles on their past experiences. There is a very fertile field for the exploitation of this group and this is being done by various groups who are constantly impressing on them the fact that the Germans are the only ones who will assure them their independence and above all not to believe the English as they will never help them gain their freedom ... As an example, they constantly remind them of Ireland and India. One thing they impress upon them is the fact that there never is any mention of Ukrainian independence by the United Nations and the only mention of them is to designate a geographical location.[75]

The basic difference in the American and British areas of concern determined the nature of their respective views on the Ukrainian nationalist community in North America. The British preoccupation with the Ukrainian "international tie-up" led them to conclude that the Ukrainian majority in North America was basically "semi-fascist or ignorant."[76] American intelligence and the State Department held a different opinion. Loy Henderson, deputy director of the European division in the State Department, who cautioned that care should be exercised not to jeopardise the cause of the United Nations among Ukrainians, dismissed those views that aimed to discredit Ukrainians in the United States or abroad. Responding to a British intelligence report, he wrote:

It seems to me in general that the author has grossly exaggerated the pro-Nazi or pro-German tendencies of the various groups of Ukrainian nationals. I gained the impression that some of his information must have come from Polish and Soviet secret service agencies which are inclined to smear any person or organisation having an interest even in the mildest form of Ukrainian nationalism.

That there are certain Ukrainian terrorists just as there are terrorists of almost every nationality there can be no doubt. During the years that I have had from time to time contact with American-Ukrainian or Ukrainian nationalist leaders and organisations, I have become convinced that relatively few of them resort to terrorist methods. There is no doubt that certain members in the United States of the ODWU [Organisation for the Rebirth of Ukraine] would have contacts with the Ukrainians in Germany; that some of them even thought that Germany might be useful as an instrument for freeing the Ukrainians. It is not believed, however, that the ODWU in this country ever sanctioned terrorist methods. Furthermore there can be no doubt that many members of the ODWU had Democratic tendencies and were in general loyal citizens of the United States although they possessed special interest in the faith of people of their own blood just as American Poles, American Irish, American Czech, etc.

It is a mistake to assume that Ukrainian nationalists are likely to be pro-Axis or anti-United Nations. It is true many are anti-Soviet and anti-Polish. You must remember at the same time however that there is no great friendship lost between certain members of the United Nations, such as between the Russians and the Poles or the Poles and the Czechs. These nationalist antagonisms, however, should not indicate that people who possess them are necessarily anti-United Nations and pro-Nazi.[77]

State Department officials were convinced the interpretation that Ukrainians were Nazi agents was overdrawn and in fact cited the source for many of the accusations in the United States as the New York–based pro-Soviet publication *The Hour*. The situation, it was felt, was also not helped "by the petty bickering among Ukrainians themselves in their efforts to gain ascendancy over certain Ukrainian-American organisations."[78]

The Canadian view on the subject was much closer to the American interpretation than to the British. RCMP intelligence continued to report that there was no evidence of Ukrainian nationalist organisations engaged in subversive activities. Moreover, the charges levelled against Ukrainian Canadian nationalists were found to emanate from the pro-Soviet Association of Canadian Ukrainians, formerly the Ukrainian Association to Aid the Fatherland. Commissioner Wood of the RCMP, in a report submitted to the Department of External Affairs on the

Ukrainian National Federation (UNF), identified the Association of Canadian Ukrainians as the UNF's persistent adversary, claiming that "the divergent viewpoint of [the UNF] to that of the Ukrainian Canadian Association [Association of Canadian Ukrainians], or communists, causes malediction to be literally 'poured out' by the latter Association against the UNO [UNF], on the slightest provocation."[79]

Despite differences in official Anglo-American opinion on the subject, there was nevertheless no doubting the utility of continuing surveillance of the Ukrainian group or of sharing information. Allied authorities, in fact, were prepared to go to considerable lengths to deal with what was generally acknowledged to be a problem. In June 1943 unusual steps were taken. An Ottawa meeting between officials from the British Security Co-ordination, its American counterpart, the Overseas Strategic Services, and senior members of Canada's Department of External Affairs was proposed to discuss the best means of coordinating the information flow on the Ukrainians.[80] In part, this proposal was in response to the heightened activity in the Ukrainian community that had been sparked by the comments made earlier by the second deputy people's commissar for Soviet foreign affairs, Oleksander Korniichuk.

In February 1943 Korniichuk issued an appeal from Moscow urging Ukrainians to engage the enemy and liberate all Ukrainian lands – from the Don River to the Carpathians. By definition this appeal meant the Ukrainian ethnographic territories within pre-war Poland as well, and it drew a strong response from the Polish government in exile. The Poles claimed that, according to the provisions of the Polish-Soviet Treaty of 30 July 1941, the status quo prior to 1 September 1939 was considered to be in force and any attempt to undermine this attitude would have been detrimental to the unity of the United Nations. Polish claims in turn provoked a reaction from the Ukrainian Canadian Committee, which held that the official Polish position, let alone the Soviet position, ran counter to the spirit of the Atlantic Charter.[81] To this end, in March the UCC submitted an official statement in the form of a memorandum to Prime Minister King outlining their concerns.[82]

The argument used by Allied statesmen to moderate some of the political consequences of the Atlantic Charter – only those nations that demonstrated political responsibility to the international community would find support for their cause – had now, ironically, become part of the Ukrainian appeals, including the appeal in the UCC memorandum. Indeed, since they sensed that it was the only leverage available and since they were cognisant of the constraints, the argument was increasingly used by Ukrainian Canadian nationalists. The Alberta Division of Ukrainian Canadians, a nationalist grass-roots organisation, for example, declared in a petition that it was the "sacred duty" of the nations concerned to ensure that the sovereign right of all peoples to self-government be recognised. Since Canada, Britain, and America were seen to be at the forefront of the movement demanding "a just and lasting European settlement," it was their hope that the Ukrainian claim would not be ignored, especially in light of the Ukrainian contribution to the Allied war effort:

Through the fifty years of our life here on this continent we have come to know England and America well enough to be able to cast our lot unreservedly on their side. And now when our Ukrainian boys in the Canadian and American Armed Forces are awaiting in the British Isles and elsewhere the signal to strike at the common foe, is it not fair and appropriate that we should expect the English speaking world to offer some guarantee of protection to our Ukrainian co-brethren in Europe?

This battle for freedom of the Ukrainians ... is no longer simply a question of some boundaries and some particular group: it is a matter of worldwide importance which is the responsibility of all liberty loving people. A sound international society can be built only on the basis of the union of free peoples united in their resistance to aggression and in determination to achieve justice for all. In the matter of justice the Ukrainian people have their claims and their responsibilities.[83]

External Affairs officials looked upon this and other nationalist appeals with consternation. Cast in the language of the charter, the appeals only served to further agitate those in favour of independence, who interpreted it as a legitimate war aim. The appeals also tended to attract the attention and ire of the pro-Soviet Ukrainian Canadians, with all the predictable consequences. The UCC memorandum to Prime Minister King, which had been made public by this time, was evidence of this. When, in a long telegram to the under-secretary of state, the newly organised pro-Soviet Association of Canadian Ukrainians denounced the Ukrainian Canadian Committee "as a body under Fascist control" and made public the accusation that the UCC memorandum was the work of "fifth columnists," the story was picked up the Canadian press. The *Vancouver News Herald* noted that the UCC proposal "word for word, letter for letter, was made for more than a decade by out-and-out Nazi puppets in Germany and elsewhere," while the *Windsor Star* charged that the UCC was not in a position to represent the Ukrainian nation, but rather, the people of Ukraine would speak for themselves "when the last invader is driven out."[84] More disturbing, it was discovered that the Soviet TASS Information Bureau in Montreal, having received a copy of the memo, wired the offending sections of the document to Moscow in a series of long cablegrams.[85]

A Soviet response was fully expected. Unwelcome at the best of times, this development was especially unwelcome now, since, according to External Affairs, "there were indications that the Germans may presently establish a puppet government in the Ukraine ... [and that] if this event takes place we may, no doubt, expect a further controversy amongst Ukrainian Canadians."[86]

British intelligence was first to alert External Affairs that a Soviet campaign aimed at Ukrainian Canadians was in the offing.[87] The department, however, already had a sense that something was underway, having been apprised by Dana Wilgress, Canada's envoy in Moscow, of news items appearing in the Soviet press on Ukrainian Canadian nationalist activities.[88] It was reported that on 13 May the leading Soviet official newspapers, *Pravda* (Truth) and *Izvestiia* (Red Star), reprinted the radio broadcast of A. Bogomolets, President of the Ukrainian Academy of Sciences. The speech lambasted the nationalist émigré community in Canada and pilloried the UCC as "traitors" whose separatist talk only inspired Germany's attempt to seize and colonise Ukraine. Bogomolets further remarked that Soviet public circles were "perplexed" that the Canadian government permitted the UCC to speak on behalf of the Ukrainian people, allegedly knowing their desire.

On 14 May an article also appeared in the same newspapers entitled "Keep Your Dirty Hands off Ukraine"; it was written by the leading Soviet Ukrainian poet and Ukrainian SSR people's commissar for education, Pavlo Tychyna. Strident and caustic, it characterised the UCC as a "Quislingite clique" that sought to sow enmity between the Allies and that with "pretended naivete exert themselves to convince the Canadian prime minister that they speak on behalf of all Canadian Ukrainians." Emphasising that after the October Revolution Ukraine was a free and equal republic of the USSR, the article concluded that it would remain so forever.[89] For Canadian officials, the importance of the propaganda lay not in the content. Of greater concern was the fact that a direct reference to an indigenous Canadian organisation had been made for the first time by the Soviet press and that this could only have been sanctioned at the highest political levels; it was an ominous sign.

Within a matter of weeks, English translations of the Tychyna and Bogomolets articles, were published by the Association of Canadian Ukrainians and released under the title *Soviet Ukraine and the Ukraino-German Nationalists in Canada.*[90] The publication was calculated to discredit the Ukrainian Canadian nationalists by capitalising on the pro-Soviet sentiment that was running high among the English-speaking Canadian public in the aftermath of the Soviet victory at Stalingrad.[91] It was clear that the effort the Canadian government had taken to contain some of the political wrangling between the Ukrainian

Canadian communists and nationalists was in danger of coming undone. More difficult still was the issue of how best to respond to Soviet authorities who, now that they were taking an active interest, were anticipated to apply even more pressure.

The concern was well-founded. Shortly after his arrival in Canada, the Soviet minister plenipotentiary, Feodor Gusev, communicated to Norman Robertson (the under-secretary of state) that the resolutions that had recently appeared in the nationalist press were unacceptable. The Soviet representative claimed the attitude in the press statements – which effectively endorsed the UCC memorandum to the prime minister of the previous March – could only be interpreted as profascist, and he failed to understand why Canada, with censorship in force, allowed newspapers to publish articles advocating the breakup of the territories of an ally.[92] The under-secretary replied to the Soviet minister that, as a matter of policy, the government did not invoke censorship to suppress editorials. Moreover, even if it were to do so, it would, in his measured opinion, "do much more damage to the general interest than would the articles themselves." Robertson asked that the Soviet Union appreciate the complexity of the problem, claiming External Affairs would equally "be happier if Ukrainians would look at the world through Canadian eyes and think of themselves solely as Canadian citizens." As he pointed out, "the process of assimilation took time." Gusev, however, was not interested in apologies. What he came to hear was the Canadian government's position on Ukrainian independence, and he was relieved by Robertson's personal assurance that "although the Ukrainians were a very large bloc in Canada ... they were not a factor in influencing Canadian government policy and too much importance should not be attached to the speeches and resolutions of the Ukrainian nationalists."[93]

In the USSR the Commissariat for Foreign Affairs also lodged a protest with Dana Wilgress. Witnessing first-hand the effects of war and moved by the suffering of the Soviet people who had until this time carried the brunt of the land war, Wilgress was not unaffected by Soviet objections. In a telegram to External Affairs, he communicated his belief that with regard to the war on the Eastern front, Ukrainian nationalists in Canada were motivated by sentiments that were hostile to the Soviet Union and that their actions could be interpreted, again, as nothing less than "pro-fascist." Because their efforts to fulfil territorial ambitions had been dashed by recent Soviet victories, he claimed Ukrainian nationalists were now seeking to promote discord between allies. The UCC memorandum to the prime minister – "a clever ruse to conceal [the] real motive which is to create discord between the Soviet Union and other United Nations" – was cited as evidence.

The issue of postwar boundaries, which was publicly addressed by the UCC in its memorandum, was an indirect cause, according to Wilgress, of the break in diplomatic relations between the Soviet Union and Poland and only served to increase Soviet suspicions of Allied intentions, which Moscow believed favoured the Polish side in the Eastern frontiers question. It was imperative, therefore, for Canada to keep clear of similar suspicions, either with regard to the Poles or the Ukrainians.[94] According to the Canadian envoy, "This would have [the] great advantage of demonstrating that we are able to follow an independent policy."[95] Wilgress argued that an uncommon opportunity presented itself now for Canada to take the lead in preserving its solidarity with the Soviet Union and that a simple, yet clear, statement denouncing the dissension and the attacks on Soviet sovereignty would significantly increase Canada's influence with that country. The minister concluded his communication by recommending the government sever its ties with those who identified with or were sympathetic to the nationalist position.[96]

Wilgress wished to emphasise the importance of the issue from the point of view of Canadian-Soviet relations and in a follow-up letter to the Canadian prime minister from the Soviet wartime capital of Kuibyshev, he would write:

It is essential that these new Canadians do not take any steps which might impair the war effort of an ally – particularly one which up to now has borne the greatest sacrifices of any of the United Nations. The separation of the Ukraine from the Soviet Union would weaken the country economically to a marked degree. It would not be much better off in the absolute sense than if it made a separate peace now with the Nazis ... One of the most effective slogans in stirring the citizens of the Soviet Union to bear the incredible burdens of the war has been "Free the Ukraine." The effectiveness of this slogan the Ukrainian Canadian Committee has sought to impair.[97]

Although he did not propose anything out of keeping with the spirit and intent of his letter to King, Wilgress remarkably ventured to suggest that since the principles of the Atlantic Charter were being used to promote territorial claims, the declaration should be abandoned by Canada for a narrower statement of war aims.

Ottawa, appreciating the gravity of the situation, responded by stating that in the event that Soviet authorities should raise further questions about the Ukrainian dispute in Canada, the Canadian minister should make it clear with the Soviets that, although both the Ukrainian Canadian Committee and the Association of Canadian Ukrainians were entitled to express their own opinions, at least within the framework of existing Canadian law, "the Canadian government [was] ... aware of [the] undesirability of any organisation or individual pursuing policies calculated to create divisions amongst the United Nations ... [and that] the situation [was] being followed from this point of view." As for Wilgress' recommendation that a statement be made in the House of Commons denouncing those efforts that aimed at creating division among the Allies, it would be followed if an opportunity presented itself in the House.[98] An opportunity was almost certain to occur, given that the long-awaited and feared Ukrainian Canadian Congress was about to take place.

The idea of a conference representing the organisations affiliated with the UCC had been bandied about since late 1941. Considerable pressure was being exerted on the UCC leadership to advance the Ukrainian independence issue, and the reluctance to do so led to scepticism within the Ukrainian nationalist community about the effectiveness of the UCC. So it was that, bowing to grassroots pressure, the executive of the UCC proposed in June 1942 to call a pan-Canadian Congress of Ukrainian Canadians under the slogan "Victory and Freedom." External Affairs was immediately informed of the proposal by George Simpson, who was in regular contact with the UCC leadership through his work in the Nationalities Branch. According to Simpson, the primary objective of the congress, postponed now until December 1942, was to give public testimonial to the war work performed by the committee. Although Simpson assumed that the Ukrainian question would be on the agenda, he was convinced any statement made could be checked informally beforehand with External Affairs for their approval, "though no reference could be made at the Conference to the fact that it had been so examined."[99]

A pan-Canadian Ukrainian congress, with its distinct political overtones, was not what was expected from the role initially envisioned for the UCC by government officials. Such a conference was considered dangerous, and the potential pitfalls were communicated to Simpson. Indeed, even if nothing detrimental was said at the event, it was argued that appearances alone could be damaging, especially in view of the new Soviet diplomatic mission to Canada, which was about to arrive. Simpson concurred that there were dangers, but he was also of the opinion that "there might be worse results if the Conference were repressed." External Affairs was not convinced and indicated that it needed to consider the matter further.[100]

It was in late September 1942 that External Affairs decided not to intervene in the congress affair, a decision undoubtedly influenced by the fact that Simpson, who in the interim had been invited to assist in drafting the congress resolutions, had shown External Affairs a copy of the draft text. Officials in the department were satisfied to the point that they had no objection to the conference proceeding as planned, at least on the basis of the material presented to them. It was made clear to Simpson, however, that extreme statements of any kind that would cause dissension and controversy between Canada and the Soviet Union had to be avoided. Advised that the department could in no way be connected with the resolutions or the congress, Simpson stated that he would try to impress upon the nationalist leadership the importance of not raising any subject that could prove politically embarrassing.[101]

Justice T.C. Davis (the associate deputy minister at National War Services), having learned independently that such a conference was being proposed, also expressed his concern to Simpson, stating that "in the light of the very great contribution being made by Russia to our freedom, it was completely essential that nothing should transpire within Canada to offend either the Russian government or the Russian people."[102] As in his discussion with External Affairs, Simpson reiterated that he would be at the congress and felt he could completely control the situation. In fact, Simpson was confident that, given the trust he enjoyed with the nationalist community, no resolution would come out of the meeting "except in the form he would dictate." But there was also the need to recognise the importance of not trying to block the initiative, since he felt that, once having committed itself, the UCC would fold unless the conference was held. More to the point, if it did fold, there was no question that the field would left "open" to the pro-Soviet Association of Canadian Ukrainians – a disastrous result in Simpson's opinion.[103] Davis agreed with Simpson that the convention should proceed, but the final decision would depend on External Affairs, and only after it had been consulted.[104] External Affairs, however, had by this time given its assent.

Simpson arranged for a discussion with the UCC leadership in Winnipeg. Communicating to them that the government did not in any way presume to say whether a congress should take place, he cautioned that there was, nevertheless, official concern that it could provide an occasion for some "irresponsible" individual to make statements that would harm Canada's relations with the Soviet Union.[105] Simpson's remarks had a profound effect, certainly greater than originally intended. Interpreting Simpson's comments as a warning and fearing they would personally become the target of security measures, the UCC executive thought it best not to convene a congress at all but to wait for a more appropriate moment to present itself, when the situation in Europe was less critical.[106] A decision to this effect was accepted at a closed session of the executive.

Justice Davis expressed satisfaction with the decision, indicating it was the most sensible thing to do under the circumstances.[107] Norman Robertson, who was keeping close watch over the situation, was equally delighted. Upon receipt of the tidings, he wrote: "I must confess that I am rather relieved at this decision, and at the same time extremely glad to learn that it had been reached independently by the members of the Executive Committee of the Ukrainian-Canadian group in Winnipeg."[108] Robertson's sense of relief, however, was premature. A heated exchange soon materialised in Saskatoon at an informal and much broader gathering of members of the various constituent organisations of the UCC. Several members were astonished that the executive, having no authority to do so without prior approval from the organisations, had presumptuously quashed the initiative. One participant at the meeting went so far as to claim it to be the work of "fifth columnists," since the fundamental issue was not the status of Ukraine, which was strictly a "theoretical question," but Canadian war work.[109] The dissatisfaction and criticism expressed with the executive compelled it to reconsider the earlier decision.[110]

A series of plenary sessions of the executive were held to discuss the matter in October 1942.[111] Contrary to the views of those who wished to limit the conference strictly to the issue of war work, it was clear that the Ukrainian question could not be avoided, since, as it was pointed out, the community itself was insisting that it be raised. The more skittish members of the committee, however, pressed for the adoption of a moderate position. Emphasizing that the Ukrainian case should be heard only on a Canadian basis, they maintained that if the Ukrainian question were to be discussed it should be done only within the framework of the Atlantic Charter and "not in its entirety." Not surprisingly, there was opposition to the proposal. Without temerity, one member of the executive questioned the purpose of a congress if the Ukrainian question was not to be addressed, since Ukrainian Canadians were already very much involved in the war effort and a conference to discuss Canadian affairs would therefore have been redundant, if not meaningless. Still another asked whether the conference was being called simply to save the UCC from fading into political obscurity. A clear and unequivocal position had to be taken, with Ukrainian Canadians aiming for nothing less than securing the same rights for Ukrainians in an independent national state as were enjoyed by others. Those who maintained this view, however, were in a minority. Conscious of government unease, the position finally adopted by the executive favoured moderation. Expressing disappointment with the decision, the representative for the hardline monarchist United Hetman Organisation would resign in early November.

A committee member communicated the outcome of the deliberations in a letter to Professor Simpson, namely, that it was not the intention of the UCC in having the issue of Ukrainian independence to the fore but that if it were raised, it would be raised only in an "incidental manner."[112] Simpson relayed the information to the deputy minister of war services and the under-secretary of state for external affairs, both of whom were pleased that the situation was still manageable. They were, however, disappointed that the idea of a conference had not been shelved, as originally planned.[113] Prudence dictated that the activities of the more militant elements be closely watched.[114]

Government officials were sensitive to the possibility of trouble, given the variable and fluid nature of the political environment, and rightly so, their fears being realised but a few short months later. The impetus was the long-simmering, but now open, row between the Polish government in exile and the USSR over Poland's eastern borders. Anxious that the question of borders not be discussed without Ukrainian interests being taken into account, the UCC executive felt it imperative to respond, at least for the record, that the "Ukrainian claim to an independent state in a free Europe should not be disregarded and the Ukrainian Question should be included in any just and permanent settlement of Europe." The response, the March memorandum to Prime Minister King, delivered by a delegation, was problematic in itself. But the subsequent public controversy that the memorandum generated and the criticism within the nationalist community that the UCC was not fully engaged forced a decision among the executive to place the Ukrainian question on the agenda at the upcoming UCC congress tentatively scheduled for July 1943.[115]

There was some reservation about pursuing this course. The ambivalence in the remarks of those present at a final special plenary session held in May disguised a deep anxiety, voiced by a few who were fearful of possible repercussions. They understood it was the government's preference that a congress not be held or that if it did take place that there would be no discussion of the Ukrainian question. Moreover, they were amply aware of the government's interest in avoiding any controversy that might "provoke Russia." There was also public opinion and the reaction of the communists to consider.

All in all, the idea of holding a congress with the Ukrainian question as its theme was not a good one, and the UCC executive understood this. But they were also aware of the impression that would have been left with the community by not following through and the consequences of this. In the end they agreed that if the issue of Ukrainian national sovereignty was to be a topic of discussion, then it was to be presented in a way that would "not threaten" the government.[116] That the final decision to place the Ukrainian question on the agenda was a difficult one was evidenced by the resignation of another key member of the UCC, Wasyl Swystun. The once implacable nationalist, now a voice of moderation, objected to the conference on the grounds that it "would deal almost exclusively with the question of Ukrainian independence and the part Canadian Ukrainians would play in achieving it."[117]

On learning of this news External Affairs were taken aback. What had initially seemed to be a situation under control now threatened to unravel. In a departmental note enquiries were made on how to contain the congress and minimise its impact. Professor Simpson was quickly asked whether he was still in a position to influence the proceedings.[118] The RCMP also increased its surveillance, especially of the Ukrainian National Federation.[119] Meanwhile, as a precautionary measure, Norman Robertson, in a hurried memo to Mackenzie King, advised him to decline any invitation he might receive and to instruct other elected officials that they do likewise or excuse themselves if they had already accepted. Robertson pointed out that "However careful and correct [the prime minister's] remarks, his presence at such a meeting would be construed as some kind of Canadian endorsement of Ukrainian nationalism, which [had] among its objectives the separation of the Ukraine from the USSR."[120] When a formal invitation was received, a telegram from the prime minister's office was sent to the UCC executive informing them that owing to Parliament being in session neither the prime minister nor any other Cabinet minister could be away from the capital.[121]

Some 600 accredited delegates and 115 guests attended the congress on 22–24 June 1943. A special undercover officer of the RCMP, who was instructed to gather information and report on developments, also managed to work himself into the crowd. Along with the proceedings of the conference, conversations and opinions were reproduced in exacting detail by the special constable, whose undercover identity was unknown to the participants. Overall, there was nothing new to report. It was observed, however, that there was an obvious note of tension and apprehension among the UCC executive, many members being unnerved by the last-minute withdrawal of a keynote speaker from the socialist League of Ukrainian Organisations, whose absence was attributed to "the fear ... that the government may not look favourably on the congress, and even take action against some of the organisations."[122]

The anxiety detected by the RCMP officer among the leadership was in fact pervasive. In contrast to the earlier bravado, there was now self-censorship, the question of Ukrainian independence being couched in terms that were carefully crafted, so as not to antagonize. Emphasis, for example, was placed on the notion that the principle of Ukrainian self-determination deserved consideration because of the sacrifices in Ukraine, the heroic struggle of the Ukrainian people against fascism in common cause with the Allies, and the selfless participation of young Ukrainian Canadians in Canada's armed forces.[123] The themes of commitment and obligation, which underpinned nearly every address, revealed not only that the leadership advocated moderation but that it also understood that only within the existing limited framework could the case of Ukrainian independence be advanced without giving offence to official sensibilities. In fact, the UCC leadership, to a man, quickly distanced itself from the few impromptu statements that went outside of the framework, disavowing any responsibility for the remarks made.[124] After all was said and done, the meeting was a nonevent.

The conference revealed the degree of uneasiness in the relationship between the community and the government. Until the last moment, despite the clear willingness of the leadership to avoid possible difficulties, there was no assurance about the outcome. In the end, the statements made did not embarrass Canada.[125] But the results could have been different. For Canadian officials, no matter how relieved they might have been, the experience proved both unsettling and unacceptable, given the potential consequences for Canadian-Soviet relations.

In late May 1943, even before the congress affair had erupted, Hume Wrong, assistant under-secretary of state for external affairs, raised the issue of restoring properties confiscated from the Ukrainian Labour Farmer Temple Association – the large left-wing mass organisation closely associated with the Communist Party of Canada and banned in 1940 as a "seditious" body. He sensed that "such an action would go some distance toward meeting the complaints of the Soviet government about Ukrainian Nationalist activities in Canada."[126]

Hume Wrong was not alone in his belief. Many of those who attended the interdepartmental meeting to discuss what action was to be taken toward the disposition of the properties – a meeting that included representatives from the Department of Justice, External Affairs, the RCMP, National War Services, and the Office of the Custodian of Enemy Alien Property – expressed the view that there was political utility in restoring the properties, especially as they related to Soviet-Canadian relations.[127] The other consideration was that this step would silence, once and for all, those who ceaselessly called for the return of the confiscated properties.[128] The problem, however, was that, ironically, nine of sixteen halls that had been sold had been purchased in judicial sales by the Ukrainian Orthodox and Catholic Churches, as well as by the nationalist organisation the Ukrainian National Federation.

It was clear to everyone that there would have to be some skilful manœuvring on the issue. It was equally clear to External Affairs, in view of what had just occurred, that those responsible for ethnic affairs at the Nationalities Branch in the Department of National War Services were incapable of dealing with the task at hand. Norman Robertson was convinced that "the right men were not being used for the job."[129]

Robertson's remarks signalled that a new phase in the government's position toward the Ukrainian Canadians was about to begin.

AN ASSESSMENT

The divide between liberal democracy and totalitarianism, which in the early war years defined for the West the nature of the global conflict, was blurred on 22 June 1941 when Nazi Germany invaded the Soviet Union and the latter was forced to join the Allied powers. For the liberal democracies, and especially Britain, whose fortunes were at their lowest ebb, the opprobrium of now associating with Hitler's former ally was beside the point. Indeed, the unexpected opportunity of gaining some relief from the German bombing of British cities was more than welcome. The question, however, was whether the Soviet Union was capable of resisting invasion, thereby allowing Britain sufficient time to prepare for the expected German assault across the English Channel.

Initial news from the Eastern front was disheartening. German forces made spectacular advances in Ukraine and elsewhere, while Soviet losses both in casualties and surrendered personnel were enormous.[130] By September, Ukraine, Belorussia, the Baltic states, and parts of Russia were under Axis control. Only when the German armed forces were on the approach to Moscow and laying siege to the city of Leningrad did the resolve of the Soviet Red Army stiffen. For senior British officials at the Foreign Office, this was encouraging news, coming as it did after the initial depressing reports from the region. It also, however, suggested that nothing should be done prematurely to undermine Soviet authority, including support for an independent Ukrainian state, which was occasionally discussed in closed circles as a possible counterweight against Nazi rule in Ukraine.

Proposals to assist in the creation of a Ukrainian national state had often been brought to the Foreign Office, but they were rejected because Ukrainian separatism was considered an artificial creation with no real evidence of popular support.[131] As time wore on, Foreign Office officials became convinced of the correctness of the strategy, if not their views. Intelligence reports indicated that because of exceptionally repressive policies in Reichkommissariat Ukraine, collaboration between the Ukrainian population and the German administration was not significant, while popular armed resistance was on the rise.[132] From the British perspective, the political nature of the resistance, nationalist or communist, was inconsequential. It was sufficient to know that it existed and was contributing to the defeat of fascism.[133] To support a Ukrainian separatist movement, whether real or imagined, would have needlessly complicated matters.

That Britain could not seriously entertain Ukrainian independence was further underscored by the difficulties it potentially posed in Britain's relations with Poland. Although there had been some discussion in 1939–40 of accommodating Ukrainian demands for autonomy in a restructured Polish state or a new Polish-Ukrainian commonwealth, the integrity of Polish frontiers was a principle from which Britain would not retreat during the critical early war years.[134] This position applied even after June 1941, and it held at least until late 1943, when de facto Soviet control over the area rendered any further discussion of frontiers moot. British commitment was not only the result of the legacy of Munich – the very integrity of British diplomacy was at stake on this question – but also reflected a real concern that any change in power relations in Eastern Europe would affect Britain's influence in the region and, concomitantly, in Europe. The strength of this commitment could be seen in Britain's firm stand during the negotiation of the Anglo-Soviet Treaty, when fierce pressure was placed on British officials to recognise the Soviet position on the frontiers question.[135] To those who cared to take note of such things, British resolve demonstrated that the Ukrainian nationalist demand for an *independent* Ukrainian state was not even a matter for discussion.

Britain's reassurance regarding Polish territorial sovereignty, which had been given to the Polish government in exile after the latter reached an accord with the Soviet Union, found its logical expression in the Atlantic Charter. Churchill made it abundantly clear to Roosevelt during the course of their historic meeting at sea that the principal aim of a joint declaration would be to set sight on the broad objectives of the Allied struggle, not least of which was to pen a statement on the *restoration* of the independence of occupied countries.[136] With this aim in view, the document was signed by both parties on 12 August 1941.

Despite the attempt to make clear that the intent of the declaration was the full restoration of the *former* sovereign rights of states, the statement was given a broad interpretation in the international community.[137] The charter was viewed as a promise of liberation not only by those nations who had been deprived of their independence under fascism but also by those who had never enjoyed self-government, including the colonial peoples of Africa and Asia and the peripheral nations of Europe. To a certain extent the ambiguity of the Atlantic Charter was reinforced by public statements made by Churchill and Roosevelt themselves, both of whom declared at one time or another that the charter had universal application to "all peoples, and especially the oppressed and the conquered."

The potential contradiction that the declaration posed was not lost upon political analysts in various capitals of the world. Not surprisingly, Nazi propagandists in Berlin sardonically asked whether it meant that Britain was prepared to divest itself of its empire. In Tokyo it was declared that, under the guise of liberalism, Britain and the United States were again intending to maintain their superior global position by reestablishing the prewar status quo. But more revealing and disconcerting for Allied officials, who instructed their diplomatic representatives to report on public reaction to the declaration, were the attitudes expressed in Helsinki, Zurich, and Stockholm. The socialist and liberal press in Helsinki spoke of the bankruptcy of the Anglo-American liberal war aims in light of Britain's alliance with the Soviet Union, stating that should "the USSR [win] the present war with [the] aid [of] England and [the] United States [then] this would signify [the] destruction of small states and peoples bordering Russia." The Finnish people, so the argument went, "were not fighting with Germany for the creation of a New Order" but against an alternate order that threatened their national existence. In Sweden analysts noted the contradiction that the Anglo-Soviet alliance posed, leading many there to make the comparison between the declaration with the Versailles agreements signed years before.[138]

This and other criticism had to be met head on, as indeed Churchill did when he implied in his first public statement on the charter that each case would have to be judged on its own merit. The ultimate criterion, he argued, would be the political and social maturity of the people in question. In this sense, British colonial policy was perceived as being very much in keeping with the political clauses of the declaration: self-rule could be granted "only when the economic and social development of a native people justify it, since in British opinion good government is as important as self-government." Harry Hopkins, President Roosevelt's special envoy, enunciated the American position, indicating that although the pledge of the Atlantic Charter offered a system of security for all nations and the real possibility for self-determination, "[this] pledge [implied] an obligation for each nation ... to fulfil scrupulously its established duties to other nations ... and to make its full contribution to the maintenance of an enduring peace."[139]

The Anglo-American interpretation of the charter had several profound implications. Without jeopardising existing bilateral relations in Europe, notably the Anglo-Soviet and Anglo-Polish agreements, it guaranteed a security coalition that fulfilled the primary objective of defeating Nazi Germany. Moreover, although the document had as its original objective a return to the status quo ante, it was sufficiently open-ended to ensure that in the event the Soviet Union became a player in the postwar period and concessions had to be made – for example, concerning the Polish eastern frontiers – they could be made with few political repercussions. Concessions were possible because the onus of political responsibility lay with those nations who aspired to "freedom." Their actions would determine their future. Only those nations fulfilling their obligation to the international community would find their rightful place in the family of nations. In the context of the global war, this condition necessarily meant contributing to the defeat of the Axis.

Unity and the commitment to the struggle of the United Nations, therefore, came to be the measure that would apply in determining legitimacy. Those who undermined Allied unity would be identified as politically irresponsible and incapable of self-government. This principle became important for relations between the dominant Allied actors and the peripheral players whose interests required the support of the former. The fear of appearing an obstinate, if not reluctant, partner, for example, was to weigh heavily in the dealings of the Polish government in exile with the Soviet Union.[140] At a different level, this same fear would also condition Ukrainian Canadian attitudes toward the war effort, as well as the relationship between the Ukrainian Canadian community leadership and state authorities. Indeed, although Ukrainian nationalist leaders privately suspected that little faith could be put in the Atlantic Charter, they felt there was no alternative but to demonstrate through loyalty and sacrifice that they were prepared to assume a share of that responsibility.[141] Coincidentally, they thought that at least in this way they could also ensure for themselves the minimum right to speak on behalf of the Ukrainian nation.

At one level, the Anglo-American interpretation of the Atlantic Charter provided Allied authorities with the means to disarm the demands of those who pressed for political change, while encouraging their participation in the war. But also on another level it ironically problematized the Allied position, made especially evident in the Canadian case. Specifically, the liberal interpretation meant that the basic thrust of the principle of self-determination for nations remained intact. Therefore, try as they might to avoid the fact, the alliance with the Soviet Union and Canada's relationship with it – considered vitally important from the perspective of its place in the postwar world – was a real problem for Canadian officials in the context of the charter. It not only threatened to expose the liberal premises of the declaration as false but also, more particularly, jeopardise the basic objective of state security by denying the legitimacy of the concerns of the countless tens of thousands of Ukrainian Canadians and other Canadians who were of the conviction that this was a struggle for a new liberal-democratic order.

The paradox and danger engendered by a situation where an alliance with the Soviet Union was both necessary and, at the same time, a liability was not lost upon some Canadian officials. Cognisant of the fact that the declaration highlighted the contradiction, a senior Canadian statesman called upon Canada to abandon the Atlantic Charter as a document guiding Canada's war aims and to replace it with a narrower statement of aims.[142] The suggestion to place political commitments above the ethical, liberal principles upon which the struggle was based, however, was impractical. It ignored a basic distinction that was being made that separated the warring powers: the distinction between liberator and oppressor.[143] There could be no escaping this distinction, for it was on this foundation that the call for sacrifice was being made and the legitimacy of the state's ability to conduct war was based.

The alternative, therefore, was to live with the contradiction. To be sure, the state's prerogative to employ force was also a possibility. However, in the case of the Ukrainian Canadian minority, neither the social nor the political conditions existed to use the kind of force that had been employed against the Japanese Canadians.[144] Ukrainian Canadians were enlisting in unprecedented numbers, and the community pointed to those soldiers who had died or were captured at Hong Kong and Dieppe as a testament to their sacrifice and their right to speak out on behalf of Ukrainian self-determination. The contradiction and the constraints under which state authorities operated were to have significant repercussions on how the state conducted itself in its relations with the Ukrainian minority in Canada. Ukrainian Canadians could only accept the Allied argument that they were assisting their own cause by advancing the cause of Canada. From the government's perspective, however, this argument alone offered no guarantee that Ukrainian Canadians would respond positively. To effectively manage the situation, state officials would continue to monitor and direct, whenever possible, the behaviour of the community, while sharing intelligence with the Western Allies, who, for security reasons, showed a growing interest in the Ukrainian Canadian "problem."

The Western Allies, however, were not the only ones who demonstrated an interest in Ukrainian Canadian affairs. Soviet authorities also kept abreast of the way Canadian statesmen were handling the persistent demands of Ukrainian Canadian nationalists. Significantly, their interest, and later their obvious consternation and protests at the way the whole matter was being handled, led to even bolder interventions by Ottawa, culminating in initiatives to discreetly inform Soviet authorities that both countries shared a common interest in seeing the Ukrainian question disappear. Concessions were made in the hope that they would demonstrate that Canada was acting as a "responsible" international actor and that the government was sincere in establishing a good working relationship with the Soviet Union, which, it was hoped, would extend into the postwar era. Living the contradiction, in effect, was not to be without costs.

4 The Nationalities Branch and the Interests of State

For the majority of Ukrainian Canadians, the period of Nazi-Soviet collaboration had offered the promise of liberation for Ukraine. Germany's invasion of the Soviet Union in June 1941, however, changed all that. No longer was the dispute over western Ukrainian lands confined to Poles and Ukrainians. The Soviet Union was now insisting that there would be no changes to the frontiers of November 1940; the annexed territories would remain forever part of the USSR. These were anxious moments for Ukrainian Canadians, who feared that the Western liberal democracies, in their effort to reconcile the two protagonists – Poland and the Soviet Union – would lose sight of the principle of self-determination for nations. In fact, Ukrainians in Canada, upon learning of the claims and counterclaims concerning the eastern borders made by both the Polish government in exile and the Soviet Union, immediately protested what was described as "this cattle-sale of nations" and called upon the Canadian government to interpret the "apparent contradiction" between the war aims of Canada and the principles of its Polish ally.[1]

Tracy Philipps, attached at the time to the RCMP, through the Department of Justice, as a specialist-adviser in European affairs, recognised the importance of the contradiction and its repercussions. For him, both the source and the resolution of the problem lay in the domain of foreign affairs. He stated that "In a wartime like this, when we are all looking back anxiously over our shoulders to our respective threatened motherlands, the interpretations or lack of interpretations of foreign affairs to the foreign-born, of our, and our allies' attitude to them, go a long way to make unity, or mar loyalty to Canada."[2]

Drawing on the experience of the recent past, Philipps believed that it was this lack of an authoritative and coherent interpretation of European events that had allowed certain of Canada's ethnic minorities to drift into an anti-British frame of mind. He cited as an example the Italian Canadians, who, although largely anti-German in their views, were becoming anti-British since "Mussolini's pro-German clique" had declared war on Britain. Although this attitude in itself was unfortunate and would require considerable time to correct, the concern was that both the community and the government were now faced with a situation where volunteer Italian Canadian enlistments were being "baited in the training camps where they [were serving] as British subjects ... [while] shop windows [were being] broken of Italians who had two sons serving as Canadians overseas."[3] Xenophobia threatened to disrupt the delicate social balance, as well as to jeopardise domestic war work. The problem called for a bold and prompt plan. But as Philipps recognised, plans were possible only when the framework into which they would fit was known.

For Philipps, it was false to assume that there were any communities that were "disloyal or even quietly discontented as Canadians." The minority communities were, nevertheless, anxious because of the current events. Recent international developments, of course, were, strictly speaking, beyond the control of Canadian statesmen. But this did not mean that Canadian authorities could remain passive. It was incumbent upon Canadian officials to provide a framework that would allow for a clear interpretation of the war aims of the Allied nations. For this reason, Philipps turned to External Affairs for their reading of the new situation in Eastern Europe, stating that "External Affairs alone are competent to give us this" and asking that they provide, at the very least, some statement to allay the growing excitement of Ukrainian Canadians.[4] Time, moreover, was of the essence, since Ukrainian Canadians were pressing the minister of the Department of National War Services to talk to them in Winnipeg "on the Russian and Polish position in reference to the world's Ukrainians, and the Canadian attitude to it."[5] Philipps cautioned, however, that care should be exercised in any statement that might be made, in view of the millions of Ukrainians in North America who were engaged both in key war industries and in agriculture. He stressed that "For Ukrainians throughout the world, this is the most momentous moment [sic] of their history. Hitler, who may be in a position to offer them the dearest object of a people's mystic dreams (just those visions for which men fight like mad-men) simply cannot afford not to try and exploit this on Ukrainians in the vital war industries of North America which are today the greatest menace to the continued existence of all he is and holds."[6]

Although the Department of External Affairs did urge the Polish government in exile on at least two occasions to make some declaration "to keep [Ukrainian Canadians] on the right lines," it avoided making a statement outlining the Canadian position on developments in Europe.[7] The issue was complicated and had to be approached cautiously, since it was not evident to the department how to deal with the issue effectively without causing greater difficulties for itself. This was not the case with National War Services. Entrusted with the domestic responsibility of dealing with "foreign-born" communities and their mobilisation behind the war effort, the department had responded immediately by recommending the establishment of a special government branch under its jurisdiction. The stated objectives of the new branch, as initially outlined by the department's deputy minister, were to conduct propaganda among the groups and implement plans that would "weave these people into the fabric of our Canadian nation."[8]

The idea of establishing a government agency to deal with ethnic issues and issues related to immigrants had been broached by Tracy Philipps in the summary report he had submitted in January 1941, upon the conclusion of his tour among the "foreign-born" communities of Central and Western Canada.[9] Philipps recommended at that time the creation of a government branch that would work with the ethnic groups and that could liase between the various groups and public officials.[10] The proposal was again put forward in a series of memoranda in May 1941, after Philipps had returned from a short sojourn to Washington, where he had gone to assess the organisational setup of a government agency that had been created for the purpose of working with ethnic groups in the United States.

Philipps was impressed by the American operation and argued for a similar agency in Canada that could perhaps work in tandem with its US counterpart.[11] Recognising the public security dimension that linked both Canada and the United States on the issue, he emphasized the need for hemispheric cooperation in the context of global war. On the basis of American and Canadian census results for 1930–31, Philipps estimated that "foreign-born citizens," chiefly of East-Central European heritage, constituted a third of the total American and a quarter of the total Canadian population, while half the labour force of North America's vital heavy industries was Slavic in origin. As a factor in the war, their opinions and concerns would matter, and any policy developed would require cross-border consultation and careful consideration.

In the specific case of Canada, however, there was an additional dimension. Unlike the United States, Canada did not posses a clearly defined national identity, which made immigrant integration a difficult proposition. An important function, therefore, of an agency like the American one would be to generate and maintain support for the country among the "foreign-born" by cultivating what Phillips termed "a consciousness of national solidarity." This consciousness was to be encouraged by reinforcing the idea of the collective purpose behind national defence and the notion that democracy was "not so much ... a fixed form of government ... as a moral concept of human relations." Of equal importance for Philipps, the historic Anglo-Celtic and French communities of Canada needed to be convinced of the important role and contribution that Canada's other ethnic communities could play in the national development of the country. Social harmony, in his view, called for mutual respect based on the implicit recognition of the equal status of all Canadians before the law. With this in mind, Philipps recognised the need to prevent discriminatory practices, especially in the workplace, which unfortunately did much to create division between peoples and within society.

Philipps was aware that a segment of public opinion in Canada, notably "old British subjects," would resist the idea that ethnic concerns had to be accommodated, insofar as this idea could be interpreted as a concession and a sign of weakness on the part of Canada. He appreciated the underlying fear, which held that this idea would heighten expectations and open the way to further demands. Philipps, however, countered by noting that the same public would undoubtedly suggest that "it was only necessary to issue authoritative orders to all the foreign-born communities that they must just become Canadians immediately, and leave it at that." This was a narrow and presumptive attitude, because it ignored the deep and heartfelt feelings that every migrant and their descendants shared, including those domiciled Anglo-Celts five generations removed who looked affectionately to the motherland with much hope, yet apprehension, in these difficult times. With his usual penchant for metaphor, Philipps was to write

As the nations of Europe melted before Hitler, they fed the river of old world nationalisms which had already started to flow again strongly here on both sides (and across) the border. Such a river can not be confined or damned without danger. The reality of its existence can not be ignored. It is therefore best to turn it to [our] account and canalise the current so that it shall not break out here and flood or disintegrate the nation's fields. With care, this rising flood can be harmonised and harnessed with our own ... If it can be fused, the current can be Canadianized and be utilised to enrich and reinforce the Nation in the process.[12]

Philipps, however, also recognised that a people's identification with their place of origin was not just a social but also a psychological phenomenon. In the case of recent immigrants, ethnicity provided an anchor in an otherwise unfamiliar world. Therefore, it was neither possible nor desirable to force newcomers to abandon what was important to them. And yet the problem remained of integrating this element at the psychological level into the public mainstream. For Philipps, the answer, therefore, was to use ethnicity as a point of reference in shifting attitudes away from "racial separateness" towards "Canadianism," in order to demystify old world identity by locating and building on the importance of that identity within the Canadian context. This strategy entailed creating a new narrative, with its own images, upon which loyalty to Canada could be based.[13] The vocabulary of the new myth would not rely on traditional and largely spurious symbols such as King and country – whose King and whose country? – but rather, would look to those principles that underpinned the liberal political and economic order of North America as the glue that would bind a divergent people together. In this regard, Philipps claimed that Canada shared with the United States both a future and a common opportunity to build a new social edifice that would combine the best of both the old and new worlds.

In Philipps' opinion, it was a mistake to ignore the pull or the significance of ethnic allegiance. In their private domain, where they sensed a world in flux, Philipps claimed that it was often to the known and tested features of family and community that immigrants turned for solace and security. In the case of German Canadians, Philipps would argue, it was possible to overestimate their Nazism, but it was dangerous to underestimate their Germanism, since the telling criterion in war was always "blood." Moreover, it was naive to assume that Nazi Germany would not try to exploit this basic emotional tie to their advantage.[14] Now more than ever, it was necessary to recognise that these communities could not be alienated or isolated. Now more than ever, it was necessary, by making them a part of the country, to secure and guarantee the loyalty of large segments of Canadian society who, through their labour, were in an immediate position to influence, and perhaps determine, the future course of the war.

The agency, then, that Philipps recommended be created was to have educational work as its principal task, promoting democracy and the idea of Canada as a society in which each ethnic community had a vital role to play. In the context of the war effort, this idea would have a precise meaning and carry with it certain obligations. It meant, above all, giving wide recognition to the contribution of ethnic groups to the war effort and conveying to them the importance of their present and future role as they participated in the life and institutions of the country. To this end, Philipps suggested that the liberal elements within each community be encouraged to take the initiative in promoting this point of view. As for the organisation of the agency, it would be small yet specialised, consisting of a director who would oversee the work of field officers and other personnel assigned to several sections that would deal with the major language groups.[15]

Justice Davis' recommended the creation of a departmental division along the lines of the agency described by Philipps in his submissions, but the recommendation was not immediately acted upon, despite the urgency with which the matter was communicated to the minister of the Department of National War Services. Philipps despaired that much of his work in establishing contacts among the large ethnic communities across Canada would come to naught. Having originally been sent to Canada by British authorities, Philipps asked Malcolm MacDonald at the British High Commission in Ottawa for an indication of direction or, at minimum, some coordination of efforts.[16] Without a mandate from the Canadian government, Philipps considered himself to be in a compromising position and claimed that he was now being regarded as a "police-agent of the government sent up to play a confidence trick to nose out the attitudes and political affiliations of [ethnic] labour."[17] Wishing to avoid a situation where he was seen to have betrayed their confidence, Philipps indicated that if he could not render any further service to the Canadian government, then he hoped that the British government would "release him from his duty" to work among the groups in North America. The gesture was premature.

The minister, J.T. Thorson, was a new appointment, and it was not until August that Phillips' idea was brought before Cabinet. In the context of the recognised need to broaden public information among the "foreign-born," the idea of a foreign languages section that would devote itself to the issue was approved in principle.[18] Philipps, still attached to the RCMP at the time, was immediately asked by Davis to draft a position paper outlining the objectives and a possible strategy for such a branch.[19] Delighted by the prospect, Philipps prepared a document that was to serve as the basis for discussion at an interdepartmental meeting scheduled for the end of October.

The position paper drew heavily on many of the ideas first outlined by Philipps in his tour report of January 1941.[20] The role of the branch, for instance, was to advise the Department of National War Services, but in keeping with his earlier prescriptions, since the work impinged on international relations, he argued that the division had to maintain close ties with External Affairs. He was also concerned that the activities of the proposed branch not only address the immediate needs of war policy but also reflect the long-term objective of immigrant integration. Press, radio, and film could be put to use in providing a Canadian viewpoint, but overall, he noted, the branch's task would be to interpret events and public policy for these groups, keeping in mind their particular background and "the special pressures to which they are subjected." Moreover, since ethnic integration was not just a Canadian concern but a North American one as well, he recommended closer cooperation with a similar organisation being set up by the United States government.[21] As for the idea, raised elsewhere, that the work of the branch be subsumed under the existing Bureau of Public Information, Philipps rejected it, reasoning that public information could be misconstrued as propaganda and widely resented as such.[22]

The interdepartmental meeting was held on 30 October 1941. Those in attendance officially approved of the creation of an administrative branch and appeared to agree in principle with the recommendations in Philipps' paper, save those that dealt with the line of authority. The branch was to be located within the Bureau of Public Information, although it was conceded that its field of activity would not necessarily be restricted to public information. Indeed, the branch was expected to make suggestions and recommendations as they related to the problems and difficulties experienced by the ethnic groups and to advise on trends of thought and policy among Canada's ethnic minorities. It was felt that branch personnel, serving in an advisory capacity, could provide much-needed information on broad developments from which policy guidelines could be drawn. The Department of External Affairs, however, wished to underline that it alone reserved the right to formulate policy insofar as it related to questions that affected the war effort and Allied relations. In this regard, Norman Robertson, the under-secretary of state representing External Affairs at the meeting, indicated there was already a full exchange of information with the governments of the United Kingdom and the United States on this matter.[23]

Other departmental officials implicitly understood that External Affairs would be the senior arbiter of policy. Justice Davis, in a memo to E.H. Coleman, under-secretary of state for Canada, indicated that the proposed section "would have to work in the closest co-operation with the Department of External Affairs as that department is the one which carries out government policy with respect to the nations from which these people originally come and in our activities among these people in Canada we must be governed by the general policies of the Department of External Affairs."[24] The willingness of the Department of National War Services to defer to External Affairs on matters of "high politics" mirrored the importance that those present attached to the international dimension of the issue. But more significantly, the jurisdictional overlap guaranteed that the branch's activities would be carefully monitored to ensure that they were in keeping with the existing policy.

Once the details had been worked out by the interdepartmental committee, a submission was made to Cabinet by the minister for the Department of National War Services, J.T. Thorson, on 27 January 1942. It recommended to the federal Cabinet the appointment of an advisory committee on co-operation in Canadian citizenship.[25] Cabinet, however, decided that such a committee might preferably be established by the minister under the powers given to him by the Department of National War Services Act of 1940. The Committee on Co-operation in Canadian Citizenship was thereby constituted under the independent authority of the minister for National War Services. Professor Simpson was appointed chairman of the committee and senior adviser to the director of the Bureau of Public Information, while Tracy Philipps was appointed European adviser.[26] Other members of the committee included political appointees and individuals who had a long-standing interest and experience in matters of citizenship and education related to immigration. Simpson, Philipps, and a small staff became the executive agency of the committee and, for departmental purposes, were designated as a separate branch with a small appropriation. The new executive agency was known as the Nationalities Branch. Simpson, retaining the title of senior adviser to the director of the Bureau of Public Information, was also appointed director of the Nationalities Branch. An editorial section, to deal with the ethnic press, was also set up almost immediately within the Nationalities Branch under the direction of Dr V.J. Kaye, Philipps' long-time associate and friend.

The Nationalities Branch, beginning operations in February 1942, was forced to work around several past government decisions, including those that had been made with respect to the disputed ULFTA halls. Several of the halls had already been sold in judicial sales. The question was what to do with the remainder, a delicate issue in view of the endless petitioning for the restoration of the remaining property.

Philipps repeated his earlier observations about the initial wisdom of having seized the halls.[27] They had been built by public-spirited individuals who had very little to do with radical politics, and it was his contention that they served primarily as community centres, providing much-appreciated cultural entertainment and enrichment for a largely isolated ethnic working class. The stated intent behind the seizure was to prevent the halls from being used for political work by the Communist Party of Canada, but, as he indicated, party organisational work did not depend on the existence of the halls. It was, therefore, a mistake for Canadian authorities to persist in identifying the rank-and-file ULFTA membership with the CPC or to fail now to support some means by which to fill the void created by the closures. As regards the mooted plan to use the unsold halls for multiethnic gatherings, he claimed this plan to be impractical, if not "utopian": "Penitent Prussians would be expected to prance with Poles. Newly naturalised Germans would jest with Jews. Hungarians would be expected to play ball with Romanians, Ukrainians with Russians, and Italians with Austrians. Rabbits and ferrets, lions and lambs, cats and dogs, would all mix and dance together, till they became good Canadians ... or till the police arrived with the ambulances on the way to the morgue."[28] Philipps cautioned that officials were in jeopardy of creating a colossal blunder if they assumed, in the spirit of good will or because the government of Canada willed it, that the various groups would set aside their historical differences and vendettas. The collage and clamour of nationalities demanded a critical appreciation of the particulars of each group, including their respective historical pasts. Only by relying on their best qualities and on the basis of a common "Canadianism," Philipps argued, could these elements be brought into the mainstream.

George Simpson shared Philipps' view that it was unwise to have seized ULFTA properties and later to have sold several of them to rival Ukrainian Canadian nationalist and church organisations. He agreed with Christian Smith, city editor of the *Saskatoon Star-Phoenix*, who privately expressed his disappointment to Simpson that the government's approach on the question of seized properties was not in the national interest and that "it was scratching deep grooves in the surface of national unity."[29] Simpson, however, did take exception to Smith's allegation that in this matter, as in other matters of government policy, "favouritism had been shown the [Ukrainian] Rightists." Simpson corrected Smith, stating that this was not the deliberate intention of government policy. The halls were disposed of according to ordinary procedure, being offered for sale through local agents and in all cases open to competitive bidding. To make sense of the situation, Simpson argued, it had to be put in context, namely that the Ukrainian Canadian communists were attempting to capitalise on their conflict with the nationalists by undermining public confidence in the Canadian government, falsely representing it as being somehow now sympathetic to fascism.[30] Such motives imputed to the government fomented suspicion and doubt. Moreover, when the nationalists were tarred with the "brush" of fascism, misunderstanding was being created between whole sections of the Canadian public. Simpson condemned these attacks, concluding that "We must not allow the rivalries of small leaders to becloud our judgment and confuse our loyalties ... In one's sympathy for the underdog, it is well to keep one's head clear."[31]

Keeping a clear head was no easy task, given the rhetoric emanating from both sides, with the Ukrainian Canadian press serving as a forum. Censorship authorities in the Department of Revenue, one of the many agencies entrusted to monitor the situation, would keep Norman Robertson at External Affairs apprised of developments, providing him with translations of the more onerous articles.[32] The Nationalities Branch, on the other hand, disturbed by the exchanges taking place, sought to diffuse the situation by suggesting to the Ukrainian Canadian Committee – the target for much of the invective – that it refrain from debating the issues, because any response could easily be misinterpreted.[33] This was easier said than done, since there was every indication a campaign was being prepared in support of the interned communists and the ULFTA.

In early March 1942, at the conclusion of a National Conference for Democratic Rights held in Ottawa, several delegations were organised to discuss with government and House members the prospect not only of releasing the communist internees but of rescinding the ban on both the CPC and the ULFTA and restoring the seized Labour Farmer Temples.[34] A Ukrainian delegation accompanied by Angus McInnis, a CCF member of Parliament, met with the Honourable Norman McLarty, secretary of state and minister responsible for overseeing the Office of the Custodian of Enemy Alien Property. Similarly, a delegation representing the National Council for Democratic Rights, a civil liberties association closely identified with the *Canadian Tribune*, spoke with the minister of justice, the Honourable Louis St Laurent. Although no commitments were forthcoming, the intervention was seen as necessary and useful because of a scheduled policy review to be conducted by a Special Commons Committee on the Defence of Canada Regulations. To this end the delegations succeeded in winning over several members of Parliament who, subsequently, would question St Laurent in the House about the seizure of the properties and the legality of the continuing internment of Canadian communists.[35] Supporters of the banned ULFTA, meanwhile, were encouraged to petition the government for the release of the detainees and to condemn it for having seized the halls – "[an] unpardonable offence against that part of Ukrainians, which built and supported the banned organisations often to the detriment of their own health and pocket" – and for "[listening] to our enemies who were germanophiles even in the last war and are now known amongst us as Hitler's agents though they mask themselves with lip service of Canadian patriotism."[36]

The nationalists were on the defensive, and, not to be outdone, they raised the spectre of a communist conspiracy in the recruiting of young men for the armed service. To counter the threat, W. Kossar, of the UNF, suggested that the commanding district officers in the military avail themselves of the organisational skills of "reliable" Ukrainian Canadians, who, he claimed, would be more than willing to contribute to the formation of Ukrainian units in the reserve or in the active army.[37] As for the moderates within the nationalist community, a few were disheartened by the divisiveness and the growing public confusion over the Ukrainian question and expressed deep reservations about continuing the polemic. The idea was even entertained that some sort of accommodation be made with the communists, if only to keep before the public eye the situation in Ukraine, which currently was at the epicentre of the European conflict and whose population was undergoing an especially difficult trial.[38] The change of heart among the moderates was also undoubtedly a reaction to the political fallout that resulted from Hlynka's speech in Parliament, which had raised the stakes by elevating the dispute to the level of international relations.[39] The speech was no small matter. Nor was the looming question of the plebiscite on conscription that was about to be held.

The issue of conscription had long been a sensitive one in Canadian politics in view of public opposition in Quebec to the idea of sending French Canadian sons to fight in "English" wars. Yet it was clear to the political leadership in Ottawa that Canada's defence needs would eventually require conscripts, and in 1942 a referendum was proposed with the hope of releasing the government from its previous pledge not to conscript.[40] Public opinion in Quebec was of primary concern, but, in light of the alliance with the USSR, the sentiment of the Eastern European communities also had to be considered. In particular, anecdotal evidence suggested that there was confusion within the Ukrainian community, namely to the effect that support for conscription necessarily meant support for the Soviet Union. These problems did not bode well. Government officials, apprehensive about the possible implications, suggested that the Nationalities Branch actively campaign for Ukrainian Canadian support on the plebiscite.[41] There was some indication, however, that this campaign would be difficult. The polls showed that even if the notion of the alliance with the USSR was successfully uncoupled from the question of conscription, there was still very little enthusiasm for conscription among Canadian farmers and the poor, categories in which Ukrainian Canadians were disproportionately overrepresented.

Recognising the potential for disaster, the Ukrainian Canadian Committee released a widely distributed communiqué before the vote, hoping to clarify the meaning of the issues involved and to encourage support for the government's position. It would also chastise those who might vote against conscription, declaring that "only those who do not care whether Canada will win this war ... or whether the enemy will defeat her and turn [her] into the same hell [that] he has created in subjugated European countries, may vote against it. Only an enemy of Canada may entertain such an idea, but we are certain that such persons cannot be found among Ukrainian Canadians."[42] Equally, the Ukrainian nationalist press, expressing confidence in the government, appealed to the patriotism of Ukrainian Canadians, urging them to vote in favour of conscription.[43]

The appeals failed. The referendum, held 27 April 1942, turned out badly for the Ukrainian Canadian community. Although Quebec and the six heavily populated Francophone constituencies outside that province were expected to vote "No," the results for several Prairie ridings, where there were large numbers of German and Ukrainian Canadians, were startling. A heavy "No" vote, for example, was registered in the "Ukrainian" electoral ridings of Vegreville, Yorkton, and Provencher.[44]

The Ukrainian nationalist leadership, unnerved by the results, explained to George Simpson that inadequate information in the rural areas in Saskatchewan and rumours regarding the implications of the vote undercut the government's position. Kossar tried to assure Simpson that "nationally minded Ukrainians were not and are not 'potential fifth-columnists.' They are loyal citizens of Canada and they have, as the people of other origins, the national sentiment of the land from which they came ... Ukrainians, in spite of the unsatisfactory result of the vote, will do everything to uphold Canada's full confidence in them. Our only hope as citizens of this country and as Ukrainians is in a victorious Canada."[45] Publicly, however, the leadership, for the most part, disavowed any responsibility for the results, blaming instead the communists, opposition parties, and the government for not appointing Ukrainians to positions of authority and for its "silence" on the Ukrainian question.[46]

Official reaction was mixed. Simpson, responding to a confidential letter from the Saskatchewan attorney general's office, which noted that the community and its leadership were insincere in their professed loyalty, rejected the view that the "No" vote among Ukrainian Canadians was intentional and deliberate.[47] Philipps attributed the outcome to a profound inability of members of the community to comprehend the issues and significance of the vote, as well as to the failure of the government to adequately prepare public opinion.[48] Others in the government, however, remained sceptical. Justice Davis would write:

It is strange that throughout all sections of the country wherein there was a rather heavy population of people who either came to Canada from lands of Europe, or who were descendants thereof, that they seemed to be able to crystallise their minds in the matter, notwithstanding the confusion, to the extent of voting in the negative on the Plebiscite. However, what has happened, has happened, and all this totals up to the fact that the situation should be reviewed ... and such action as can be properly taken to deal with the problem which now confronts us.[49]

The "problem" to which Davis was in part referring was that the results of the plebiscite gave further cause for animosity between the nationalists and the communists. In Fort William, Ontario, an area with a significant ethnic Ukrainian concentration, representatives of the local Association to Aid the Fatherland, identified the nationalists as fifth columnists and demanded the municipal government exercise its authority in the quarters over which they had jurisdiction.[50] The pro-Soviet newspaper *Ukrainske zhyttia* (Ukrainian Life), identifying the culpable role of nationalists in the referendum, noted that hoping to prevent Canada from aiding the Soviet Union, they voted "No."[51]

Elsewhere, the results of the plebiscite provided the necessary backdrop for William Kardash's *Hitler's Agents in Canada*, a publication whose title was designed to attract an already suspicious public. Contemptuous of all nationalists but reserving his harshest criticism for the Ukrainian National Federation, Kardash pointed to the results of the plebiscite as evidence of the work of this fifth-column group. Urging Ukrainian Canadians "to expose the quislings in their midst," he insisted the government conduct an immediate investigation of the organisation. "It doesn't sound logical that we can fight Hitlerism abroad," the uncompromising Kardash argued, "and encourage its friends at home." Demanding a stop to the "anti-soviet/pro-nazi" activity of the nationalists, he ended his charge to the government with the final words, "Do it now."[52]

Meanwhile, the perception that Ottawa was negligent in shielding the nationalist community from this and other attacks fuelled the view among the nationalists that the government was abandoning the community and retreating from its professed role of preserving national unity. One prominent member of the leadership, now left to fend for itself, indicated that if the government did not do something to stem the flow of public invective, the nationalists would take the matter into their own hands, and then "the fat will properly be in the fire."[53]

Contrary to this opinion, government, and especially the Nationalities Branch, was doing all it could to temper the influences on both sides. Philipps, who sketched out much of the branch's strategy, stated that more attention and a large part of the division's resources were being devoted to the problem of the foreign-language press. Believing the material published in the ethnic press was the source of much of the controversy, Philipps suggested that a short-handed way to deal with the situation was to replace it with "responsible" news and information.

Although the branch's existing editorial section received, by and large, the co-operation of the ethnic press, understaffing severely handicapped its ability to provide the necessary information to redirect the focus of ethnic groups from issues that tended to disunify. Philipps pointed to the United Kingdom foreign-language material, which was created originally for European audiences and was received by the Nationalities Branch for its use, as an example of the type of written copy that was unacceptable because it was largely insensitive to the Canadian scene.[54] Philipps was convinced that if a Canadian viewpoint was to be conveyed to the communities, it had to be prepared by Canadians and produced in the mother tongue of ethnic groups. It was Philipps' contention that their "Europeanism" had to be used as a "point of departure ... and a base from which to work away, towards Canadianism." As he would argue, "Many of them speak English well enough. But it is usually narrowly confined to a limited vocabulary sufficient to meet the simple needs of their daily work. But for general purposes they do not yet think in English. For any profound and proper understanding, it is essential to a man's needs to have things presented to him in the language in which he thinks."[55] Providing the material and then having it presented in the various mother tongues required specialised personnel. Philipps, consequently, recommended increasing the staff of the branch with this goal in mind.[56]

Philipps also pushed for a policy of systematic foreign-language broadcasting among the larger ethnic groups of Canada. A memorandum was prepared urging that the federal broadcasting agency, the CBC, implement a program that would see a Canadian interpretation of the news from the various motherlands and introduce talks that would address, among other things, such topics as the rights and responsibilities of Canadians. He reiterated that the formula on which such a policy had to be based was one of winning the war, as well as building and unifying the Canadian nation.

In every immediate and temporary act, we must not lose sight of the ultimate and permanent aim. Therefore great care has to be exercised that every temporary stone we lay in our emergency shall not be merely a stepping stone towards immediate safety. It must be so selected and so laid as to be able eventually to serve also to broaden the foundations of the ultimate and permanent edifice of the nation.[57]

Philipps claimed that it was in the interest of Canada to institute a program of communication in the various languages since the enemy was broadcasting in them and they were the mother tongues of the minorities in Canada. The idea was not to counter propaganda with more propaganda but to provide a defensive measure to "immunise or reinforce" the attitudes of the various minorities toward a national conception of Canada and toward winning the war. This strategy, however, did not mean that what was wanted in the way of personnel were "lip-service parrots or quick-change artists ... but well informed, good citizens by conviction," individuals who understood the institutions and political culture of Canada and could speak to the contribution of Canada's ethnic communities in the making of a nation.[58]

According to Philipps, since these ethnic groups were in a unique position to give moral encouragement to the nations that were resisting Hitlerism in Europe, there was an additional advantage. Speaking directly to the issue of democracy, Canada's minority communities were best equipped to answer across the seas, not through what Philipps described as "controversy or insinuation," but by describing their daily lives and giving voice to their expectations. The Axis powers, on the other hand, understood the importance of the ethnic bond and were using it against "the domination of what they call the 'contemptuous' Anglo-Saxon peoples." He pointed out that radio broadcasts, exploiting every possible discontent, were encouraging the rancour of early Ukrainian settlers to Canada, whose treatment had left many of them embittered. To counter this sort of propaganda, Philipps argued it was necessary to assume a position that would allow Canada's ethnic peoples to speak to their ethnic kindred in the homelands and to describe in their own words and in their own language the social, political, and economic conditions in Canada:

[to tell them] of his day's work here, of his freedom from fear, of his fair returns, [emphasising] just those things of which their ethnic kindred over there have been deprived by German occupation. Such simple and unadorned activities of everyday life will do more to carry conviction to the common man, whose war this is, and to restore hope to the hopeless, and to show that these specific liberties still exist in the everyday world and are worth fighting for, than most of the militarily necessary half-truths of our news and than most political talks on abstract Freedom and Liberty, with capital letters.[59]

Working this line of argument, Philipps informed the director of public information that a favourable opportunity had recently presented itself by which the contribution of Canada's Ukrainian minority to the war effort could be made known to their Soviet allies. In a surprising move, Philipps observed, the Soviets were now sending news telegrams to the nationalist Ukrainian Canadian press for the purpose, it was presumed, of seeding the notion that a common ground existed between the two. An exchange of information through Ukrainian Canadian newspapers was now possible. The benefits were twofold. On one level, the "news of the exploits, *as Canadians*, of their brother Ukrainians over here" would solidify the Canadianism of Ukrainian Canadians. On another level, it would also demonstrate to the Soviets the sincerity of Canadian intentions; that Canada was fully cognisant and appreciative of the fact that the Soviet and Anglo-American cause was one and the same. Philipps noted that "The publication over there for [Soviet]-Ukrainian [consumption] of this Canadian-Ukrainian news would be for Canada and the Allies a triumph of public information in a hitherto closed field, where the motives of our capitalist democracies are still suspect. This is not a recommendation. This is a suggestion of possibilities ... In helping Russia to understand and appreciate our contribution, we are also helping ourselves."[60]

The other aspect of the equation, selling the USSR as an ally to the nationalist community, was also crucial. As Philipps himself reported in a summary statement of the activities of the Nationalities Branch, more and more time was being spent "sympathetically clarifying" the alliance with the Soviet Union. This tactic was necessary in order to abate the "violent inter-racial controversies which [were] distracting ... recent citizens from quiet concentration on their war work and war services."[61] However, according to Philipps, it was increasingly pointless, given the disruptive nature of the pro-Soviet element. Philipps wished to be clear. He, personally, supported encouraging the communists and their press if they were to show signs of concentrating on the interests of Canada or putting Canada's interests first. However, as he noted, the pro-Soviet press all too frequently appeared to be devoting "unlimited time and space" to attacks on the Ukrainian Canadian Committee, *Ukrainske zhyttia* (Ukrainian Life), with its incessant allegations that the UCC was a Nazi organisation, being cited as a principal offender.[62] Since the UCC had on various occasions declared that it would avoid controversy for the sake of the war effort, Philipps claimed that it was now leaving itself open to "the danger" of being discredited and that the government was left open to the charge that it was deliberately permitting such attacks. Philipps asked that steps be taken to curb or discourage the endless innuendoes and the barrage of groundless accusations.

In addition to countering the untrammelled attacks against the nationalists in *Ukrainske zhyttia*, there was also a desperate need to introduce some sort of balance in the news coverage in the pro-Soviet press. Material with a decidedly European bent constituted the core of the news being reported, much of it reprinted from Soviet sources repeating to Ukrainian Canadians many of the Soviet criticisms of the Western Allied war effort. Moreover, coverage of the war was exclusively confined to developments in the Soviet Union. "Although [*Ukrainske zhyttia*] purport[ed] to be a Canadian newspaper," Phillips underlined that "it contain[ed] very little about, or for Canada."[63] A Canadian point of view, in effect, was not being conveyed to the part of the community that looked to this publication for its information. Consequently, because they lacked a Canadian perspective, it was virtually impossible to bring them out of their isolation. More effort had to be directed in this area if the Canadian interest was to be preserved and the Allied position reinforced.

The inordinate emphasis on foreign affairs in the press pointed to a deeper, underlying problem that was endemic to both the pro-Soviet and the nationalist elements in the community, namely, that their allegiance was located outside Canada. In Philipps' opinion, this problem needed to be confronted, because it undercut the national conception of the country and worked against efforts at creating a national identity. But it was also dangerous in the context of the conflict, especially where there was no clear indication of what might occur if circumstances were to change. This danger was particularly worrisome in the case of the pro-Soviet Ukrainians. Philipps argued that attacks by the communists on the government's war policy, which had been so prevalent in the early years of the war, had ceased, but not because Canada had changed its policy or because of any misgivings about the relationship of the Communist Party of Canada to the Canadian government. Rather, the Communist Party depended on the fortunes of a foreign country that, having been attacked by Canada's enemy, found itself now on the same side as Canada. "Their support of Canada at war," he claimed, "is dependent solely on the changeable and temporary policy of a foreign State." The difficulty was that "If these citizens of dual allegiance have changed their face towards Canada, they can change it again with equal ease."[64] From the perspective of Canadian interests this possibility was intolerable, unacceptable, and, indeed, potentially dangerous, according to Philipps. There was, of course, the concern that any criticism of the pro-Soviet element could be misinterpreted as an attack on an ally, the Soviet Union. But Philipps argued differently.

Philipps asserted that if the situation were to be properly understood, a distinction had to be made between the Communist Party in Canada and the Soviet Union.[65] The Soviet Union, "state-capitalist and national if not nationalist" in its political makeup, was no longer in his estimation a revolutionary power. Moreover, as doctrine marxism-leninism had lapsed into the unenviable role of dogma under Stalin, while revolutionary politics was no longer tolerated – trotskyism, for example, represented "counter revolution" in the Soviet Union. According to Philipps, the Soviet Union had assumed a traditional political role.[66] Moreover, as an ally it was more concerned with maintaining the alliance than with the welfare of communists and fellow travellers abroad. Only in this way, he explained, could the recent and dramatic shifts in Soviet foreign policy be understood, especially with respect to the movements the Soviet Union had previously controlled through the Comintern. As evidence Philipps pointed to the tacit approval of the Soviet Union of the "liquidation" of communist bands by the Serb General Mikhailovich, who was commanding the Allied Forces in Yugoslavia. In Canada, equally revealing was the recent series of telegrams that had been sent directly to the Ukrainian Canadian nationalist press by the Soviets, circumventing the pro-Soviet Ukrainian press altogether.[67] If the Soviet Union had been motivated by ideological concerns, then, he argued, these developments would have been entirely out of keeping with its alleged program.

The point was that these actions were symptomatic of the transformation that had taken place in the Soviet Union. In this regard, it was essential to differentiate between the Soviet Union as a traditional ally and the communists in Canada, whose disunifying activities threatened the very alliance. Philipps urged that action be taken to curb this element, which the Soviets were not in a position to control, so that the Soviet Union and Canada were not "embarrassed" as allies by their disruptive tactics.[68]

In assessing the Soviet's new policy of initiating contacts with the Ukrainian nationalist community, Philipps concluded that it was but part of a larger strategy to cultivate Ukrainian nationalist sentiment both within Canada and within Ukraine itself. The direct communication with nationalist newspapers – including those that advocated Ukrainian independence from the Soviets – and the cabled articles expressing a "strong nationalist sentiment" were in Philipps' view an attempt to build on pan-Slavic solidarity. The intent, he believed, was to capture the goodwill and sympathy of a population that normally would buck the idea of supporting the USSR but that was inclined to support their ethnic kindred in the Soviet Union.

For Philipps, the idea of fostering pan-Slavism among Canada's various Slavic minorities was in itself an unwelcome, if not dangerous, proposition. He argued that "We may, not unreasonably, question the advisability of a foreign government, even if Allied, being allowed to make a political penetration and to organise its influence among its ex-nationals who are now Canadian citizens and thus seriously retard the process of their becoming part of a Canadian nation."[69] The success of Canadianization depended on the public's identification with the idea of Canada as a nation with its own interests; pan-Slavism served to draw an important segment of the Canadian population away from that concern.

Philipps, however, also observed that pan-Slavism was being encouraged and designed as a pressure point that would be able to exert some influence on the Western liberal democracies. The war on the Eastern front was going badly for the Soviet Union, and Philipps surmised that the initiative taken in promoting pan-Slavism was prompted by the Soviet desire to see a second front opened up as soon as possible to alleviate some of the pressure. Pan-Slavism offered an opportunity to mobilise public opinion with the possibility of influencing the direction of the war policy of the Western Allies. Philipps cautioned, therefore, that steps had to be taken to prevent the movement, around which various committees were now being created, from assuming that role. Indeed, in case of Soviet collapse he believed the Western Allies would be in an untenable situation, since the movement, with its foreign orientation, could be used to undermine their ability to carry on with the war.

Philipps argued that there were three options available to Canadian authorities: discourage what could not be prevented ("To make the organisers aware that the movement is considered unnecessary and undesirable"); exercise a certain amount of orientating and guiding influence ("making clear that their Slavism can only be set within the unifying framework of Canadianism"); or do nothing. If the government decided to stand aside, then it also had to recognise the consequence that the "basic organisation, in substance though not in appearance, [was] bound to fall by degrees into the hands of outside influences which [were] first and foremost not Canadian."[70]

Philipps' thoughts on the pan-Slavic movement in North America were submitted as a memorandum to Justice Davis. Aware that External Affairs would look unfavourably on any decision that would appear to violate the arrangement that saw that department responsible for matters directly affecting questions of foreign policy, Davis sent a copy of the Philipps memo to External Affairs for their reaction, enquiring what course of action should be pursued.[71] External Affairs, however, had already received a copy of Philipps' report before the Davis correspondence and had had sufficient time to digest its contents.

The response at External Affairs was twofold. Philipps' report contained what was thought to be an "over-emphasis on the repercussions of a Russian defeat, and an under-emphasis of the importance of finding ways and means of supporting the general war effort."[72] Saul Rae, a special assistant assigned to the office of the under-secretary and tasked with assessing the Philipps memo, indicated that there was evidence of support for the movement in certain quarters and therefore that it was unlikely that it could be prevented, even if the government was so inclined. Moreover, Rae remained unconvinced that there was sufficient reason to interfere, since he felt that this was the beginning of a new phase in cooperation among the various Slavic groups and that there could be some "useful implications" for Canada. He stated that

Mutual suspicion between the Slavic countries of Europe was one of the central reasons for the breakdown, prior to 1939, of collective resistance to the threat of German aggression. From the point of view of our supreme present interest, viz., the defeat of Nazi Germany, and from the point of view of a post-war system built on the mutual confidence of the countries of Europe, we should think twice before assuming that this attempt to create a basis for common action should be dismissed as "dangerous" merely because the USSR has been a moving spirit in the plan. If a feeling of Slav unity will help our Canadian Poles and Ukrainians, Czechs and Slovaks, Serbs and Croats to see that they have a common interest in the defeat of German aspirations, then this feeling should be utilised and guided.[73]

Rae did not wish to underestimate what the results might be if the movement was to be used by the pro-Soviet left. But it was also important to consider the recent European developments that allowed for a coalescence of interests to emerge between the various competing nations of East-Central Europe. He believed such collaboration in Europe could only have a positive effect on the Slavic groups in Canada, whose many quarrels stemmed precisely from their preoccupation with politics in the homeland. Given the prospects for a postwar European system that would be based on mutual trust and confidence, it was in Canada's interests to promote the collaboration of Slavic peoples in Canada. Rae therefore suggested that there should be no attempt to thwart the tendency that would either see a strengthening of the cooperation between these peoples in the war or that would reduce the tensions between the various ethnic factions and minorities in the Canadian community.

With respect to Philipps' analysis, Rae contended that it was based mostly on opinion. Instead of searching for ways and means to enlist the cooperation of ethnic groups, Philipps, he argued, concerned himself with the hypothetical effects of a Soviet rout. Pointing to Philipps' use of the Ukrainian Canadian Committee as an example of the possible negative effect that a pan-Slavic movement might have on public opinion, Rae claimed the illustration was selective, conveniently fitting into Philipps' interpretation. In this regard, Rae suggested that there were other groups, such as the Czechs, who were inclined to support a pan-Slavic movement, inferring that only those groups, such as the UCC, that had strong "ideological" objections to the Soviet Union would be opposed to a movement of this nature. Rae attributed Philipps' views to an anticommunist bias but stopped short of recommending that Philipps' position be terminated. He did however call for more able people to provide the necessary field reports, reports that he hoped would contain, in his opinion, more in the way of fact and less of fiction.[74]

Philipps, who, as of September, had not yet received a reply to his memorandum on the pan-Slavic movement, arranged to meet with George Glazebrook, a senior officer in External Affairs, to discuss the subject and ascertain the department's views. Glazebrook, briefed by Rae, was quick to point out that there could be no policy that might be interpreted as supporting or opposing what were essentially private organisations. If advice were given, it was to be separated from any comment on the value of the pan-Slavic movement as such. But Glazebrook also went further, declaring that he did not share Philipps' view that a distinction could be drawn between Soviet and Canadian communists and that as a result the government could not support what in his opinion was "an anti-communist Canadian group against a pro-communist Canadian group." As Glazebrook asserted, "it would not be difficult for them to make a case that they are simply representing the interests of Russia and arguing that an attack on Communism was, by inference, an attack on Russia."[75]

Philipps found the conversation astonishing, if not incomprehensible, musing that if the government made no distinction between "Russian and Canadian communists," then was it Canada's intention to offer the soon-to-arrive Soviet emissary the same accommodations provided the eighty communists still interned at Camp Petawawa and the Hull gaol?[76] It was, of course, a rhetorical question. Philipps was neither for nor against communism, and the issue was not about ideological conflict. Rather, Philipps' concern was whether Canadian interests were at risk, given the orientation of a group that owed its allegiance elsewhere.

The release of the Canadian communist internees was a matter that had been raised periodically with the government from the time of the German invasion of the Soviet Union. Yet nothing was done because, contrary to Glazebrook's opinion, the government did differentiate between the Communist Party of Canada and the Soviet Union as an ally. From the point of view of the alliance, the internment of Canadian communists was clearly awkward. But it was also regarded as justifiable, given that the CPC's policies of "unity" and the "continuation of the class struggle" were considered "incompatible inasmuch as it [was] impossible for unity to exist at one and the same time as class struggle." Indeed, so long as the CPC continued to conduct its activities on the basis of what was described as a "Dr Jekyll and Mr Hyde policy," the official inclination was to treat it as a threat to state security.[77] That position, however, could not be maintained in face of mounting public pressure, forcing a change, if not in official attitudes, then at least in policy.

The growing political storm over the internment of antifascists was leaving the impression that the government was not doing all that it could to win the war. Senior officials expected that the CPC would continue to put more pressure on the government to secure its legality, as indeed it did. Individual petitions to the government and representations from supporters, comrades, and next-of-kin pleading for the release of interned party members and the lifting of the ban had by the summer of 1942 translated into a full-scale effort. Organised to coincide with a review by a parliamentary select committee of the Defence of Canada Regulations, the campaign was bolstered by the support of a number of high-profile personalities who expressed dismay over the contradictory nature of the government's position.[78] Opposition from the anticommunist lobby was still in evidence, but the overall effect was a shift in the public's mood on the question of releasing the political prisoners.[79] Consequently, a decision to parole the internees could not be postponed without political consequences, and the process of their release was initiated in September. The parliamentary committee's recommendation, on the other hand, which approved lifting the ban on the CPC and other left-wing associations, was ignored.[80] The campaign to reinstate the outlaw organisations and to restore the ULFTA properties would therefore continue.

Philipps' candour and persistence did not endear him to External Affairs. In fact, the senior officers there were clearly agitated. But they were prepared to ignore him insofar as he did not interfere in matters in which the department had a proprietary interest. They were not to do so, however, for long. In the summer of 1942 Philipps journeyed to Washington to discuss technical matters with officials at the Foreign Nationalities Branch in the U.S. Office of Strategic Services and to exchange views with members of the State Department with whom he had previously been in contact. Soon thereafter, in discussing the pan-Slav movement in North America with Adolph Berle, U.S. assistant deputy secretary of state, Lester Pearson, Canada's minister counsellor in Washington, communicated to Norman Robertson that he had learned that the State Department had already been apprised of the position of the Canadian government. Led somehow to believe that Canada was inclined to take an "unfriendly" view of the movement, Berle pointed out that although the United States government was not in a position to dictate the foreign policy of an ally, the Canadian stand ran counter to the American position. Despite American reservations about its potential, the United States, he remarked, did not necessarily take an unfavourable view of the movement.[81]

Norman Robertson explained to Pearson that Berle's remarks were intelligible only on the assumption that the view that Canada was inclined to take a negative attitude toward the pan-Slav movement had been expressed to State Department officials by Philipps during his recent trip to Washington. Robertson noted that there was no justification for this view. He instructed Pearson to make this clear with Berle, so that the State Department understood that Canada still subscribed to the principle of a "community of purpose" in Allied policy. As for Philipps, he had finally exceeded his authority by directly challenging the determination agreed to at the time of the creation of the Nationalities Branch, which stated that External Affairs alone was responsible for matters that impinged directly on foreign relations. Robertson concluded rather cryptically in his letter to Pearson that "This particular example gives point to the views expressed in my confidential letter of September 26th, to Mr Justice Davis, a copy of which was forwarded to you."[82] Robertson no longer had any use for Philipps. What remained was to eliminate him from the public service.

In October and November demonstrations were organised in various centres by the Canadian left in support of lifting the ban on the CPC and other organisations, culminating in a mass rally at Toronto's Maple Leaf Gardens. Sponsored by the Civil Liberties Association, it was attended by thirteen thousand people, who heard several prominent speakers, including Mitchell Hepburn, Ontario's premier, urge the government to implement the earlier recommendations of the parliamentary select committee. It was an impressive event. The momentum in support of the banned organisations paralleled a further escalation in the rivalry between the pro-Soviet and nationalist Ukrainians. Disruptions at community gatherings, for instance, were commonplace, resulting at times in street brawls that ended only after the police were called out.[83] Increasingly fierce and unbridled attacks had also become standard fare in the Ukrainian Canadian press. From the government perspective what was especially troubling was that the past caution exercised by the pro-Soviet Ukrainian press in criticising government policy was now being dispensed with. Whereas before, the government of Canada was criticised for its inaction, it was now charged with directly protecting "pro-fascists."[84]

The agitation in the Ukrainian Canadian press, which threatened to drag the government into the political fracas, featured in the official decision to establish policy guidelines with respect to "foreign-born groups" especially those originating in "the borderlands of Russia." At External Affairs George Glazebrook was given the task of setting out some general guidelines. In the working paper that was finally tabled, Glazebrook suggested that in principle, recognition could not be granted to independence movements (with the exception of the Free French movement) because of the long-standing practice and belief in international diplomacy that it was politically unwise to make such commitments. It was also seen as desirable for Canadian policy to be consistent with that of the United States and Britain, which necessarily meant establishing a working relationship with the Soviet Union. According to Glazebrook, this relationship was necessary not only from the point of view of the conduct of the war but also with a view towards postwar relations. Since the controversy on the homefront threatened to jeopardise movement in that direction, Glazebrook broached the idea that it might be necessary to suppress the groups in question. By his own admission, however, he thought "[this action] would be difficult to defend and do more harm than good."[85] Instead, he recommended censorship rulings that would put the government in a stronger position to deal with the situation and called for increased surveillance and warnings when the groups "stepped out of bounds."

The Department of External Affairs began also to consider how to deal with the situation in National War Services. Although concerned about the activities of Philipps and the Nationalities Branch, External Affairs was proscribed from directly interfering in the work of other departments. Nevertheless, Robertson communicated to the associate deputy minister of national war services, Justice T.C. Davis, that there had to be more coordination and delineation in the responsibility for the work between the two departments on the issue. Davis agreed, stating that "The functions of our committee [Nationalities Branch] and the officials thereof should be clearly defined, particularly, in order that there may be no conflict whatsoever with the activities and view-point of your department."[86] External Affairs, however, had much more in mind in light of the reorganisation of public information services.

On 9 September 1942 the newly organised Wartime Information Board (WIB) superseded the Bureau of Public Information. As a consequence of the abysmal performance of the latter in modifying opinion on the plebiscite vote, it was absorbed into the WIB, which was under the direct authority of the prime minister's office.[87] The reorganisation had raised the question of the future of the Nationalities Branch and, more specifically, whether it was to be transferred to the WIB. The policy of the WIB was to establish a minimum of administrative staff, but it was also reluctant to assume responsibility over an advisory committee and a branch whose work "was more political than informational." It was suggested that the branch remain with War Services, although operational connections would be established for purposes of coordination.[88]

Aware of an opportunity, however, External Affairs called a meeting of all departments that maintained and operated news clipping services, including clippings of the foreign-language press, to discuss the operation. The recommendation at the meeting, after it was evident that there was considerable administrative overlap, was that the activity of the various departments dealing with the press, including the foreign-language press, would be centralised in the press division of the WIB. Moreover, in the case of the Nationalities Branch, there was some consideration being given to the thought that "it might be more advisable to transfer the whole thing to Wartime Information."[89] Although there was no confirmation that this would be done, the statement was a hopeful sign that the problem would be resolved in External Affairs' favour.

In contrast to the manœuvrings of External Affairs, Philipps, in his own words, was "working more carefully and harder" than ever before, and his mind and energies were being "stretched to the limit." The equation upon which he operated was that "half the war would be won in the mines, shipyards and factories of North America," where the influence of ethnic labour was most pronounced.[90] Success here would require overcoming the prejudice of those individuals who regarded Anglo-Canadians as unsympathetic and arrogant and overcoming the defeatist element among the ethnic communities who subscribed to the view that their respective homelands were permanently in the grip of Hitler and that their kindred could be saved only by coming to terms with the Germans. For Philipps, then, the challenge was to ensure that ethnic labour, working in industry and producing food in the Canadian West, would not lose heart, to tie them so securely to the idea of Canada and its institutions that, come what may, their support and allegiance could be counted on.

Philipps believed that it was the foreign political orientation and activity of both the right and the left that was the principal cause behind the controversy among the ethnic populations. Moreover, these foreign influences only served to rekindle historical animosities and suspicions, while helping to incubate attitudes that, by their very nature, allowed these communities to retain their European orientation, or, as Philipps described it, "to think 'foreign.'" Although this in itself was not necessarily incompatible with a passive loyalty to Canada, it was insufficient.

There was a need to instil among ethnic communities an appreciation of their contribution to Canada as Canadians, which, by Philipps' account, was the "only and real proper ground" for their integration. It was Philipps' view that consolidation of the Canadian nation was retarded by these foreign influences, which, no matter how well meaning, tended to fracture communities along political lines and according to old vendettas. "Consolidation as a nation," according to Philipps, "can only be attained by the natural process, agreeable to all groups, of abating their feeling of neglect by attracting, as a whole, each 'foreign-born' community from the outside edge of the nation towards the centre of the nation's heart, which is [its] government."[91]

Philipps believed the Nationalities Branch had an important role to play in the "Canadianizing" process. The contacts with the various ethnic communities made by branch personnel were already well developed, and through them there was an opportunity to access the foreign-language press. But in meeting this task, Philipps was keenly aware that the branch was inadequately staffed. Ironically, Philipps was renewing his proposal that additional personnel be hired on to meet the needs and workload of the editorial section under Dr Kaye just as the WIB was attempting to assume control over the Nationalities Branch. To support his claims, Philipps pointed to the number of staff at the Foreign Nationalities Branch of the U.S. Office of Strategic Services as an indication of the shortcomings of the Canadian operation, even when population differences were accounted for. Philipps repeated his plea for additional staff on several occasions, playing up the importance of the foreign press angle.

There is only one thing that all these groups of our citizens have in common. They have in common their Canadianism. This is the only leadership and common ground upon which they can unite. Foreign-language newspapers of Canada are divided again by two very important differences, (a) those whose interests are derived from, and centred in Canada, and (b) whose interests are overwhelmingly abroad. If group (a) can be strengthened and group (b) be induced to change its fundamental policy, a very constructive step forward would be made for Canada.[92]

Philipps, of course, was aware that the government was anxious to avoid any semblance of pressure on or even guidance of the press because of the sensitive nature of free speech in an open society. But he also recognised that if a Canadian interpretation of events and news were not provided, the various groups would get their information from "un-Canadian" sources that would both revive their Europeanism and retard their Canadianization. In contrast to the Canadian

effort, he noted that the Germans were broadcasting daily over short-
wave to Canada, while Serbian Canadians were getting their material
directly from the Yugoslav legation press service in Washington and
Moscow was radioing material that, once in Canada, was being edited
and chosen for different aims. "We," wrote Phillips, "in our small
Editorial Section, cannot make bricks without straw ... When our
straw, our raw material, is (as now) so colourless, so scanty and so
belated, we on behalf of Canada simply cannot compete."[93] Philipps
recommended that more material should be provided, notably, up-to-
date news items acquired from the Overseas News Service or the Allied
Labour News, which could then be translated and given a Canadian
perspective by branch staff. Distributed to the major foreign-language
groups in Canada for their use, he believed these news sources could
be used effectively as a counterweight to the foreign influences.

The issue of foreign influence came up again when Philipps felt
obliged to respond to a memo from Hume Wrong, the assistant under-
secretary of state, which questioned his analysis of the pan-Slavic
movement in North America. Defending his position, Philipps argued
that pan-Slavism was a political movement whose ostensible design
was to act as a pressure group on Allied war policy. He repeated his
claim that the key consideration was that the Soviet Union was not
using the movement for "revolutionary" ends, as some observers
speculated, but simply to advance its own state interest, which was
principally its survival.

It was Philipps' contention that the Soviet Union was now a traditional political actor, the Soviet leadership both understanding and
abiding by the basic principles governing international relations,
including the principle of state sovereignty. Therefore, Canadian officials were in a position, and in the right, to make clear to their Soviet
counterparts that Canada could and would not tolerate political pressure through indirect means. Philipps sought to impress upon Hume
Wrong that Canadian officials could head off the movement, if they so
desired, without fear of repercussion, because the Soviets themselves
made the distinction between the alliance and the activities of the CPC,
which was behind the movement. To illustrate his point, Philipps indicated that during his years of work in Turkey at the time of the Turkish-
Soviet Alliance, when close co-operation existed between both governments, anyone who advocated either fascism or communism ("civil war
or class war") was summarily dealt with as a matter of detail "without
clouding the amicable relations between the Allied powers."[94]

For Philipps, however, there was more at stake than the simple
matter of foreign interference. At issue was its effect on the process of
Canadianization. Pan-Slavism by definition was European-centred and

not Canadian-centred, and because its focus was European it would never be able to overcome the historical animosities that had informed past ethnic behaviour and motivations in Canada. Pan-Slavism was an illusion that could not assist but only further impede the process of Canadianization. To ignore this was to avoid the tasks that lay ahead in promoting a Canadian alternative.

Pan-Slavism however delusively promising it may seem, has never been (and can never in our time be) a unifying influence. It always, on the contrary, proves a disintegrator ... Pan-Slavism, except in a vague cultural sense, is as illusory a political mirage as pan-Arabism. It is worse than useless to us as a unifying force.

In all conscience, the interests and security of the English-speaking nations would be well served if ever any real political solidarity of the Slavonic-speaking peoples could be created to contain the Teutons on the East.

But it is a stark impossibility that pan-Slavism could, especially with the present embitterment of historic hates, unite Serbs and Croats, Bulgars and Serbs, Russians and Poles, Poles and Ukrainians, even in the Americas. Even when the peoples of Slavonic speech see each other at a distance they, so to speak, already make "long noses" at each other. The closer they are tied-up together, the more sure they are to cut each other's noses OFF. The inevitable break up of such an attempted tie-up will create for more discord and disunity and distraction from our effort for the war than if this disingenuous and delusive foreign political movement had never been launched among Canadian citizens at all.[95]

Philipps repeated that if his diagnosis and prescriptions were correct, as he firmly believed them to be, then the Canadian government "should regard coldly any attempts by 'foreign-born' groups to get together among each other on any foreign un-Canadian basis directed from outside Canada." He was convinced that the Canadian government could only afford to encourage an "all-Canadian" movement, by exerting more positive encouragement to those newer citizens who derived and centred their interests in Canada.

In mid-October 1942, the deputy minister of national war services informed Philipps that a decision had indeed been made to transfer the editorial section of the Nationalities Branch to the press division of the WIB. The reasoning of Norman Robertson, the under-secretary of state for external affairs, who was the principal architect behind the move, was also made known to Philipps. Philipps strenuously objected to the move, no doubt motivated in part by the need to protect the branch and the relative autonomy it now enjoyed as an independent body within National War Services. But more to the point, he claimed that External Affairs failed to understand the role and function of the editorial section, since it identified its purpose as simply reporting on the foreign-language press. The work of the editorial section was "positive and constructive," supplying material that had a decidedly Canadian angle to it. Monitoring the ethnic press, Philipps argued, on the other hand, had no positive value. He noted, for instance, that the Directorate of Censorship was translating many of the same articles that had been provided by the editorial section of the Nationalities Branch to the foreign-language press and sending them back to the branch as a "scoop." This was a credit to censorship, but ultimately, in his opinion, a waste of effort. The point was not to report on the groups for fear of what was being said but to provide a Canadian perspective and, through that perspective, necessary direction.

If, in the first generation and a half of these great Canadian communities, we do not furnish news of their motherlands, to which all average Canadians (except perhaps average French-Canadians) anxiously and naturally look back in time of war, then they will tend to get copious and often un-Canadian news and articles on the motherlands from press sections of foreign Legations in the U.S. or direct from Europe coloured or interpreted in a foreign way. These sources revive old nationalisms and retard Canadianization. If we do not ourselves provide a picture of the motherlands set in a Canadian frame, then they will continue to get it in their homes [and] in their mother tongues on the air direct from their motherlands which are under direct or indirect enemy control. The salient fact is that, in any case, these 'Europeans' want it and will get it somehow. Since this is so, the picture had better come to them in a Canadian frame, from a Canadian and Canadianizing source.[96]

Given this objective, Philipps argued that there could be no place for any of the work conducted by the Nationalities Branch in the Wartime Information Board, which to the recent European immigrant had "the suspicious smell of a 'Propaganda-Ministerium,' a vague german-cousin to a Gestapo or a Cheka." Propaganda should not be the aim of the branch, he claimed. Rather its purpose was to make available information about Canadians for Canadians, so that they may know who they were and what they might yet become. In Philipps' opinion, it was a mistake to assume that because the function of the branch was to deal with information and publicity "they had anymore to do with propaganda then a chestnut horse [had] to do with horse chestnuts."[97] More importantly, if the editorial section were to be transferred, Philipps argued the remaining work of the Nationalities Branch would be seriously jeopardised. The deputy minister, to whom the plea was made, was unmoved, convinced as he was that the most appropriate place for the editorial section was with the WIB. Moreover, he informed Philipps that he was giving thought to the possibility of having the entire branch transferred over to the WIB or that there might be some association with External Affairs.[98]

Justice Davis was influenced in his decision to deal with the Nationalities Branch by the fact that he had been appointed as the Canadian high commissioner to Australia. In view of both his pending departure and the escalating controversies within the Ukrainian ethnic press, he thought it would be prudent for the management of the Ukrainian Canadian situation to be turned over to those who were acquainted with the issues and could keep close watch while providing more immediate policy direction. For Davis and other officials there was some urgency in the matter because of the news that the nationalists were planning to stage a conference that would, by every indication, lead to a "premature" discussion of Ukrainian affairs in Europe and result in an embarrassing situation for Canada.[99] In fact, Justice Davis informed Norman Robertson that he was going to discuss the matter of transferring the entire branch to the WIB with the minister for national war services. Davis also indicated that he would approach the minister to appoint a new director, since Professor Simpson was retiring from the position for reasons of health, and that the appointment would be secured from the list of candidates waiting for positions in the Department of External Affairs. Robertson was elated by the prospect that the branch would finally be transferred and that a member of his department would be appointed as its head. He could not have been pleased, however, with the deputy minister's recommendation that the services of Philipps be retained, regardless of his assurance that Philipps, as per instructions, would not take any more trips outside Canada as a representative of the Canadian government.[100]

Justice Davis' recommendation that Philipps be kept on was premature. News reports, widely circulated, began appearing that described both Philipps and Kaye as having rather unsavoury pasts. Both were identified as having extensive contacts with "fascists" in Europe and North America, but Philipps, in particular, was singled out as an intimate of the Cliveden group, a prewar group of appeasement advocates. The source of the allegations was the pro-Soviet American weekly, *The Hour*, which, having been alerted to Philipps' Washington trip, listed him "as one of our enemies at home" and reported that he was an adviser and frequent visitor to the State Department. The judgment of U.S. official involvement with Philipps was questioned, as was the wisdom of the Canadian government in having men of "this calibre and this stripe" in its employ.[101]

The news item, copied in précis without verification in the mainstream American periodical *The New Republic*, appeared as a leader in the *Globe and Mail*. Immediately, the editor of the *Canadian Tribune*, the press organ of the still-banned Communist Party of Canada, gave notice to the newly appointed minister of national war services, General L.R. LaFleche, that the paper was under pressure to pursue the issue of Philipps' past associations and his relationship with the government, unless that relationship was fully explained or the charges proven groundless.[102] Despite the fact that Philipps had taken the initiative to refute the allegations in the *Globe and Mail* and *The New Republic* and had received formal apologies from both papers, the *Tribune*'s stated intention to continue its investigation, with the prospect of even more unwelcome debate, was disconcerting.[103]

The desire to head off the controversy prompted a "disinterested third party" to suggest that Philipps meet with one of the principal critics of the government's "position," the freelance writer Raymond Arthur Davies, a frequent contributor to left-wing periodicals and newspapers. Philipps was hopeful that a casual and informal conversation would clear up the misunderstanding. He was mistaken, however, Davies being motivated by the journalist's desire for possible additional information to be used in a forthcoming exposé. Placed on the defensive, Philipps argued during his brief meeting with Davies that his interest was strictly "Canadian" and that he had no quarrel with the Soviet Union. Nor had he made any criticism of communism in the Soviet Union, both because "it was not his business to do so" and, more particularly, because communism, at least from his reading of Marx, did not exist in Stalin's USSR. "Such an illusion would therefore have been both out of date and off the point at a time when ... It was the duty of all good citizens to avoid controversy and to seek unity in Canada."[104]

The meeting served only to pique Davies' interest, and he began to enquire among government officials about Philipps and the activities of the branch.[105] Philipps, on the other hand, privately found the conversation depressing, having learned that a government source was behind the damaging reports in *The Hour* and the pro-Soviet Ukrainian-American weekly *Narodna volia* (People's Will).[106] Expecting the allegations in the press to continue and feeling increasingly isolated and daunted by the idea that there were individuals within government who were actively working to discredit him, Philipps tendered his resignation to the deputy minister of national war services. In view of the press reports and the controversy being generated, Justice Davis accepted it.

To finalise details of the transfer of the Nationalities Branch to the WIB before he was to leave for overseas, Justice Davis called a meeting of the WIB and External Affairs officials. Those in attendance agreed that the WIB would work closely with External Affairs, "which would formulate policy and consider in particular the question of direct contacts with foreign language groups other than through their press."[107] As for branch personnel, Davis informed the representatives that Philipps had tendered his resignation and that it had been accepted. Regarding Kaye, the consensus at the meeting was that it was best to release him from government service because he was "so tarred with the Philipps brush" that his usefulness was in doubt.

On 13 November 1942, the deputy minister recommended to the minister that the Department of National War Services relinquish control over the Nationalities Branch and that the latter be transferred to the WIB, which would be working in close cooperation with External Affairs on the problem. Justice Davis recommended that certain functions – contacts with leaders of foreign-language groups and "weaving these people into the fabric of Canadian life, to think in terms of Canada ... and to get the greatest support out of them" – be the responsibility of External Affairs. Davis emphasised that the overriding importance of the external relations factor underscored the need for these tasks to come under the supervision of the Department of External Affairs. Indeed, the department's contacts with "Ministers and Consuls and similar groups in other lands from outside of Canada" led Davis to conclude that External Affairs was "most closely allied to the problem we are trying to handle here in Canada" and therefore logically suited to offer direction, while outlining requirements.[108]

George Simpson, still chairman of the citizen's advisory committee to the Nationalities Branch, wished to go on record before Davis departed that he felt the attacks on Philipps and Kaye were unjustified. In his opinion, there were no two individuals who had been more sincere in their aim of promoting Canadianism, although Philipps had clearly been handicapped by the frequent charge that as an Englishman he was in no position to promote a Canadian identity. Furthermore, Simpson claimed that it was unfortunate both were withdrawing under "the attack of mud," because it gave the impression the charges were true. In any case, Simpson thought that Philipps' ability and training made him an invaluable political ally and that it would be "difficult to find anyone with similar experience and talent."[109] Davis indicated he would relay Simpson's views and concerns to the WIB, where the editorial section was to be transferred, and to External Affairs, which would be responsible for the other activities of the branch.[110]

Reaction to the rumours of the expected transfer of the branch and the dismissal of Philipps and Kaye was varied. Donald Cameron, an academic and member of the advisory Committee on Co-operation in Canadian Citizenship, expressed relief at the departure of the two, conveying to Justice Davis that he had objected to the appointment of Philipps and Kaye from the start because of their "outlook."[111] Others acquainted with the work of the committee, however, were not of the same opinion.

John W. Dafoe, the outspoken editor of the *Winnipeg Free Press*, felt that Philipps had been treated unjustly and communicated as much to him in a letter. Replying, Philipps confessed that he considered his ouster to be unfair, believing that he and the liberal elements of the ethnic communities working toward unity were targets of concerted campaigns waged by both the right and left, which sought control of the debate. The pro-Soviet Ukrainian faction were especially "determined that any unity among Ukrainians in North America should not lead to any Chicago or Pittsburgh Agreements which laid the foundations for other subject peoples who, in the last world war, thus broke up another empire, that of Austria."[112] Characterising them as "wolves" pressing in on the liberal centre, Philipps said they busied themselves with "distracting the well-intentioned but ill-informed North American public opinion into controversy, confusion and disunity." As for the government, Philipps claimed that "The temptation for governments, as we all know, is that, if the wolves howl loud and long enough, a government tends to feed to the wolves first its servants and then its friends in order to distract attention from itself." Thanking Dafoe for his vote of confidence, he concluded his letter with the words *Verbum sapienti est.*

Before his departure and as a final act Philipps felt inclined to leave a note for the file so that there could be no misconstruing his position. He resented the allegation that the work being done in the branch was "anti-Soviet," arguing that all was on record, and it would show the branch's work was practical in its program to aid the Soviet Union by attempting "to clear the public mind of misconceptions and prejudices." As for the various ethnic organisations that were working within their communities, Philipps denied the allegation that they were creatures of the branch, intentionally set up for narrow political gain. He argued that their creation and the interests they represented were the natural response of individuals who hoped to organise themselves to meet the perceived needs of living and coping in an alien environment. To deny or ignore the deeper meaning of this phenomenon was to fail to fully appreciate the difficulties encountered by immigrants and to recognize that if they were not chanelled into the positive aspects of Canadian identity, they would become ghettoised and continue to be suspect.

The suggestion seems to be that if we adopt a negative or passive policy, all their and our desires will just come true. The truth, which it needs moral courage to face, is precisely the contrary. It is mainly because, for lack of adequate organisation, we ignore them and make little attempt to penetrate them gently and friendly from within, that the minorities ... are (as in Europe) becoming the prey of mutual misunderstanding. By the extremes of their foreign-language press, by their motherland radio under enemy control and by what seems to them Anglo-Saxon contempt and neglect, they may in any afterward confusion become less, instead of more, assimilable or a seed-bed for extremist experiments.[113]

At the end of 1942 Justice Davis left for Australia with a clear conscience that his work was complete. He could not have foreseen, however, that authorisation for the transfer of the Nationalities Branch would in fact be denied, despite his recommendation. In a surprising turn of events, Philipps and the others were asked to remain on staff, at least for the time being, in order for the new minister of national war services, General LaFleche, to get his bearings. Given the record of change in the department and confronted by the prospect of over-seeing an even further diminished portfolio, LaFleche wanted a complete account of the origin, aims, and functions of the branch.[114] No premature decision regarding transfer of responsibility or reorganisation would be made until there had been a preliminary assessment.

Within weeks of the reprieve, a rejuvenated Philipps submitted a report that had been requested by the minister, in which he outlined the objectives of the Nationalities Branch, indicating that it had been hampered in its activity and mandate because many of its policy recommendations had failed to receive necessary departmental authorisation.[115] He also indicated that the ineffectiveness of the branch was due in part to the opposition of the passive, yet extreme, right, "who refused to co-operate," and to the counterproductive pro-Soviet left, who were more interested in confronting their political adversaries. This made for difficult work among the large ethnic liberal majorities that were associated with either the cultural and fraternal societies or their respective churches. Philipps reiterated that the best strategy in dealing with the situation – one that he recommended LaFleche should pursue – was to reinforce the liberal centre in each community through encouragement and participation in a program that actively promoted a Canadian perspective. This strategy, according to Philipps, had been employed in the field in the past. As he pointed out, the underlying theme that he often used in communicating with those communities was that they should always ask whether what was being done was in the interests of Canada and, by extension, in the interests of the

Allied nations at war. Philipps conceded "This by no means answers all the questions but, while awaiting the answer, it puts the emphasis where it ought to be."[116]

Within the community, events appeared to be coming to a head, and the political damage had to be minimised. In response to a UCC plan to issue a press release that rejected a proposal to cooperate with pro-Soviet Ukrainians in an Aid to Russia campaign, Professor Simpson had confidentially informed the executive that it was not a good idea because the intent "could be misunderstood in some quarters."[117] Meanwhile, at External Affairs, Norman Robertson found himself replying to objections raised by the pro-Soviet Association of Canadian Ukrainians over the presence of the Ukrainian republican flag at various parades. Violent street confrontations, often resulted and Robertson urged that the opposing groups should put their differences aside, because "there was another factor that had to be borne in mind … in the present struggle against the Axis powers in which Canada is engaged, it is the common responsibility of all Canadians, and of all residents of Canada, to oppose the enemy's efforts to create disunity by exploiting the differences of outlook between various groups."[118]

Such minor details were easily dealt with. But it was the international developments and their implications for controversy in Canada that were running ahead of the government's ability to cope with the Ukrainian Canadian problem. The Polish and Soviet claims on the eastern frontiers question and the Ukrainian Canadian response in a memorandum of March 1943 to the Canadian prime minister were a case in point. Similarly, the growing interest of the British and American governments in Ukrainian Canadians created a sense of unease among officials in Ottawa, inasmuch as it was thought that their inability to manage the situation was being interpreted abroad as a sign of unreliability. And of course the Soviets protests could not only not be ignored but could be expected to continue, insofar as a steady traffic of cablegrams was being sent to Moscow by the Montreal-based TASS bureau informing authorities there of developments within the Ukrainian Canadian community.[119]

Especially damaging from the viewpoint of the government – whose censorship agencies were intercepting the cablegrams – was the TASS transcript of the R.A. Davies publication *This Is Our Land: Ukrainian Canadians against Hitler.*[120] Chastising the government for its role in creating tensions within the Ukrainian Canadian community, Davies claimed that it had shown partiality toward "pro-fascists" and "fascist" organisations such as the UCC, "which, though set up with official backing, has concentrated its work not on war tasks, but merely on combating the communists and attempting to split Canada away from her allies." Davies insisted that the government should take steps to correct the situation by returning the sequestered ULFTA halls and checking "the pernicious anti-allied and fascistic influence of those Ukrainian leaders and groups that are pro-German." Singled out for "its anti-Soviet, anti-Polish and anti-Czechoslovak agitation," the UCC, in particular, was identified as a major offender, and nothing less than a ban on the organisation would suffice. More damaging, however, from the government's perspective was Davies' recommendation that the services of Philipps and other "experts" advising Ottawa who were characterised as "fascist" in outlook and working, with official blessing, against the Allied cause be terminated.

With the new set of allegations, the situation had arguably reached a climax. Closely monitoring events, the RCMP indicated that the enmity that existed between the Ukrainian communists and nationalists – each considering the other as "deadly poison" – was now without parallel.[121] At External Affairs officials feared that in the absence of moderate opinion amongst the Ukrainian Canadian leadership, the community would fall into the hands of the extreme elements of the left and the right.[122]

Philipps, recognising the volatile and potentially disastrous nature of the controversy, assured Professor Simpson that the branch was keeping its distance and would not involve itself in the current polemic.[123] He also communicated to Simpson that the branch was all but inactive, since the new minister had not given authorisation to proceed with the fieldwork. Philipps had sensed that ministerial paralysis was the result of an unwillingness, under the circumstances, to engage in this politically sensitive work but was concerned that, without any reasonable guidance, events would take their course. As for the other government departments, he confided to Simpson that he doubted whether they could provide direction, since he felt their views were based on dated knowledge and archaic notions, akin to the old views and prejudices that historically had informed the British mindset and failed British policies in Africa and India. Describing the premises upon which such ideas were built as antiquated and out of step with reality, he concluded that "In such conditions, only time can (as it will) prove us right. Time alone, and near future time, will also prove the worth of our work. Meanwhile, we shall only irritate and precipitate the destruction of our work, if we try to see or reason with the obstructers [other department officials] who quite naturally think that they are right. One of the truest of the catchword half-truths is that 'to govern is to foresee.'"[124]

Emboldened by External Affairs, which had already once tried unsuccessfully to bring the Nationalities Branch under its authority, WIB officials, under the aggressive leadership of its new director, John Grierson, began to exercise greater initiative in pulling the branch within their orbit of activity.[125] In late March, the WIB, considering that "it [was] the logical authority under which this work [was to be] carried on," proposed to appoint an individual to head up the branch and negotiate after the fact with the Department of National War Services for control of policy. Officials in the WIB recognised that normal protocol was not being followed in this instance. But the intransigence of National War Services and its inability to act on what was perceived to be a worsening situation convinced the WIB "that the only way to solve the problem [was] to secure the required personnel, and announce to the Department of National War Services the intention of the Board to invade this field of work."[126] In May, the necessity of acting on the so-called Philipps Committee became a matter of urgency. Philipps, following up on an earlier recommendation, urged the CBC to liberalise its programming to include broadcasting in the mother tongues of the major language groups in Canada, inasmuch as "it [was] Philipps belief that such broadcasting might have a useful effect upon such groups in giving them a sense of solidarity with the Canadian people at the present time."[127]

External Affairs, to whom many of the WIB memos were directed, concurred with the opinion expressed within the WIB that something had to be done – and done quickly. Recognising that he had an ally in John Grierson, Norman Robertson proposed again to call a meeting of all agencies "monkeying" with the foreign-language issue. The idea was that after some discussion, these agencies would see the necessity of concentrating policy in the Wartime Information Board. Although this strategy had been used once before, External Affairs appeared to demonstrate greater resolve this time, in that there was every indication that the department would follow through on the decision to have the Nationalities Branch transferred over. As for the WIB, Robertson informed Grierson that the assumption by his agency of responsibility over the Nationalities Branch would require the careful selection of personnel for this "treacherous" job, since, in Robertson's opinion, this line of work attracted individuals who were apt to have "axes to grind." He also concluded that, all things considered, Grierson would find the Ukrainian question in Canada to be the most difficult. Robertson felt that there was an important job to be done by the WIB and believed that "it [was] one which [had] to be planned pretty carefully."[128] Robertson's cautious admonition to Grierson revealed that he believed the way ahead was still fraught with danger.

AN ASSESSMENT

Within days of the German invasion of the Soviet Union, the associate deputy minister of the Department of National War Services, Justice

T.C. Davis, submitted a memorandum to the minister, alluding to the growing problem that confronted Canadian authorities. Davis believed that the recent global realignment created confusion among the Canadian public, especially among "that section of our Canadian population who were either born in Europe or whose origin [was] European." France was collaborating with Germany, while Hitler's former partner, Stalin, had now become an ally of the liberal democracies. In view of the changed situation, Davis recommended that a division within the department be created whose duty would be "to direct and give leadership" to these people.[129]

Justice Davis' views are significant for several reasons. First, he distinguished between those who knew what the national interest was and those who did not. Second, the notion of providing "direction" also implied that despite the changing political landscape, some individuals had an absolute knowledge of what constituted the national interest. By inference, the suggestion was that it was the government official and not the public who knew what constituted the national interest, because the national interest was a constant, existing independently of the political environment. As Davis pointed out, yesterday's enemy could just as well become tomorrow's friend; the particulars could change but the national interest did not, and although the public could be confused, the official was not.[130]

Davis' comments capture a particular understanding of politics, one that is derived from the "vocation" of holding office and an allegiance to the office and from the duties and obligations that accompany the role. This understanding recognises that the official, functioning as a steward, not only provides for the operation of the state but, in the context of the perceived anarchy of the political environment, is responsible for its security and very survival. State preservation is the overriding interest by which policy and political action is determined. And since that interest is impermeable, it serves as a constant. As Davis' remarks reveal, alliances may change, but the central national interest, the security and survival of the state, remains the same regardless of political change. This axiomatic principle is understood best by officials who must deal with the affairs of state.

The principle of state security, however much a guideline informing the political realism of the official, does not operate outside a context. Decisions pertaining to the security of the state are often made on the basis of information and intelligence. Although the bureaucracy is adept at acquiring and processing information, it frequently commissions outside "specialists" to assist and advise, either because they have an intimate knowledge of particular issues or because they can offer problem management. The difficulty, however, with inviting external actors to participate in the policy process, even in a passive role, is that they do not share the same vision as the career official or the same understanding of the state agenda, because their role, unlike the role of the career public servant, is not defined by loyalty to office. Furthermore, since they are not constrained by the notion of allegiance to office, the principle of hierarchy, so central to the decision-making process, is usually ignored. This can and does on occasion complicate the policy process or the conduct of state affairs.

These problems clearly arose when Canadian officials, in their effort to deal with the ethnic and, particularly, the Ukrainian Canadian "problem," called upon the services of Tracy Philipps. Phillips was acting in an advisory capacity, and his views, in time, would be looked upon with suspicion and his activities considered divisive. The disagreement, however, between Philipps and senior government officials was neither personal nor ideological; rather, it was much more fundamental.[131] As a self-described "dollar-a-year man," by temperament and disposition, Philipps was not a career civil servant.[132] He shared neither the civil servant's sense of commitment to office nor the civil servant's political conservatism. His view of politics was characteristically open-ended and pragmatic; he approached political problems with few preconceived ideas and no predetermined model for political action. In a sense he was radically different from his associates, notably those in External Affairs whose preoccupation with a narrowly interpreted definition of state security led them to approach political issues in a very precise and doctrinal way. Nevertheless, Philipps was not unappreciative of the political concerns that animated Canadian officials. On the contrary, deeply committed to the Allied cause, he clearly understood, for example, that the alliance with the Soviet Union was absolutely necessary to bring about the defeat of fascism. Furthermore, Philipps also recognised that national unity was critical from the perspective of Canada's war effort and an Allied victory. From these points of view, Philipps appeared little different from his peers. But he did differ in the questions he continually put before himself as reference points: On what basis would victory be won? And on what basis would national unity be achieved?

Philipps, like his counterparts, understood that there were two essential tasks in dealing with Canada's ethnic minorities: minimise any internal threat that these groups might have posed to the Canadian war effort and secure their loyalty.[133] In the context of national mobilisation, the loyalty consideration depended not only on making a clear distinction between fascism and democracy but also on making explicit, in the context of the war, the needs of the state in relation to the individual. Loyalty, conditioned by conflict, was an expression of the recognition that the needs of the state transcended the needs of the individual. Disloyalty was a tag reserved for those who failed to acknowledge the transcendant needs of the state, and the state's prerogative to use force to minimise potential threats to its own security was predicated on this understanding. Yet Philipps recognised that loyalty under these conditions is fleeting and that the only guarantee of security is the collective trust that, like loyalty, emerges from a shared sense of purpose. Only within the context of the historical task of nation building were the intertwined issues of loyalty and security to be resolved. For this reason, the idea of nation building, a process Philipps described as "Canadianization," assumed a central role in his views.[134] Indeed, what in Canada's case was being tested in the war was not simply its economic and military might but the very idea of Canada as a nation. Therefore, the real challenge for Canada at this most crucial time, according to Philipps, was to lay the political foundation for the future integration of Canadian society.

In his memoranda and reports, Philipps emphasised the nature of the tasks at hand: loyalty and security. Both objectives, he suggested, could be secured only by both promoting the integration of the "foreign-born" on the basis of the existing political culture, while emphasising the common referents that existed among the divergent groups. Indeed, the nature of liberal democracy, Philipps argued, afforded an opportunity to accommodate ethnic particularism while still providing the basis for the construction of a new social edifice, one that would neither be riddled with social and political contradictions nor be saddled with past prejudices. He would argue that the values associated with liberal democracy and their acceptance would lead to the resolution of political differences among ethnic groups and the eventual disappearance of the animosities that had been brought to Canada like so much unwanted baggage.[135]

Officials within the senior levels of the bureaucracy intuited the nature of the tasks at hand. Indeed, the ethnic minorities question was to assume a wider importance than one would have expected, and not simply for reasons of state. Yet senior policymakers arrived at qualitatively different conclusions than Philipps did concerning how to deal with the minorities question, because the philosophical reference point and point of departure for the official was entirely different. For Canadian authorities, whatever minimised risk would be the basis on which victory would be won, while a strategy that avoided contentious issues would be the basis for promoting national unity.

This strategy was directly related to a very particular understanding of both the political environment and Canada's role and ability to deal with the changing political landscape. The Soviet alliance, for example, was necessary from the point of view of winning the war but also vital from the point of view of Canada's responsibility as a player in a new international order where the Soviet Union was emerging as an important global actor. In this sense, situations had to be avoided that would jeopardise Canadian-Soviet relations and Canada's role as a "responsible" player in international relations. This emphasis on political obligation, conceived of in realist terms, would affect the government's dealings with the Ukrainian Canadian minority and condition its views on the Ukrainian question. But more significantly, the strategy would deprive the state of the basis with which to further integrate Canadian society, while exposing state officials to the charge of political cynicism in their conduct of the war and their understanding of Allied war objectives. The publicly embraced principle of national self-determination, central to the political objectives of the war, for example, would fall by the wayside as the dictates of "high politics" demanded that state officials assume their prescribed role.

For state officials this contradiction was both dangerous and problematic, since the critical element of public trust that legitimised the official's claim to act in the national interest was being eroded. State behaviour toward the Ukrainian minority, therefore, would be conditioned in a very profound, yet subtle, way. Indeed, since the views and concerns of the Ukrainian Canadian nationalist community could not be dismissed nor its leadership suppressed, given that their views were being expressed in terms that officials themselves publicly subscribed to, it remained to manage the group, so that those concerns and views would not jeopardise political obligations or find their way onto the wider public agenda.

By necessity, managing the group required information. Consequently, the collection of intelligence on Ukrainian Canadians and their organisations became a central and prominent feature of government activity in dealing with the community. Senior officials looked initially to the Nationalities Branch to fulfil this role but increasingly relied on other traditional agencies, such as the RCMP and Postal Censorship, for more detailed and reliable information on attitudes within the community.[136]

Critically, information gathering substituted for policy as a means of dealing with this particular group, if only because a positive, comprehensive policy could not be developed in light of the contradiction. Indeed, since the state agenda demanded that officials be informed of internal community developments to offset and/or lessen the repercussions of potentially damaging political situations, the need for detailed and up-to-date intelligence was paramount.

In due course the idea that the Nationalities Branch could fulfil the function of an agency entrusted to provide specialised information proved doubtful. Because over time there was more emphasis being placed by branch personnel on providing direction to ethnic groups than collecting information, the branch soon came to be seen as a liability, especially by the Department of External Affairs. The problem was that political direction implied policy, and since a coherent policy could not be formulated in the context of the contradiction, no direction could be given and no plan approved; it was difficult enough, as one senior official put it, to keep "the trimming from interfering."[137] Indeed, the growing tension and anxiety that arose from trying to deal with the Ukrainian Canadian "problem" increasingly put into question the utility of maintaining the Nationalities Branch. The result was the extraordinary situation in which other departments placed pressure on National War Services – under whose jurisdiction the branch lay – to curtail its activities and remove the personnel who were complicating matters.

In this regard, the decision to dismiss Philipps from the ranks of government service was inevitable. Yet there was much uncertainty before that decision was finally made. In some measure this uncertainty was a consequence of the arguments Philipps himself employed, which addressed and underscored the contradictions in government policy. These contradictions included defining the role of the Nationalities Branch, the government's handling of the so-called left-right split within the Ukrainian Canadian community, and, in general, its understanding of the problematic nature of ethnicity.

On another level, government indecision with respect to Philipps reflected the peculiar official approach to what was described as the Ukrainian Canadian problem. In the absence of policy, a piecemeal strategy to problem solving was adopted. And insofar as the problem did not get out of hand, Philipps' activities were tolerated. In fact, the dissatisfaction expressed with Philipps' work in the Nationalities Branch centred not on what his work should be but rather on what it should not be. More importantly, in the absence of a tangible policy his work was tolerated so long as it did not serve to "aggravate" the situation. Once the problem did escalate and once the newly reorganised Wartime Information Board expressed interest in this line of work, Philipps' fate as specialist-adviser was no longer in doubt. But it was simply not enough to dismiss Philipps. The work in the ethnic area was considered too important to be left unattended. Moreover, simple monitoring and the occasional intervention were no longer sufficient. Work among the ethnic minorities would require guidance and that, it was to be hoped, would come from the new vision of John Grierson and his Wartime Information Board.

5 Unencumbered Statecraft: Dealing with the Ukrainian "Problem," 1943–1945

In order to strengthen the government's overall information services, a decision was made in September 1942 to establish the Wartime Information Board (WIB), which would replace the Public Information Board, the agency that had failed so miserably in modifying opinion in the conscription plebiscite. Attached directly to the prime minister's office, the objectives of the WIB were to facilitate and stimulate the domestic flow of information by improving the movement of information to the public, streamlining the whole process, and increasing accessibility. The WIB was also tasked with promoting a wider knowledge of the Canadian nation at war both within Canada and abroad. Specialised public information programs and agencies would continue to operate in other departments. The WIB was to coordinate its efforts with these agencies but was proscribed from exercising authority over them. News and publicity focusing on the concerns of other departments was to flow directly from their agencies and remain under their jurisdiction.[1]

Organisational problems and personnel changes would lead to a false start at the WIB. However, once John Grierson, a well-known and respected producer of documentary films, assumed management, the WIB not only became more serious in its endeavour but also took on a distinctive character.[2] That character was reinforced and complemented by the small coterie of dedicated professionals and technicians Grierson would gather around him, individuals who would bring to their work the same passion and enthusiasm as their mentor. His missionary zeal was infectious, and they too, in time, would become articulate advocates of the Grierson thesis and the Grierson ideal.[3]

Grierson was an unorthodox sort who had a strong belief in the role that public information could play in moulding opinion around political goals. Public attitudes toward specific issues affecting national mobilisation, he believed, required cultivation and instruction through the systematic use of art, film, and the printed word. For Grierson, traditional and spontaneous, but largely unsophisticated, displays of "patriotic tub-thumping" were no longer sufficient, effective, or even necessarily desirable. Rather, the complexities of modern war demonstrated the need for coordination and planning if public opinion surrounding the war effort was to be mobilised and citizen participation increased. For this goal to succeed, public information had to be not only clear and forceful but, more importantly, responsible, functional, and purposeful. Above all, it had to educate, inspire as well as convince.[4] Grierson insisted that the old laissez faire approach to government information

is no longer a tenable government attitude in a complex world of contradictory interests and forces. Initiative in planning, ordering and securing national results has progressively been forced upon governments. We need not argue the advantages and disadvantages of this development. The historical fact is that it has happened, and happened of necessity. It has happened where a laissez-faire policy has failed to secure order, co-operation and harmony in the body politic. In most cases public opinion has forced the power of initiative upon governments.

Obviously, governments cannot take upon themselves the responsibility of community planning unless they exercise the power to inform and instruct the people on matters of state. Information services – propaganda services, if you like – follow inevitably in the wake of government initiative. They are inseparable as Siamese twins, whether you are dealing with departments or governments as a whole. Once you have given the power of initiative, you must in all reason give it the power to persuade people so that national plans may become effective.[5]

Grierson was only too aware of the liabilities of such a program. There was, for instance, the public suspicion of propaganda, which was readily identified with state control, and of course its incompatibility with liberal notions of society and politics. However, in his opinion this was one of the great paradoxes of public information in a democratic polity. It was also in the very nature of democracy, he argued, to produce such contradictions. In the end, the success of public information and the role assigned to it would depend on "faith in the process" and the "good will" of men who knew and would do what was both "right" and in the "public interest." Armed with purpose, conviction, and the results of in-house surveys and public polls, Grierson set out to shape opinion in support of government policy and objectives.

If moulding domestic public opinion was one aspect of the new information program, the other was to publicise and make clear Canada's voice in the international community, while helping to promote the idea of its relative importance in foreign affairs. "The war," Grierson argued, "has given to Canada a degree of international significance she did not have before. She has developed ... into a power to be reckoned with in any country's language ... A young nation like Canada, feeling her new strength and new importance in the world, obviously does not want to be taken lightly or, as they used to say, taken for granted ... Her place at the council table and her place in the world, materially and spiritually, depend on the predisposition of other nations to hear her voice, understand it and respect it. That carries with it the duty of a great deal of prior work in creating that predisposition."[6] Part of the new information program, therefore, was to assure other states that Canada understood its international obligations and that the country was willing to accept this responsibility as it prepared to sit around the table with those who would set the course of the new postwar order. For Grierson, there was a tremendous sense that the future brought with it certain challenges but also opportunities. In this regard, half measures and a half-hearted approach would not do. Moreover, distractions would not be tolerated, a view increasingly shared by other government officials.

Relations between the wib under Grierson and the Nationalities Branch at National War Services were strained almost from the outset. Philipps had proposed in December 1942 that directives setting out guidelines for editorial content in the foreign language press, be sent to the various ethnic newspapers.[7] A confidential draft of the recommended directives was forwarded to the wib for its approval. Grierson, however, declined to act on the proposal, indicating the directives were more appropriate coming from Censorship.[8] Philipps replied that Censorship had informed him that this activity was outside their field of operation and recommended that the wib was best suited to handle it. He added, however, that if the wib felt they could not authorise the directives, then perhaps they could simply indicate "agreement on the general terms" that would allow directives to be issued from the office of the minister of national war services.[9] An officer with the wib, A. Dunton, informed Philipps that his suggestion had again been vetted before Grierson but that the latter was uninterested.[10] Having received no satisfaction, Philipps dropped the matter.

Grierson's reticence in committing the wib to Philipps' proposal stemmed from his growing interest in the question of unity among

Canada's ethnic minorities.[11] A cursory examination of the situation suggested, in his opinion, that too much emphasis had been placed on the "particularism" of these communities, ignoring what he considered were the more obvious and serious divisions within the groups. In Grierson's estimation, "the political factor" was being ignored. He claimed, for example, that "the Right-wing Ukrainians were closer to the Right-wing Poles than they were to the Left-wing section of their own community and it was leading to a violence of feeling between the opposing factions in each of the groups."[12] He argued that to avoid partisanship, efforts at resolving political differences between the groups should not be channelled through individuals or organisations, as had been done in the past and was still being advocated, but directed through the WIB.

Grierson's suggestion clearly stepped outside the bounds of the original WIB mandate, which called for jurisdictional autonomy and noninterference in the work of existing agencies dealing with specific issues of wartime information. That the WIB was investigating the possibility of providing material for wider distribution among Canada's minorities meant the work of the Nationalities Branch would be made redundant. This, however, was the intent of the move.

In late March 1943, an internal memorandum was prepared underscoring the view that the WIB considered itself to be "the logical authority" to supervise the work being performed in its field. It also proposed "to appoint a man to have charge of that branch [Nationalities] and to negotiate then with the Department of National War Services for control of policy." Grierson admitted that the approach was "unorthodox," but he also believed that current circumstances warranted such action.

The inside story appears to be this: that the present Committee [Nationalities Branch] did not conduct propaganda in this field in a manner calculated to induce better relations among the various national groups ... It is now the opinion of the Wartime Information Board that the only way to solve the problem is to secure the required personnel, and announce to the Department of National War Services the intention of the Board to invade this field of work. [The WIB] is not properly concerned with the orthodoxy of this proceeding, but it is thought that in reporting to the Treasury Board in connection with the establishment of a position of Chief, Foreign Language Groups Section, the redundancy should be pointed out.[13]

The aggressiveness that Grierson demonstrated in this and, still later, in other attempts to bring the Nationalities Branch under the authority of the WIB in part arose from Philipps' increasing involvement in work that Grierson considered regressive. Grierson was informed, for example, that Philipps had independently approached the CBC with the suggestion that the agency include broadcasting in the mother tongues of several ethnic groups in Canada. On the basis of the success of a similar project in the United States, Philipps argued that this suggestion would give the groups a greater sense of solidarity with the rest of the nation in the current struggle.[14] From Grierson's point of view, the proposal would only promote undesirable ethnic particularism, since catering to the needs of ethnic communities, he observed, only served to reinforce existing attitudes. Initiatives encouraging further sectarianism were not needed. What was required was a policy that would help shape appropriate attitudes among these communities, such that they would think of themselves as less foreign and more Canadian and be reminded of the advantages and benefits of being Canadian – of their economic welfare, social security, and the political rights they enjoyed. The sentiment was shared by External Affairs, whose officials were anxiously keeping watch over the activity at National War Services. Not surprisingly, a natural empathy soon developed between External Affairs and the WIB on resolving this mutually important question.[15]

For External Affairs, the proposed national UCC congress, the political tensions within the Ukrainian Canadian community, and the obvious and growing interest of the Soviet authorities in the activities of the nationalists, all pointed to the urgency of trying to wrest control of the Nationalities Branch away from National War Services. The shared interest between External Affairs and the WIB in achieving this result produced extensive joint discussions on the matter. Norman Robertson (the under-secretary of state), in fact, conscious of the work Grierson was doing to condition Canadian public opinion toward the Soviet Union as a postwar ally,[16] would soon channel information to Grierson on the external relations angle of the Ukrainian problem, focusing in particular on the recent Soviet diplomatic protests. He stressed in his correspondence with Grierson that the WIB had an important role to play:

The Ukrainian Question has been, for a good many years, a source of irritation in our relations with Poland, against which Ukrainian irredentism has been primarily directed. It now looks as if it may become an even more troublesome factor in our relations with the Soviet Union. One important aspect of this question is its treatment in the Canadian foreign language press, Ukrainian, Polish and Russian. I have felt for a long time that we should be receiving prompter and more objective summaries of political comment in the foreign language press ... I am hopeful ... the Wartime Information Board will effect a real improvement in the present position which will be of use to the Press Censors and to this department, as well as to WIB. The latter, I think, has a special and positive responsibility in relation to the foreign language press which, in the past, has been worked over and interfered with from time to time by three or four different agencies of the federal government, none of which has ever been given any clear directives in policy and none of which has really been equipped in respect of personnel or authority to do durably useful work in this field.[17]

Encouraged by External Affairs, Grierson and the WIB began to move more confidently in bringing the Ukrainian situation under control but also in dealing with Philipps at the Nationalities Branch. A position paper was drafted by the WIB outlining broad objectives in handling the Ukrainian affair.[18] The paper urged the necessity of devising a uniform policy on the Ukrainian question, pointing to the seriousness of the anti-Soviet attacks in the nationalist press, Soviet diplomatic protests, and the UCC's recent plea for Ukrainian self-determination, which had been submitted in a memorandum to the prime minister. The campaign among pro-Soviet Ukrainians for the return of the sequestered ULFTA halls also had to be considered, especially since Canadian public opinion was being widely mobilised in favour of the return of the properties.

The paper recommended, therefore, that all the efforts taken to date by the various departments working in the area should be inventoried, a uniform policy for the foreign language press defined, and a standing interdepartmental committee authorised to supervise the implementation of that policy. The WIB was to be the central agency coordinating policy affecting the press and other issues relating to the group, while those aspects of the problem pertaining to external relations would be handled jointly with the Department of External Affairs. The paper concluded that the nature of the propaganda to be directed at the nationalist community would be "tackled later on," after jurisdictional authority had been established. External Affairs and Press Censorship officials, to whom the paper was sent and vetted for their approval, were in agreement with the recommendations as outlined. External Affairs, in fact, argued that when National War Services was informed, it would see the logic of the recommendations and would have to consent to the guidelines as described.

With the tacit approval of External Affairs and Press Censorship in hand, the only remaining issue for the WIB was how to deal with the Nationalities Branch, which still had responsibility for the area, and with Philipps, who was bound to object. Malcolm Ross, a WIB official, was entrusted with looking into the matter. After some research into the details of the legislation that initially set up the agency, Ross concluded that there were provisions in the original order-in-council that would have allowed for the transfer to the WIB of powers that related to public information under the 1940 National War Services Act. Believing that there were technical grounds for the WIB to have effective "control over Philipps" and the branch, he enquired what action was to be taken.[19]

Encouraged, Grierson immediately called a special WIB meeting attended by senior board and censorship officials, as well as by Norman Robertson representing External Affairs and the clerk of the privy council, A.D.P. Heeney.[20] The discussion at the meeting centred on the WIB's expressed desire to assume more responsibility for the ethnic press. Pointing to the confusion and duplication in the area, Grierson proffered the idea that it would coordinate the existing activities and efforts. Although careful to avoid the impression that it was intruding on other jurisdictions, a passing reference was made to the legislative mandate that identified the WIB as the agency commissioned with overseeing the government's public information program. Those in attendance agreed that the WIB should assume a greater role and responsibility for the area. The problem of the Nationalities Branch finally appeared to be resolved. Indeed, shortly after the meeting Robertson would write to the former deputy minister of national war services, Justice T.C. Davis (in response to a friendly inquiry from Australia as to Philipps' whereabouts), that Grierson at the WIB was developing plans for work that had until then been covered by the Nationalities Branch and that "Philipps, of course, has no place in these plans."[21]

Within a matter of weeks, Grierson wrote to Heeney, who was secretary to the cabinet, asking that the resolution adopted at the special WIB meeting, calling for "the amalgamation within WIB of existing agencies dealing with ethnic information services," be conveyed to cabinet at this time.[22] Heeney, however, hesitated because the language of the resolution now being submitted for government approval by Grierson seemed to differ from what was originally agreed upon.[23] Tasked with drafting government policy statements for cabinet, Heeney was reluctant to accept responsibility for any action that might create artificial divisions between departments that were working on the general question of war information or that could possibly undermine the authority of another department, in this case National War Services.[24] Before he would submit the resolution to cabinet, Heeney asked Robertson for his recollection of the decision arrived at during the meeting.[25]

Robertson confessed that "amalgamation" of other departmental agencies within the WIB had not been discussed, admitting that such a decision would have required the agreement of all parties concerned,

including National War Services.[26] Grierson was subsequently
informed of Heeney's decision that the resolution would not go forward as drafted. Discouraged, Grierson, however, would not be denied.
The episode simply underscored the difficulties involved in dispensing
with Philipps and the Nationalities Branch, a matter that would be
made more difficult when the minister of national war services was
apprised of the efforts outside the department to gain control over the
Nationalities Branch.

External Affairs, in the meantime, had become increasingly concerned with the possible effects that Ukrainian nationalist activities
would have on Canada's external relations. George Glazebrook, the
department's designated liaison with British Intelligence, informed A.J.
Halpern, of the British Security Co-ordination in New York, that the
conflict within the community was escalating and that there was
considerable material there for "embarrassment."[27] Indeed, the
appointment of Oleksander Korniichuk, a Ukrainian, to the position
of second deputy commissar for Soviet foreign affairs was interpreted
by Dana Wilgress, Canada's minister to the USSR, as "significant from
the point of view of Ukrainian nationalism," and he felt that the
appointment was not to be taken lightly in Canada.[28]

Although the conclusion drawn by Wilgress was speculative, there
was other evidence to suggest growing Soviet interest in Ukrainian
nationalist activity in Canada. Within a few months of settling in as
the new Soviet minister to Canada, Feodor Gusev protested against
the activities of the nationalists, which he claimed had been inspired
by the March memorial of the UCC to the Canadian prime minister.
He urged the government of Canada, in particular, to curb the statements appearing in the nationalist press.[29] Wilgress, who had earlier
asked that he be advised promptly of any developments that could
have a bearing on Canada-USSR relations, was informed of the protests. His own view was that the Soviets, sensitive to Allied intentions
and motives, were being watchful, and he cautioned External Affairs
not to be misled or taken in by the nationalists. Suggesting that the
anti-Polish character of the UCC memorial was simply a "clever ruse
to conceal [the] real motive ... [which was] to create discord between
[the] Soviet Union and [the] other United Nations," Wilgress concluded
that it was bound to increase Soviet suspicion of "hostile influences"
affecting policy towards the USSR. Therefore, if some propitious steps
were taken by Canada, he felt that they would go far "in preserving
solidarity with the Soviet Union which is so important both for the
war effort and for future peace."[30] In Wilgress' opinion, a good
beginning would be for Canada to distance itself from the Atlantic

Charter, a document that, as the UCC memorial amply demonstrated, needlessly promoted territorial claims. Canada, he argued,

is a country which has solved successfully the reconciliation of two peoples or alien cultures within the bosom of one state. We should be one of the last countries to deny the success which has attended the efforts of the Soviet Union to accord cultural autonomy to the different peoples composing its population. This is particularly striking when applied to the Ukrainians because of the close cultural affinity existing between Ukrainians and Russians – a circumstance not present in the case of the two principal races of Canada.

Since coming here I have seen evidence of the Atlantic Charter being used to promote territorial claims put forward by the Russians, Poles and Ukrainians. When the voices of the countries of Eastern Europe now fighting with the Axis are added to this chorus, the impossibility of achieving harmony from this refrain will become more obvious. It is my hope that the peaceful atmosphere of Ottawa may permit the drafting of a statement of war aims less likely to be used to promote disunity than the document drafted on the stormy waters of the Atlantic.[31]

Some observers shared, if not Wilgress' understanding of the problem, then at least the general view that there were advantages in outlining Canada's position on postwar policy. Arnold Smith, a political secretary at the Canadian mission in the Soviet wartime capital of Kuibyshev and Wilgress' junior colleague, was one such individual. Indeed, he had written a working paper on this very subject that Wilgress subsequently sent to Prime Minister Mackenzie King in the hope of making more clear what was in fact being proposed.

The working paper began by indicating that an important obstacle in considering Canada's ambitions to have a voice in postwar policy was that very little was known about what, if anything, Canada stood for in world politics and about the kind of general policy it would be likely to support or initiate in the future. Moreover, there was widespread opinion among the foreign councils that Canada had little or no point of view. Indeed, there was a sense that Canadian representation in any international committees would at best be pointless, or at worst that it would be seen to give one more vote to the position of the United Kingdom or the United States on any subject under discussion. To dispel this impression, Smith proposed that King promote a slogan that would "ignite world opinion" and catch on like Roosevelt's Four Freedoms or the Atlantic Charter. It was necessary to advance a slogan that would avoid the problems of the Atlantic Declaration, a document that in Smith's opinion "misfired through its over-emphasis of traditional nineteenth century sovereignty, and the increasingly obvious fact that it largely fails to correspond to the real policies of the Great Powers."[32] Smith called on Prime Minister King to put forward the idea that "Prosperity is Indivisible," a concept that had much to commend it. As Smith argued, the slogan was sufficiently vague so as not to commit its proponents to anything definite, yet the policies it suggested were eminently practicable and therefore likely to be initiated. Smith explained:

Internally, in Canada and the United States, the connotation is full employment, good profits and larger exports. In Europe the connotation is in no sense incompatible with the socialist aspirations of Left-wing groups, yet the slogan takes no explicit sides in the important disputes which exist and will probably spread in Europe over this issue. And throughout most of Europe and all of Asia and Africa the slogan suggests economic development, the large-scale investment of capital which is the greatest need of these parts of the world and an indispensable condition for full employment in the economic system of the United States. In other words the slogan suggests both international economic collaboration and solidarity, but also, internally in every country, the vital importance of social solidarity and recognition that the well-being and prosperity of the mass of the common people is essential to the well-being of the world.[33]

The slogan, it was hoped, would strike a universal chord. More importantly, if properly handled, it would give the country the political "meaning" it sought – catapulting Canada to the centre stage of world politics as an advocate of a new and prosperous future.[34]

King thanked Wilgress for Smith's most welcome and "valuable" suggestion. The proposal reinforced in his mind the value and importance of the public information program being developed at WIB. The Atlantic Charter, the prime minister concluded, had in fact encouraged unnecessary and harmful discussion about aims and objectives that complicated relations with the USSR.[35] Promoting a progressive but noncontroversial alternative vision of the future would go a long way to resolving some of the current difficulties and tensions in Allied relations. It would also establish Canada as a bona fide and credible partner in the postwar deliberations.

The dispatch from Kuibyshev, with its attachment, was but one of a growing number received by the prime minister from Wilgress in the spring and summer of 1943. Having been posted early on as a Canadian trade commissioner in Siberia and with some experience in trade negotiations with the Soviet government, Wilgress, who had come over from the Department of Trade and Commerce to accept the diplomatic appointment in External Affairs, was considered the government's resident expert on Soviet affairs.[36] Coming from an authority of sorts, his dispatches were always read with interest and appreciation. Wilgress' appointment as Canada's envoy to the USSR, however, was unfortunate, since Wilgress demonstrated an unusual tendency to conflate his desire to understand the Soviet Union with empathy for the Russian people, to the point where the two were seen as synonymous.[37] In his attempt to promote confidence in Canadian-Soviet relations, Wilgress would often provide highly speculative, if not misleading accounts, based on preconceived notions of Soviet motives and their rationale.[38] His accounts not only gave a false sense of actual conditions but also served to raise the level of anxiety in Ottawa.

When Wilgress learned of the proposed UCC congress through Norman Robertson, he quickly informed the Canadian prime minister not to accept an invitation to attend, advising that acceptance could be interpreted as an endorsement of Ukrainian nationalism.[39] Everything possible needed to be done to allay the suspicions of the Soviet Union, which if isolated, Wilgress contended, would turn inward and away from the West, with dire consequences for all.[40] It was suggested, therefore, that perhaps an overture could be made in the form of the return of the ULFTA halls, the status of which would soon have to be decided anyway. Not only would this step remove a "source of friction" with the Soviet government, but it would also signal to Soviet officials the desire that Canadian-Soviet relations not be clouded by the irredentism of the militant Ukrainian Canadian nationalists, which was likely to increase.[41] Confident that a favourable decision would be made by an interdepartmental committee examining the issue of the restoration of the properties, George Glazebrook proffered the idea that news of the decision be sent to the Soviets before it was made public. This news, it was thought, would not only serve as a goodwill gesture but also help to ease Wilgress' growing anxiety "about the impression being created amongst Soviet officials by our Ukrainian nationalists."[42]

Although the view among External Affairs officials was that the extreme element within the nationalist community would continue to press for Ukrainian independence, there was some room for optimism. Mr T. Kurban, of the Federation of Russian Canadians, in a conversation with Leo Malania, a political officer at External Affairs with extensive contacts in the Russian-Canadian community, reported that he had observed some interesting trends among the nationalists. The resignation of W. Swystun, a leading figure, from both the UNF and the UCC, for example, demonstrated that even within the hardened nationalist core there was division of opinion on the wisdom of holding a congress. Kurban also claimed that the perception among the moderate element was that the UCC was incontrovertibly within the hands of the militants, which explained the ambivalence of the moderates toward that body and their willingness to cooperate with members of the Association of Canadian Ukrainians and other pro-Soviet organisations.[43] It also accounted for their participation in the Aid to Russia relief drive against the objections of the extremists within the community. But perhaps more importantly, impressed by the rate of assimilation among the Ukrainians, Kurban noted that Ukrainian Canadians were showing signs of being increasingly in accord with mainstream public opinion and that, shortly, their interests and the national interest would be one and the same.

Kurban's views were confirmed by R.G. Riddell, a senior External Affairs official, who, during a visit to Winnipeg, enquired about the situation there. He reported to Ottawa that the general impression among those acquainted with Ukrainians on the prairies was that they were being rapidly assimilated, a process accelerated by the group's propensity toward exogamy. There were, of course, exceptions, notably those "isolated rural communities where Ukrainian groups live by themselves and where few ideas native to this continent have penetrated." More significantly, although the majority of Ukrainian Canadians were nationalist in their political orientation, the feeling was that their views were not taken seriously by those who were familiar with them. Although there were a few staunch advocates, the political objective of securing an independent Ukraine "would seem to be largely academic." Moreover, the belief in local Winnipeg political circles was that they "would not deliberately embarrass the government or betray the interests of the country as a whole for the purpose of supporting Ukrainian independence."[44]

External Affairs officials were encouraged by the reports. But it was also evident that the onus was on the department to ensure that the more egregious statements made by either extreme in the community be kept in check. This was especially necessary in view of the upcoming Ukrainian Canadian congress, which it was feared, would turn into a "free for all." That there was some cause for concern was evident in the UNF booklet *A Program and a Record*, which had just been released.[45] Although the booklet was a seemingly innocuous statement outlining the organisation's political program and activities, the final pages however were sharply critical of the Ukrainian Canadian communists, describing their campaign to discredit the nationalist cause as "slanderous in form, dishonest in substance and predatory in aim." Claiming the high moral ground, the UNF condemned their rivals for their slavish attitude toward the USSR and unprincipled stand in the early years of the war.

The publication could not have appeared at a less opportune time. Having just met with the Soviet envoy, who complained bitterly about the public statements of the nationalists, and with the UCC congress scheduled to be held in a matter of weeks, Norman Robertson felt compelled to pen a curt and unusually firm response. Noting that the current difficult period demanded the united effort of all Canadians, Robertson expressed his disappointment "that your association should have found it necessary to discuss at such length within the pages of this formal statement of its activities, the differences which separate it from other societies of Canadian Ukrainians. There are many in Canada who think that, at so critical a time in our history, it is perilous to pursue questions which separate us either from our allies or from our fellow-Canadians."[46] Nevertheless he was still hopeful that he would be able to persuade the UNF executive and others to desist from issuing any further statements that could only inflame passions, especially in the context of the proposed congress. Indeed, appealing to the patriotic sensibilities of the organisation, he concluded his letter by stating that "I know that your association is one which places great loyalty to this country first among its objectives and that its members would not willingly act in a manner that they thought to be against the better interests of the country as a whole. It is because of this confidence that I take the present occasion to mention the matter of your relations with other groups."

Ukrainian Canadian activity leading to the congress and the meeting itself had become the subject of much American and British interest. In April 1943 the American consul general in Winnipeg informed the United States secretary of state of the deteriorating situation in Canada. Underscoring the point that the Ukrainian influence on political life in Canada was the largest of the non-Anglo-Saxon races – not including the French – he concluded that "They are organising skilfully to be ready to bring pressure on the post-war settlement of Europe in favour of Ukraine."[47] When the congress did take place in June 1943, the consul general considered it sufficiently important that he submitted a full and detailed report to Washington.[48]

The attention devoted to Ukrainian Canadian activity by the United States consul general was in keeping with an earlier directive by the U.S. secretary of state requesting that any suspicious activities of Ukrainians abroad be reported to the State Department.[49] It also, however, paralleled the efforts of the Overseas Strategic Services and the British Security Co-ordination to keep abreast of Ukrainian developments in North America and to coordinate information on the Ukrainian issue. Since the focus was on Canada's increasingly active

Ukrainians, the Department of External Affairs felt that the matter should not get away from them. The most logical approach in dealing with the issue was to bring together the specialists from the BSC and the OSS to discuss the Ukrainian situation in detail.[50] Furthermore, because the problem had bearing on Allied security and hemispheric defence, Canadian officials thought it best that relevant information, including sensitive intelligence, be passed on to their security counterparts. It was a move inspired in part by the British, who began to take an increasingly dim view of what appeared to be a revival in the political activity among the Ukrainian nationalist communities in North and South America.[51]

Of particular concern to security officials at the BSC was the role in Canada of Tracy Philipps, who appeared to be at the centre of much of the controversy, suggesting that it would be in everyone's interest if he simply retired from the scene. But the BSC noted that "The facts about Philipps are remarkable ... [Canadian] External Affairs officials say they would be very pleased if he would go home [to Britain], but for some reason which remains unexplained, they have been able to do nothing about him. Even when the plans were set on foot for the [UCC] Congress, in which Philipps was certainly a – if not the – leading mover, and the potential dangers of which External Affairs fully realised, no action could apparently be taken either about Philipps or the Congress."[52] Aware of Philipps' British connection, the BSC disclaimed any responsibility for him. By implication, the problem was a Canadian one, and if something had to be done, which was certainly the case, then it was up to Canadian officials to act and act quickly.

The "potential dangers" referred to by the British were more than apparent to Dana Wilgress, Canada's minister to the Soviet Union, who was dealing with Soviet officials on a daily basis. In a conversation with the second deputy commissar for Soviet foreign affairs, Oleksander Korniichuk, the subject of the UCC memorandum of March 1943 to Prime Minister King – Ukrainian self-determination – was once again raised. Responding to Soviet criticism of Canadian inaction, Wilgress outlined the government's position on censorship and noted that the activities of such groups as the UCC had to be tolerated so long as their behaviour was "within the law." Korniichuk, however, insisted that this was the "typical" work of the Germans who, by raising the question, were trying to create dissension among the Allied nations. Wilgress countered by telling him that there was "no evidence that the Ukrainian Canadian Committee had any connection with the Ukrainian organisations formerly in Germany, to which he [Korniichuk] replied that German agents had ways of stirring up agitation of this kind without giving the suspicion that they had a hand in it."[53]

Wilgress thought it best to change the subject. It was clear to him, however, that the activities of Ukrainian Canadians, in which Soviet authorities had developed a keen interest, served to complicate Canadian-Soviet relations or, at the very least, acted as a serious obstacle in any further movement in improving relations. Indeed, it was his view that the activities of Ukrainian Canadians distracted Soviet officials and severely undercut Canada's ability to alter Soviet ambiguity towards Canada or its perception of Canada's limited role in international affairs.

The Canadian diplomat was not far off the mark. Although Soviet embassy officials had the distinct impression that "the Ukrainian problem was an embarrassment to the Canadian government," they were equally convinced that the Ukrainian community "exerted influence on the internal and foreign policies of the Government of Canada" and that in the official Canadian attitude there was "a clear orientation toward the reactionary faction of the Ukrainian immigration." Soviet officials concluded that "the attitude among the leading government agencies towards the Ukrainians revealed the existence of reactionary elements and forces hostile to the USSR in the governing circles." Highlighting the importance of lending assistance to the progressive Ukrainian organisations in their struggle against the nationalists, embassy staff recommended that not only should materials on German-occupied Ukraine and the significant contribution of the Ukrainian people to the defeat of fascism be provided but also that "the more interesting aspects" of Ukrainian Canadian community life be publicised in the Soviet press. As for the organisations advocating Ukrainian separatism, it was further recommended that pressure be brought to bear on the government of Canada to suppress these groups "whose activities were incompatible with our diplomatic relations with Canada."[54]

Among External Affairs officials there was a clear and immutable sense that any improvement in relations with the Soviet Union would require some propitious steps to be taken, especially as regards the Ukrainian question. The degree to which this was possible, however, would become significant as the Soviet Union, hoping to advance its postwar position, began to explore whether several Soviet republics – Ukraine, Belorussia, Moldavia, and the Baltics – might be given separate representation on various international postwar tribunals, in particular the War Crimes Commission. Importantly, in its request the Soviet Union argued that the right of the Commonwealth nations to participate on the commission would be met on condition that a similar right was extended to Soviet republics that had suffered immeasurably under German occupation and whose populations were fighting valiantly in the ranks of the Soviet armies for the common Allied cause.[55]

It was an extraordinary request, politically loaded and with enormous implications. For Britain, agreeing to the condition would have implied de facto recognition of the proposed political changes in the East and, ergo, the dominance of the Soviet Union in Eastern Europe.[56] This, Britain was not yet prepared to accept. Canadian resistance, on the other hand, would relate directly to the question of its own postwar status.

In its deliberations with Britain, the Soviet Union had insisted on a similar right of participation for its republics not only as a matter of principle but also of fair exchange. For Canadian officials parity was unacceptable because it brought into question Canada's constitutional and international legal status. As was pointed out, Canada and the other dominions had long enjoyed full international recognition, and to draw a parallel between the Ukrainian SSR, for example, and Canada was to misunderstand Canada's constitutional status and international position.[57] Soviet Ukraine, in law and in fact, had no individual international status, and although the case could be made that it was "evolving," this point was moot under the circumstances. Canada's independence was indisputable, a point that had to be made clear to the Soviet leadership.

For Canadian statesmen, Canada's political independence vis-à-vis Britain was central to the issue. On different occasions and in different ways Canadian officials had raised with Soviet officials the subject of Canada's independence, whether in its foreign policy or its stand on other matters of importance.[58] Indeed, Wilgress went to great lengths in his first encounter with the first deputy commissar for foreign affairs, A. Vyshinsky – "the best of the Soviet officials ... to appraise the independence of our foreign policy" – to emphasise this aspect of Canada's political character. Then, as later, Vyshinsky offered no comment, mirroring the USSR's ambivalence about Canada's international role.[59] But now the matter had come to a head. To equate Canada with Soviet Ukraine and to leave that equation unchallenged was to undermine Canada's future political prospects. Noting that not clarifying the issue now "would lead to further difficulties later," Wilgress was instructed by External Affairs to "clear up the misunderstanding." To conciliate Soviet officials while trying to strengthen Canada's hand in the deliberations, Wilgress was also advised to communicate that the government of Canada "did not attach a great deal of importance" to its involvement on the War Crimes Commission, except in those cases affecting Canadian nationals: "You should assure the Soviet authorities that Canada is prepared to accept limited participation for that reason. This will mean attendance at only those meetings of the Commission when [it is] constituted in [a] final form where matters affecting Canada are discussed. It should, however, be made clear that such limited participation is not – repeat not – connected with Dominion status."[60]

A meeting with V. Molotov, the Soviet foreign minister, to personally communicate Canada's position was arranged.[61] The discussion was critical from the point of view of Canada's national interest, and Wilgress attempted to make the best possible case. Claiming that Canada and the other Commonwealth nations exercised a substantial degree of sovereignty, Wilgress insisted that Canada's participation on the international war crimes tribunal could not and should not be conditional on the right of Soviet republics to similar participation. Molotov replied that the government of the USSR did not question the independence of the dominions. Nor did he imply that the Soviet republics enjoyed similar status. He did, however, repeat the view that the republics had the strongest moral claim to be represented on the commission because of the suffering of their people.

From the perspective of international law, Molotov further argued that there were no obstacles in the way of granting the Soviet republics the right of representation in foreign relations independently of or equally with the USSR and that the formal juridical objections concerning the participation of the republics in the War Crimes Commission did not apply in this instance. When Wilgress pointed out that this position ignored provisions in the Soviet constitution whereby all questions of foreign policy and economic planning were centred in the all-union government, the Soviet minister stated that Soviet officials were "the best interpreters of the Soviet constitution." When further pressed, Molotov, tired of the banter, indicated that the official position of the USSR was outlined in an *aide-mémoire* delivered to the British government, to which Wilgress was directed for further information.

Working on the assumption that the Soviet government's claim was motivated by strategic ambitions aimed at improving the USSR's postwar position, British officials, with whom the USSR was negotiating, continued to resist. Unimpressed and clearly annoyed, the Soviet Union responded by declaring that the Soviet republics were sovereign states in no less a degree than the British dominions and that their sovereignty depended solely on agreement between the republics and the USSR.[62] The United Kingdom government therefore concluded that there was no working with Soviet government on the issue and that if there was general agreement among the other Allies, then the War Crimes Commission should proceed without Soviet participation.[63] Canadian officials agreed to the proposal. The overriding consideration from the Canadian perspective, given the implications for Canada's international status, was that "Their [the Soviet] claim for representation of constituent republics is based on indefensible grounds about which it is impossible to compromise."[64]

The issue highlighted the difficulties Canada faced in asserting its international role. Its status was questioned as a result of the political power play between the Big Three – the United States, the United Kingdom, and the Soviet Union. To Wilgress, Britain, in particular, showed lack of leadership in its inability or unwillingness to meet Soviet interests in the East.[65] This intransigence, he believed, had the unfortunate consequence of forcing the Soviet leadership to employ a diplomatic tactic that profoundly affected Canada and the other Commonwealth nations. Wilgress urged the government of Canada to impress upon London the view that unless Britain changed its position or at least made some other accommodation with the USSR, Canada's voice would continue to be dismissed and its independence questioned by the Soviet leadership.[66] Within this context, when British officials, hoping to preempt a possible Soviet request for a diplomatic exchange with the Ukrainian SSR, communicated to Canada that such an exchange would have profound implications for Poland and the Baltic states, External Affairs responded by suggesting that it not be dismissed entirely out of hand. The claim of each Soviet republic, External Affairs suggested, had to be judged on its own merits. Since Ukraine was the world's second largest Slavic state and held an important place in the world economy, a case for recognition could be made in this instance.[67]

The shift in the Canadian position was based on several increasingly salient factors that were hard to ignore with the march of time. Canadian officials understood the logic behind the original British position. Diplomatic exchange with Soviet Ukraine, which now included annexed Polish territory, would have signalled British acceptance of a new postwar order. And although Britain was showing signs that it was prepared to accept certain changes, including perhaps a compromise on the frontiers question, it had not entirely abandoned the idea of a new balance of power, with a view to a continuing role in Eastern Europe. This, however, had to be negotiated.[68]

From the perspective of Canada's Department of External Affairs, on the other hand, British strategy was increasingly untenable, given the rapidly changing military situation in the East. By late spring/early summer 1944, the Soviet Red Army was in the process of recovering nearly all the disputed territories. In this regard, the incorporation of the Baltic states into the USSR was seen as a given, while the disagreement over Poland's eastern frontiers was a foregone conclusion. Britain's adherence to the principle that no concessions should be made until the peace settlement was only postponing the inevitable. Arguing that "it is undesirable that this question should become a matter of controversy during the peace settlement, where it might easily serve to side-track more important issues, and be exploited to divide the United Nations to the detriment of their permanent interests," Canada voiced what was clearly becoming obvious – that Britain's traditional support for Poland and the Baltic states was no longer viable.[69]

For Canada, there was also a growing need to assert its own interest in the evolving context. Soviet influence over developments and, ultimately, control in Eastern Europe was increasingly accepted as a fait accompli. The issue, therefore, was how best to adjust to the expected realignment in global power that would see the Soviet Union playing an important future role. Now more than ever, Canada's ability to respond politically to the USSR would determine in part whether it would be received as a partner and player in the postwar system. Accommodating the Soviet request for diplomatic exchange with the Soviet republic of Ukraine, Canadian officials concluded, might be conducive to Allied unity. That conclusion did not mean, as was pointed out, that Canada or the other Allies should either hasten recognition or the exchange of diplomatic representatives. Nor did it presume that the Soviet government would receive a favourable reply. This, ultimately, would depend on several factors. Canada's interest, repeatedly made clear, was that the issue of its own international status had to be resolved first. Canada would accept a decision favouring international recognition for the Ukrainian SSR only if it was not interpreted as a matter of reciprocity and a political distinction was made between the status of Canada and the Soviet republics.

There was, finally, an additional and not unimportant consideration in Canada's assessment of a possible diplomatic exchange of representatives. From the point of view of the Ukrainian controversy in Canada, the under-secretary of state for external affairs, Norman Robertson, believed the effect of Canada's recognition of the Ukrainian SSR would be positive. Sensing an opportunity here and casting an eye to the future, Robertson felt that recognition "in the long-run ... would drive from [the] minds [of the Ukrainian nationalists] the mirage of absolute Ukrainian independence and in this way ... hasten the process of their assimilation. Once the question ceases to be a matter of controversy, it is also to be expected that the most important source of the division among Ukrainian-Canadians will be removed and both Right and Left-wing elements may be induced to co-operate more effectively in the interests of Canadian citizenship."[70]

There were some obvious and useful benefits to be derived from a move granting Ukraine *de jure* international status. Recognition of Soviet Ukraine, however, was, for the time being, hypothetical. Such a decision – if it ever was made – would have to be made jointly with the other Western powers.

The question of the assimilation of Ukrainian Canadians had been on the minds of External Affairs officials for some time. In May 1943, before the UCC congress, the head of the department's legal division, assistant under-secretary of state John Read, hoping to allay the anxiety of Soviet officials, had argued in response to some pointed remarks about the nonconforming nature of the Ukrainian immigration in Canada that "Ukrainians in principle were good Canadians" but that the process of assimilation would take time. He was of the view that eventually all the uncertainties associated with the group, as with others, would be taken care of in due course, as they became assimilated.[71] In the wake of the UCC congress, however, it was evident that assimilation would require some assistance, inasmuch as passions were being fuelled from outside the community. As George Glazebrook, External Affairs' point man on Ukrainian affairs, remarked, "If Grierson proposes to deal with the [Ukrainian] problem, he may well start with the non-Ukrainians" – especially those in the Nationalities Branch at the Department of National War Services.[72]

This approach, however, was easier said than done. The new minister of national war services, General L.R. LaFleche, when informed of the efforts by the WIB and External Affairs to assume control over an agency in his department, expressed surprise. Under the circumstances, the recommendation that had been proposed earlier by Justice Davis to transfer the Nationalities Branch over to the WIB was ignored. Hoping to get a better sense of what was going on, LaFleche asked his newly appointed deputy minister, Charles Payne, for his assessment of the work being performed by the branch. In reply, Payne indicated that he was unsure of where things stood because of the uncertain nature of Philipps' role but that until he could get a better handle on the situation, Philipps would be instructed not to leave Ottawa or issue any statements.[73] In the meantime, Payne stated that he would cooperate in any way the minister saw fit to put "this Division on what may be termed a rational basis."

The restrictions imposed on Philipps with respect to both travel and contact with ethnic communities proved frustrating. Moreover, passive obstruction on the part of External Affairs was becoming increasingly apparent. The jeremiad Philipps, sensing something was amiss, declared that perhaps nothing should have been done at all with respect to the foreign-language communities, since a false impression had been given that the federal government was prepared and willing to listen to their concerns,

to understand their difficulties which (in the first generation and a half) are most wholly of European origin, to remedy the many discriminations against the equality of citizenship and to help them attain full-fledged membership of the nation ... which means everything to them. They are being led to expect understanding, guidance and positive help. So far, wherever we have contact, we have got (and deserved) confidence. Since we no longer get support and are being passively obstructed, we are now betraying, involuntarily & in the name of the Govt., the confidence which we had gained.[74]

He concluded that public officials either had no interest or, alternatively, no plan except to criticise those who offered some direction.[75]

When Philipps learned, however, that External Affairs had all along been engineering the transfer of the entire branch to the WIB, his frustration turned to resentment. Claiming that officials in External Affairs were completely ignoring the concerns of the "foreign-born" workers – who "are tired of being called (and used) as bloody bohunks and damned dagoes" and who "intend to fix their after-war position now while the Anglo-Saxons *need* them" – he accused the department of acting irresponsibly. He argued that department officials, unable to resist pressure from members of the pro-Soviet left who were becoming increasingly vocal in their condemnation of both the government and the branch for its handling of the "foreign-born" question, were taking an expeditious course that in the short-term satisfied certain "limited goals" but that in the long-term would have serious consequences.[76] Philipps was not alone in his views. Others, equally disturbed by recent developments, showed their lack of confidence in the government by resigning from the public service. Dr Kaye, who had been working as chief of the editorial section, left. So too did the congenial George Simpson, who had chaired the advisory board associated with the branch, ending what he personally described as an "embarrassing situation."[77]

The resignations of Kaye and Simpson followed immediately on the heels of the recommendation of the deputy minister, who, having been told that under no condition would the minister of national war services allow the Nationalities Branch to slip away from his department, suggested after a cursory review of its activities that there was an "urgent need ... for expert and intelligent guidance, both as to policy and reorganisation."[78] This would become an important matter for the minister as pressure began to mount.

Grierson, hoping to gain headway with the minister over policy, had informed LaFleche that he had recently met with the Canadian Unity Council, a nonpartisan body representing a diverse number of ethnic organisations. The council, Grierson relayed, complained bitterly of the activities of both Philipps and the branch. He noted that they objected to Philipps' "sanitising" the country, arguing that his presence was both divisive and resented. Grierson repeated the council's demand that nothing short of Philipps' immediate removal from a position of authority would suffice. Believing "that a formula could be devised which would secure a healthy co-operation," Grierson concluded his missive to the minister by stating that "There is only one matter of which I am doubtful. If the situation is as now suggested and it, because of past history or for one reason or another, the influence of Mr Philipps is [more] divisive than unifying, a co-operative understanding in the matter of information could not be implemented while he remains a negative force within the setup."[79]

The Canadian Unity Council was not the only group interested in the goings-on of the branch and its personnel. A campaign among pro-Soviet organisations and the pro-Soviet press went into full swing once the Davies book, *This Is Our Land: Ukrainian Canadians against Hitler*, became available. More editorial space was given to publicising the "pro-fascist" activities of the Ukrainian nationalists and to questioning the motives of those in the government who, it was alleged, openly supported and encouraged the activities of the nationalist organisations. The pro-Soviet Russian Canadian newspaper *Vestnik* rhetorically asked, "Is it possible to allow wolves to watch over a herd of sheep? Can the Russian Canadians approve of a committee [the Nationalities Branch] directed by the most bitter enemies of their native land and agitation for the dismemberment of Russia? Would not the revival of the committee, as at present constituted, prove an insult to Russian Canadians ... to the Canadian people, [to] our great ally?"[80] There was also resentment that a government agency was dictating to hyphenated Canadians where their Canadianism lay, and the Liberal government was accused of using the agency as a vehicle to advance its narrow party interests among certain ethnic voting blocs.[81]

From the perspective of the minister of national war services, the situation was getting out of hand, and although he "believed that 'salutary neglect' might on the whole be better than attention," this was no longer a viable strategy. Even backbenchers within the Liberal party urged the minister to do something. Foreseeing the potential embarrassment if the parliamentary opposition were to latch on to the controversy as a possible means to discredit the King government, H. Winkler, a Liberal member of Parliament, wrote to General LaFleche:

The reports I have received on the committee [Nationalities Branch] would not add up very creditably to the work of the committee; not perhaps because of the committee's intention, but to the fact that it is wholly inadequate in its genesis to meet the situation. What group of people would want to be guided by a man who is not known to them as being either qualified or even distantly connected with any institution [on] which their faith is grounded. Certainly I, as a Canadian born of the fifth of sixth generation, would not welcome leadership from a condescending person or group of persons who would put me on the straight and narrow path of Canadian citizenship. I think the same would apply to any other Canadian-born, regardless of antecedents. When we ask for leadership, we want leadership of our own choosing.[82]

The minister replied that everything possible was being done to straighten out the problems with the branch but that, despite the rumours, he did not intend to disband the body or its advisory committee. LaFleche felt confident that there was a real need to continue the initiative because there was much that needed to be done in the area. The solution to the problem, he claimed, would be to ensure that the work was being done properly.[83]

Censorship reports of the negative ethnic press coverage of the branch and the alleged fascist connections of Philipps and Kaye came into the possession of Grierson, who forwarded the material to A.D.P. Heeney in the prime minister's office. Grierson also sent copies to Robertson, to whom he communicated that, since the documents revealed a situation that was dangerous and not improving, they should perhaps be brought to the personal attention of the prime minister. In the attempt to get the branch "into Grierson's hands," Robertson obliged.[84]

King, however, was already aware of the situation. With the publication of the Davies book, left-wing Labour Progressive Party members of Parliament were now making inquiries about the branch and its handling of the foreign-born question. Hoping to avoid a full-blown and potentially embarrassing debate on the floor of the House of Commons, King instructed LaFleche to exercise immediate control over his department and deal with the problem.[85]

LaFleche needed no more to be said. In January 1944 the advisory body to the branch – the Committee on Co-operation in Canadian Citizenship – was immediately called to Ottawa to meet and discuss the functions of the branch. Reorganisation was the topic of discussion. Those in attendance did not resist the minister's request that the organisational structure of the division be revamped, its functions more precisely defined, and a new director hired, one who would both be an employee of the department and have the requisite knowledge to reorganise the branch. An agreement was also effected at the time with the WIB stipulating that routine requests for information from the foreign-language press to the WIB would simply be dealt with directly by the WIB as a matter of course. Furthermore, requests for general information sent to the Nationalities Branch would be sent to the WIB for direct action, and when the Nationalities Branch, through its contacts with the foreign-language press, discovered facts of conceivable value to the functioning of the WIB's information service, these facts would be communicated to the WIB.[86] Requests to the WIB from the foreign-language press for information that had political overtones, however, would still be referred to the branch for special treatment.

The overtures to the WIB were obvious attempts to satisfy officials at the board, notably Grierson, who, ironically, would resign from the WIB in January because of his own political difficulties.[87] But these overtures were courtesies only and did not amount to a transfer of responsibility, indicating that the minister was not about to relinquish control over the most sensitive aspects of the operation and function of the branch. At a certain level, LaFleche was personally interested in the problems of integration and citizenship and had strong opinions on the matter.[88] On another level, however, the principle of political prestige and authority had to be considered. As a former deputy minister in the Department of National War Services and now cabinet minister, having successfully run as a Liberal candidate in a by-election, LaFleche was not prepared to have policy in an area with which he was acquainted dictated from outside the department.

The recommendations adopted at the January meeting of the Citizenship Committee were elaborated upon and incorporated into a comprehensive report submitted to the department by Dr Robert England on 12 June 1944.[89] England, who had been a member of the same committee until his resignation in 1943, had been commissioned to undertake a thorough investigation of the Nationalities Branch. His instructions had been to recommend steps that would see to the proper functioning and reorganisation of the branch – at least within the parameters of the framework defined by the minister. The result was mixed.

In his report, England, using such words as cooperation, inculcation, integration, and assimilation interchangeably, suggested that the Nationalities Branch be reorganised as a division of citizenship that would introduce an extensive program aimed primarily at the foreign-born, one "that would attach them closely to Canadian ideals and aspirations in the interests of their own peace of mind, and of the future welfare of their children." He stressed the need to promote citizenship, since in his opinion, like the opinion expressed earlier by the WIB, there had been too much emphasis in the past on the ethnic particularism of Canada's minorities and on European developments that tended to distract these same peoples. Specifically, he underlined the importance of and opportunity for cultivating a spirit of civic-mindedness and for developing a sense of Canadian identity through film, literature, and radio. The new citizenship division would, in this regard, cooperate with the National Film Board and the CBC to produce documentary films and create programming that would assist in generating greater mutual understanding. On the critical question of social-economic rights, he further recommended that the division work to lessen segregation and end discrimination in obtaining housing.

Less promising, but perhaps more revealing, were several other seemingly random suggestions. For instance, England recommended translating English and French literary classics – Shakespeare and Balzac – for "New Canadians," so that they might have a better sense of the country, and he proposed that the division partner with the

Department of Fitness and Health in promoting mass displays of folk dancing as a way of encouraging fitness and well-being. England also endorsed the idea that the legal procedure for name changes be simplified "to enable use to be made of the root of the name, except in the case of those who served a term of imprisonment for a criminal offence." For England, the concept of Canadianization had a distinct, if not limited, meaning, pointing to the difficult years ahead for the task of articulating a clear idea of Canadian citizenship.

Significantly, in formulating several of the proposals contained in the submission, England had consulted Grierson and his remaining colleagues at the WIB. The report was less than was hoped for by WIB officials, but it was still satisfactory, if only because a major obstacle had finally been removed.[90] That is, during the evaluation process, England suggested that Philipps be released from public service because of the controversy that had centred on his activities and person. Philipps, according to England, had used the wrong approach in dealing with the problem: "Being familiar only with the European pattern, [Philipps] placed his emphasis on the political problems in Europe rather than on the cultural contribution of these groups to Canada." The results were dangerous because, instead of channelling attention away from Europe, he tended to promote a framework that resurrected European ideas and, sometimes, aspirations. "The objections to this," England remarked, "are obvious."[91]

Notwithstanding pressure from the WIB and other quarters to dismiss Philipps, the minister – on the preliminary recommendation of England and before the report was submitted – asked Philipps for his resignation. Philipps resigned on 12 May 1944 and immediately left for Europe to assume a position with the United Nations relief organisation UNRRA. Philipps, however, had already surmised that his role was ending. In March 1944 he placed on record with the deputy minister his version of the situation. Faced with difficulties in dealing with the "foreign-born," the government, he pointed out, had approached him initially for assistance and had invited him to work on the question. Subsequently, however, after the immediate crisis had dissipated, it had done nothing further to help, offering him no encouragement and little support in either putting the question on a balanced footing or developing a framework that would prove both beneficial and enduring from the perspective of building the nation. This was unfortunate, he claimed, since not only was an opportunity lost but the suspicion of government among ethnic communities had also deepened. In the effort to integrate those who would become Canadians, the government had failed miserably. He believed it would require a generation to forget and still yet another government to recognise what needed to be done.[92]

Simpson, upon learning of Philipps' dismissal, expressed his regret and offered personal thanks to Philipps for his work, or, as he put it, "for holding the bridge over a difficult period." He communicated to Philipps that it was his hope that those who succeeded him in the branch would bring to the project the same energy and understanding as did he. Philipps, in kind, expressed his thanks to Simpson for having devoted so much of himself to the work at hand. "It was," Philipps wrote, "an unalloyed pleasure to work with an unselfish and generous minded man who never tried to avoid being found on the side of the weak against the strong, be they represented by intriguing Mandarins or myopic Meanies." As for Philipps, "Let me ... write on this chapter, as it closes my temporary and tiny contribution, the old mortal epitaph VSLM, *Votum Solvit Libens Merito*."[93] External Affairs, informed of the changes at National War Services, received the information with satisfaction, if not relief.[94]

The military situation had by this time improved markedly on the Eastern front. Indeed, by July 1944 Soviet forces were systematically pushing back the invader all along the line, and although casualties were high, the prospect of recovering all the territories of 1940 was in sight. To the extent that the reunification of the Ukrainian lands was a principle from which the Soviet leadership was unwilling to retreat and that the Allies were increasingly prepared to accept, Ukrainian autonomy in Poland, let alone independence, became an impossibility. Among American and British security officials there was evidence to suggest that this development was having a quietening effect on the nationalists. Reporting on the setbacks, u.s. intelligence, for instance, described Ukrainian Americans as "resigned but pessimistic."[95] A.J. Halpern, of the British Security Co-ordination in New York, observed the same trend among Ukrainian Americans, commenting that "More and more people have come to the conclusion that a strong united Ukraine has only one chance for survival as an independent cultural and national entity, and that this chance lies in its union with Russia."[96] He further noted that insofar as American Ukrainians were not "absorbed by American culture, [they] will have to orientate themselves towards Russia," a fate, he believed, that similarly awaited the Ukrainians in Canada.

Halpern's observations were presumptive. Ukrainian nationalists were beginning to accept the geopolitical reality, but this did not mean that their interest in Ukraine or its future had in any way diminished. It had simply been redirected as the practical problem of war relief now began to overshadow all other considerations. Recalling the experience of Ukrainian refugees in the wake of the First World War, the nationalists in Canada as well as the Untied States were convinced of the need to create relief agencies that addressed the particular needs of those who, for a variety of reasons, refused to be repatriated to the USSR. To secure approval and support for the creation of a subsidiary body that would solicit aid for Ukrainians in Europe, a UCC delegation, for instance, was sent to meet with officials from both the Department of National War Services and External Affairs. The discussions, which were perceived to go well from the perspective of the Ukrainians, prompted the UCC to prepare a formal statement on the formation of a charitable agency tentatively called the Ukrainian Canadian Refugee Fund. The statement, which took the form of a memorandum, was submitted to the prime minister as well as to External Affairs for their support.

The memorandum declared that Canada, like all the other Allied states, was already making arrangements for the rehabilitation of displaced persons and that every effort was being made to assist, through various international charitable bodies, people who had contributed to the Allied cause. These organisations, composed mainly of official representatives of the Allied nations, would operate through the medium of their respective Allied governments. Ukrainians, however, according to the UCC memorandum, were confronted with a unique problem: "Due to the conflicting political claims over the sovereignty of the territory in question, they are finding themselves in the position of being claimed to be the citizens of two countries. In reality, however, it gives them a status of stateless and homeless refugees."[97] It was argued that for political reasons a great number of Ukrainian refugees scattered throughout the liberated countries of Europe, Africa, and the Middle East would remain in a state of "homelessness," and it was to these people, the memorandum claimed, that Ukrainian Canadians hoped to bring aid.

Although the UCC was aware of the existence of several international relief organisations channelling aid to the regions affected, the committee observed that the funds collected by ethnic groups in Canada for those agencies were being distributed by the respective governments on territories from which these groups originally came. Since Ukrainian refugees represented a special type of refugee for whom effective aid could not very well be administered, because there was no constituted Ukrainian national government, Ukrainian Canadians wanted to supplement Western government aid through an organisation set up specifically for that purpose. The idea was to create an agency that would address the needs of Ukrainians and whose funds would be administered by an international body such as the Red Cross.

An application to the Department of National War Services was enclosed with the memorandum for consideration and support. However, upon receipt of a copy Norman Robertson immediately wrote to the director of Voluntary and Auxiliary Services at National War Services, advising that the application be rejected. While Robertson agreed that aid to displaced stateless persons could best be rendered by an international organisation such as the Red Cross, he thought it "inadvisable" to register the Ukrainian Canadian Refugee Fund as an auxiliary unit. Robertson's own view was that the UCC claim, which stated that persons from Western Ukraine were in a position of statelessness because the territory was in dispute, had no merit. The statement, he contested, would be accurate only if neither of the two states concerned – Poland and the Soviet Union – wished to accept them as citizens. In Robertson's opinion, "There is no evidence at present that this is the case. It is quite probable that before the end of the war an agreement will be reached between the authorities concerned, which would allow these persons to opt freely for the citizenship of either state."[98]

There were, however, other concerns. As Robertson pointed out, any action of the Canadian government authorising a Ukrainian refugee fund was likely to be "misconstrued" by both the Polish and Soviet governments. The two governments in the past had accused certain Ukrainian groups of collaboration with the Germans. Therefore, the proposal would appear to Soviet and Polish authorities "as an attempt to rescue Ukrainian collaborationists, especially since the Committee [the UCC] has been severely criticised by both Poles and Russians as representing, as far as their aspirations for an independent Ukraine are concerned, the views of the Ukrainian groups which have allegedly assisted the Germans."[99] Although Robertson acknowledged that the loyalty of the UCC and its war record were above reproach, he made it clear that the international implications of the proposal "would prove to be a source of considerable embarrassment to the Canadian government." The UCC had to be persuaded to abandon the project and told that only by unconditionally supporting the Red Cross would they be doing all that was possible to assist their compatriots abroad.[100]

The question of directing Ukrainian aid through authorised agencies to the USSR was for the longest time a singularly volatile and hotly disputed issue among the nationalists.[101] Although the Red Cross was viewed as an agency worth supporting, there were strong objections to the independently run Canadian Aid to Russia Fund (CARF), which was soliciting aid among Ukrainian Canadians.[102] The nationalists objected to the campaign because, although CARF was working closely with the Soviet Red Cross and Red Crescent, the Soviet organisation was not a member of the International Red Cross. Moreover, since International Red Cross officials were not allowed on Soviet territory, which would have provided for independent confirmation of distribution, soliciting aid under false colours was seen as a gross misrepresentation of the nature of the enterprise. The underlying principle, the critics argued, also needed to be considered. If CARF was entitled to canvass for funds under a charitable license granted by the government, then a request for a similar license to operate an independent Ukrainian aid agency was correspondingly legitimate. This was especially so since the Ukrainian organisers considered the CARF appeal within the Ukrainian community – "Help our Brothers and Sisters in Russia" – to be disingenuous, insisting rather narrowly that "We have no brothers and sisters in Russia; our brothers and sisters are in Ukraine."[103]

The criticism, publicly voiced, led CARF to call upon the government to undertake disciplinary action.[104] The authorities, however, were reluctant to intervene, since the objection raised regarding the relationship between the fund and the Red Cross was essentially true, although the Canadian embassy in Moscow reported, on the basis of information gathered, that the aid was in fact being distributed among various centres that included the Ukrainian cities of Poltava and Kharkiv. The impolitic utterances were nevertheless disturbing, complicating, as they did, the government's efforts to cultivate an atmosphere conducive to further improvement in Canadian-Soviet relations. The National Council for Canadian-Soviet Friendship, to which the Department of External Affairs looked to facilitate the promotion and exchange of public information on the Soviet Union, for instance, was being sidetracked by members of the council's executive who wished to challenge the statements attacking CARF. Malcolm Ross, seconded to the society from the WIB to act as chair of the organisation, indicated through regular contact with External Affairs that under the circumstances it was a strain to keep the project from digressing or running adrift.[105] It was his belief that the only way the government could get a handle on situations like this was for controversial issues to be diffused right from the start, before they could erupt.

It was in this context that the chief press censor of Canada brought to the attention of George Glazebrook at External Affairs an editorial published by the Yorkton-based Ukrainian Redemptorist biweekly *Buduchnist natsii* (Nation's Future). Censorship characterised the article as "vicious," especially in its personal attack on Stalin, and asked the department what action should be taken.[106] Glazebrook recommended that the chief censor contact the editor, quoting the relevant passages of the Defence of Canada Regulations. Following the suggestion, censorship wrote to the editor, stating that section 39A, subsection a, of the regulations "provides that nothing should be published which is likely to prejudice the relations of His Majesty's government with any friendly foreign power."[107]

In its reply to the government, the newspaper remained unrepentant, and since no offer was made to retract the statement, John Read, the assistant under-secretary of state for external affairs and head of the department's legal division, was consulted about the prospects for a prosecution.[108] Although Read believed it was "undesirable" to implement administrative action under the Defence of Canada Regulations, it was his considered legal opinion that a strong enough case existed to bring the matter before the courts under Section 135 of the Canadian Criminal Code.[109] The matter was subsequently turned over to the Department of Justice for prosecution. Justice, however, felt that the editorial did not warrant legal action, either under the Criminal Code or the Defence of Canada Regulations. Their opinion was that it would do more harm than good, creating greater controversy among this segment of the population. The decision was regretted by External Affairs, which felt that prosecution would have had "a healthy effect" on those papers that tended to follow the same line.[110] Since Justice was responsible for criminal proceedings and showed no interest in moving on the case, External Affairs considered it pointless to pursue the matter any further.

The problem of cultivating a healthy atmosphere in which to promote Canadian-Soviet relations was also hampered by the unresolved issue of ULFTA properties, which was again enjoying a resurgence. Correspondence directed to the prime minister was assuming "the proportions of a campaign," and it was clear that the issue could no longer be indefinitely postponed.[111] An earlier decision by an interdepartmental committee advising Prime Minister King to return the properties prompted King to appoint a special commission to examine the question in detail and propose practical recommendations. The commission agreed in principle with the original findings of the interdepartmental committee, noting in particular the importance of the international aspect of the question, which had been impressed upon the commission members by External Affairs during the deliberations. Although claiming the effect of the decision would be indirect, External Affairs pointed out that

there could be no question that the USSR was concerned about Ukrainian nationalism wherever it existed in the world. [The Soviets] regard the Ukrainian Nationalist organisations which existed in Canada as in other countries as part of a movement for the partition of the USSR which before the war had its centre in Germany. We had been made aware by the articles published last May in the Soviet Union that they regarded the Canadian Ukrainian Nationalists with suspicion. If, therefore, decisions were made in Canada, which seemed to favour the Nationalists at the expense of their friends amongst Canadian Ukrainians, the Soviet government would be at least puzzled if not offended.[112]

Moreover, since this controversy usually led to indiscreet statements by competing factions which were often "misunderstood" by foreign governments, it was also communicated that "anything which could be done to remove the cause of any dispute was all for the good." External Affairs would not be disappointed; the commission recommended the return of all the halls.

Acting on the commission's recommendation, Cabinet authorised the allocation of $100,000 from the Enemy Alien Custodian's Administration Fund for the purpose of repurchasing seven halls that had been sold in judicial sales.[113] Not all the Ukrainian nationalist organisations in possession of ULFTA halls, however, were prepared to relinquish their title to the properties. Therefore, the final decision reached by Cabinet involved not only the repurchase of the halls at Lachine and Winnipeg, which had been successfully negotiated, but seizure under the War Measures Act – with provision for compensation – of the remaining properties in Toronto, Hamilton, Saskatoon, Edmonton, and Vancouver. The net deficit to the Office of the Custodian of Enemy Alien Property as a result of the entire fiasco was $74,000.[114] The issue of ULFTA halls was finally laid to rest.

The decision on the halls and the recommendation in January 1945 by External Affairs to ignore any further appeals by the nationalists on the question of Ukrainian independence revealed the extent to which the government was prepared to accept any possible consequences.[115] The government position was influenced by the growing sense among officials that the nationalists were finally resigning themselves to the reality in Eastern Europe.[116] Further petitions, External Affairs concluded, were simply the work of extremists. In fact, reports showed that even the most militant of the Ukrainian nationalists in Canada appeared to be reconciled to the fate of Ukraine within the Soviet Union. The public statements of the former UNF nationalist leader W. Swystun were of special interest in official circles because they originated with a person who had some stature within the community, potentially signifying a real change in the traditional position of the nationalists.[117] It was not known, however, how broad and sincere this sentiment was in the overall community.

Motivated by a genuine and sincere desire to maintain some connection with Ukraine, Swystun's public remarks urging Ukrainian Canadians to reconcile themselves to the Soviet Union did strike a chord with other leading nationalists. Michael Stechishin, an executive member of the Ukrainian Self Reliance League, for instance, would express "full agreement" with Swystun. Furthermore, echoing Swystun's position, he would privately indicate to his brother, also an official with the USRL, that he was inclined to write an open letter recommending that the nationalist leadership adopt a more conciliatory policy toward the Soviet Union, "not because I want to cease to be a Ukrainian, but because I do not want to see the Ukrainian people in Canada cut off from the source of our nation in the old country."[118] Stechishin argued that little could now be done to alter the situation in Ukraine and, therefore, the task among Ukrainians in the emigration was to maintain some form of contact with Ukrainians in the homeland. Cooperation with the current Soviet regime, he believed, was therefore a prerequisite.

This attitude, however, was in the minority. Moreover, when raised publicly, it was interpreted as capitulation and dismissed. The counterargument was made that the issue was not whether the nationalist community could succeed in affecting the political outcome in Eastern Europe. Rather, Canadians of Ukrainian descent, able to express views and opinions where others could not, were obligated to protest the oppressive nature of the regime in Ukraine.[119] In keeping with this sentiment, Anthony Hlynka, the Social Credit MP and former UNF executive member, repeated, in the context of the House debate on Canada's participation at the upcoming International Security Conference in San Francisco, his earlier and rather unusual proposal that "the submerged nations of the USSR be represented by those who could speak on their behalf." The proposal was dismissed by the *Edmonton Bulletin* as "outrageous," while the *Edmonton Journal* characterised it as nothing short of "preposterous."[120] As for the "disloyal" Hlynka, he was roundly chastised for imperilling Canada's security and putting it in an "impossible" situation. "This is Canada," he was told, "– no hyphens."

For Ukrainian émigré nationalists, the San Francisco conference offered the last real opportunity to present the case for Ukrainian self-determination. It was a forum, however, where unsolicited views were not particularly welcome. The conference agenda, with its emphasis on security defined within the framework of great power relations, meant that there could be no room for what were considered largely peripheral and inconsequential issues. The Ukrainian nationalist delegations, from Canada as well as the United States, implicitly understood this and reluctantly couched their appeals in language that they felt would at least be acceptable and that might still have some effect.[121] They were wrong.

Based variously on the Atlantic Charter and Roosevelt's Four Freedoms and presented with reference to the Universal Bill of Human Rights, the petitions made no impression. Rather, regarding them as an annoyance, the public liaison officer for the United States delegation communicated to the Ukrainian representatives that it was neither the time nor the occasion for such appeals. As he pointed out, although the interest of the United States in the welfare of peoples who felt oppressed was well documented, "it would not serve anybody's interest to create an impression that the United States government was the unreasoning champion of the disappointed." He further made clear the official U.S. position by declaring that "It is necessary above all at this time to work out a friendly accommodation with the USSR. Nothing should be done to disturb that effort."[122]

The Soviet response was even more to the point. When the UCC delegation telephoned the senior Soviet representative in the hope of securing an audience, they were told that if they did not desist from this and other such activities, the local municipal police would be called in to deal with them as a public nuisance.[123]

The inability to be heard, let alone exert any influence on the San Francisco proceedings, prompted the UCC to redirect its energies towards the more limited, yet still pressing, problem of refugees. There were in total an estimated five million Ukrainian refugees in Europe, of whom approximately one fifth, it was believed, would be opposed to repatriation to the USSR. In view of Soviet demands for the return of all former inhabitants of the territories east of the Curzon Line, which was finally accepted as the new Polish-Soviet border, the UCC appealed to the Canadian government to do whatever was possible to prevent their return.[124] The problem of prominent European Ukrainians involved in the anti-Soviet struggle who were now faced with the prospect of repatriation was especially acute. And it was on their behalf that the UCC made several special inquiries about possible government intervention.

External Affairs, however, thought it was inadvisable to intervene on behalf of the refugees or to make representations to the British occupation authorities in Germany with reference to specific cases raised by the UCC. Dana Wilgress, Canada's ambassador to the USSR, who had the occasion to comment on the subject, pointed out that "It would be prejudicial to our relations with the Soviet Union if we were to make representations to the United Kingdom authorities that prominent Ukrainian nationalists should not be handed over to the Soviet authorities. The Soviet government regards these people as 'Fascists' and our interest on behalf of such men would be misunderstood as an unfriendly act towards the Soviet Union."[125] Wilgress further concluded that "From the purely strict legal point of view it is also no business of ours what happens to these Ukrainian nationalists, although this could not be very well used in reply to representations submitted to us by the Ukrainian Canadian Committee."

Wilgress' view was one that echoed in External Affairs. "It is certain that the Soviet authorities will consider any assistance to these persons as an attempt to shield them from punishment for their anti-Soviet activities [and therefore] Under the circumstances, it is proposed that no further action be taken in connection with the representations of the Ukrainian Canadian Committee."[126] Appeals thereafter were answered briefly and noncommittally.[127]

By early December 1945 the problem of repatriation had become especially urgent. The military government in the British occupation zone of Germany had ordered all displaced persons from territories now under the control of the Soviets to be sent to Soviet repatriation camps in Neunkirchen and Stuttgart. The Americans also threatened to send the refugees back. Panic ensued among the refugees, resulting in scores of suicides and numerous cases of self-inflicted wounds. The likelihood of even more deaths alarmed Western occupation authorities, who ordered a stay on further repatriation. The Ukrainian Canadian Committee, in the meantime, had frantically appealed to the Canadian government to intercede.[128]

Twenty-five members of Parliament, convinced of the necessity of Canadian government action, collectively sent a telegram to Ottawa urging the prime minister personally to intervene in the matter. External Affairs, however, viewed the request with scepticism notifying Prime Minister King that the government had received numerous petitions with respect to the forced repatriation of Ukrainian refugees. After inquiring in Washington and London, they had concluded that there was no evidence to suggest that Ukrainians were actually being repatriated against their will. Norman Robertson told King that "The whole question of displaced persons is ... one of great difficulty at the moment. I would suggest, therefore, that we make no reply to any of the representations we have received concerning Ukrainian refugees and that we follow this policy even in regard to the telegram from the twenty-five members of Parliament."[129]

George Simpson, who continued to maintain contact with the UCC, sympathised with the attempts of the committee to render assistance, but he also knew that as long as the Soviet government considered Ukrainians in Western Europe a potential security threat, it would make every attempt to have them repatriated. Since international law supported the USSR in making this claim, only the humanitarian side of the plight of the refugees could possibly make a difference. Moreover, except for collecting relief funds, nothing could be done safely, for as Simpson pointed out "the present temper in Canada" was favourable to the Soviet government as a state that had helped save the Allied cause and whose cooperation was essential to global security. Anything other than collecting relief funds would only provoke a negative reaction.[130]

The "temper" in Canada, at least officially, was indeed in favour of the Soviet government.[131] Stanley Knowles, CCF member of Parliament and a Canadian delegate to the Preparatory Commission of the United Nations, when replying to references by the Soviet delegates to "the pro-German intrigues of the Ukrainian refugees and ... the anti-Soviet Ukrainians in Canada," had indicated that the anti-Soviet statements of Ukrainians in Canada were deplored both by the Canadian government and by large sections of the Canadian population. In an effort to deflect further criticism and circumvent an embarrassing situation, Knowles communicated that, although not a matter for the public record, he too found the political activities of the Ukrainians in Canada objectionable. Canada, however, represented a form of democracy that allowed people to hold and express such opinions. Pointing to himself as an example, he noted that as a socialist critic of government policies, his adversaries not only tolerated his views but had also appointed him to the prestigious Preparatory Commission. It was, in Knowles' opinion, one of the great virtues of both liberal democracy and good government that "extreme views" such as his could be tolerated, a practice the Soviets might do well to adopt.[132]

Knowles' illustration "greatly amused" the delegation. Soviet officials, however, were still concerned. It was within this context that a meeting was held between Leo Malania, a newly appointed third secretary at External Affairs with responsibility for Soviet affairs, and Dmytro Manuilsky, the Ukrainian SSR commissar for foreign affairs, to discuss Soviet-Canadian relations, with specific reference to Canada's Ukrainians. The Soviet minister noted that relations between the two countries had been satisfactory in the past. But Manuilsky also conveyed to the junior secretary that in the new era of postwar relations, Canada could greatly improve its status with the Soviet Union if a favourable and unequivocal statement were made outlining the Canadian government's position on Ukrainian nationalism.

Malania, mindful of the department's sensitivity on the subject, reiterated that undue importance should not be attached to the "sentimental" views of Ukrainians in Canada. Although Ukrainian nationalism was still much in evidence, he stated that its attraction would eventually be reduced by assimilation. The Canadian official urged Manuilsky and his colleagues to be patient, claiming Soviet authorities only hindered their cause when "so powerful a country as the USSR, took such vigorous notice of their activities."[133] Moreover, Malania indicated that the situation had to be understood from Canada's point of view, namely, that the effect of any further controversy was only to keep Ukrainian nationalism alive and well and thus to retard the process of further Ukrainian assimilation. The meeting was concluded on a satisfactory note, both parties appearing to agree that there was common ground for understanding on the issue.

The conversation between the two diplomats was followed shortly by an extraordinary development. On 6 September, clutching a handful of secret documents and with a young family in tow, Igor Gouzenko, a lowly cipher clerk at the Soviet embassy in Ottawa, defected. In exchange for political asylum in Canada, he offered evidence of an espionage network that had been working actively to acquire secret information on the new atomic device that was being developed. The prime minister and senior officials at External Affairs were taken aback by both the evidence and the implications for the future.[134]

As expected, the controversy soon began to shape the events to come, among which there were a few poignant, but fleeting, moments. In his last meeting with the Soviet Ukrainian foreign minister, Leo Malania had offered the observation that the best mutually beneficial strategy for dealing with the Ukrainian question was "to develop good all around Canadian-Soviet relations."[135] The irony of those final few words could not have been lost on the junior diplomat, since shortly after the disclosure of Gouzenko, Malania, finding himself personally compromised by the affair, was forced to resign from Canada's diplomatic corps.[136]

Neither was the meaning of the Gouzenko affair lost on Norman Robertson. Revealing his profound sense of betrayal a few short days after the defection, Robertson would write: "I think of the Russian Embassy being only a few doors away and of there being there a centre of intrigue. During this period of the war, while Canada has been helping Russia and doing all we can to foment Canada-Russia friendship, there has been ... spying."[137] So much for good all around Canadian-Soviet relations. So much for the Ukrainian "problem." A new phase in global politics was about to begin.

AN ASSESSMENT

By mid-1943 the turning point in the European theatre of the war had come and gone. The decisive victories at El Alamien, Stalingrad, and Kursk were already behind the Allies. The Western powers, in fact, were preparing for an assault on Fortress Europe, and victory, if not assured in the year to come, was at least in sight. But final victory would not come without further sacrifice. The tempo of production on the home front as well as the level of public enthusiasm for the war also had to be maintained. In Ottawa both issues were paramount in the minds of public officials.

Of equal concern, however, was the question of the postwar political order. Canada had entered the war as a junior player but was now proving its mettle as a military and economic power in its own right. Nevertheless, in foreign circles Canada was still considered something of a colonial appendage. The uncertainty that resulted from this disjuncture in its role as a major economic producer of war goods and a minor political broker was translated into the issue, and still later yet the preoccupation, of where Canada would stand in relation to the dominant powers after the war. The question of postwar peace and, specifically, Canada's place in the global political structure supporting that peace was as important to Canadian officials as the conduct of the war itself.

The implications of both demands – maintaining industrial/civilian morale while politically defining Canada's future international role commensurate with its current economic and military status – were to have some profound implications for policy that were not entirely incongruent with the realist perspective that continued to inform the views of Canada's statesmen. Indeed, the need to portray Canada as a "responsible" ally – whether in its domestic or foreign policy – was rooted in the perspective of the statesman as realist. Canada had to legitimise its right to participate in the crucial peace negotiations. If it were unable to do so, it would become politically marginalized. Consequently, new strategies were in order, including a change in the nature of Canadian domestic propaganda.

That propaganda was to be repackaged to draw the exhausted population within the ambit of state activity itself. A new format, in effect, was applied. No longer was the emphasis on simply defeating the Nazis and restoring "democracy" and "freedom" to Europe. These were old clichés that by the fourth year of the war were showing wear. What mattered was conditioning the Canadian public to see itself as a creator of its own destiny and to view the state as a guarantor of social welfare and public security. In effect, the interpretation and explanation of state programs and policies replaced the time-worn propaganda of laissez-faire liberal politics. The notions of production, efficiency, and solidarism were promoted and presented as vital ingredients in the successful prosecution of the war, supplanting the more abstract and nebulous concepts of "liberty," "democracy," and "obligation."[138]

The shift in the character and content of the propaganda had some distinct advantages. As George Glazebrook of the Department of External Affairs, mindful of the Soviet alliance, explained, it was not wise to pursue too far the distinction between democracy and totalitarianism.[139] In this way the conundrum posed by the alliance was neatly circumvented. Second, Canada would have to define its international status not only in relation to its Western partners but in relation to the Soviet Union as well. Canada was entering a new phase in its relationship with the USSR, and the problem of at least dealing with, if not reconciling, the dilemma between the liberal ideals that had ostensibly governed the war in the West and taking advantage of postwar political opportunities had to be addressed. Ultimately, given official assessments, what was needed here was some movement toward selling the Soviet Union not just as a wartime ally but also as a potentially important postwar political actor that Canada would have to deal with in a responsible manner.

This requirement was conventional wisdom for officials who were dealing with matters of "high politics." Those at the policy level who did not understand the necessity would have to be removed. At the level of public opinion it was hoped that public education programs would put this point of view across. And if education failed to work, then it was always possible to claim that this point of view was a matter of national interest and state importance. Significantly, by elevating the issue of postwar relations to the level of "high politics" and by repeating the view that there was no room for public discussion or input in matters of state, the officials who were dealing with the problem neutralised those who had hoped that their concerns – which were consonant with the declared war aims of liberal political democracy – would be accommodated.

The strategy that was implemented was distinctly state-centric in character. The incongruity between the philosophical underpinnings of liberal democracy and the state interest was effectively resolved as officials played on the shared interests and values between state and society, attempted to minimise the perception of divergence between the two, and sought also to alter the perception that divergent interests and values even existed. The failure, however, to influence and alter the perception of the Ukrainian Canadian nationalist community, which was putting forward claims in keeping with the liberal philosophical premises upon which the struggle was based, prompted state authorities to employ an alternative strategy and set of options. Specifically, unable to dissuade the nationalists from engaging in further "embarrassing" and potentially dangerous controversies, Canadian government officials sought to diminish their role in various ways on several issues.

John Grierson, formerly of the National Film Board, was selected to head the newly organised Wartime Information Board and was authorised to provide the new direction to domestic propaganda. He brought to the job not only zeal but the conviction that the nature and actions of civil society could be shaped through mass suggestion. As a biographer of Grierson wrote, "He orchestrated a system whereby the state was to act as the diffuser of information over all aspects of society ... he intended to build national consensus and national will ... a process he would call 'being totalitarian for the good.'"[140] Grierson's goal was to mould a Canadian identity from above. By definition, his perspective could not accommodate the dissenting views of Tracy Philipps, whose approach to the nation building task was entirely different. It was not surprising, then, that Grierson and his circle would assist in Philipps' removal. In this step they were encouraged by External Affairs. Indeed, External Affairs not only considered Grierson an ally in settling the Ukrainian "problem" but also confided in him as an individual who shared a similar understanding of the needs and role of the state, albeit at a different level.

The attempt to have the Nationalities Branch transferred over to the WIB failed in the final analysis because officials in the Department of National War Services resisted. Significantly, however, their resistance was not predicated on an alternative policy vision. Rather, it was determined by more mundane considerations, notably the minister's interest that the portfolio, which earlier had undergone changes, not be further diminished by a reduction in responsibilities. This interest did not mean that National War Services could ignore outside pressure. Indeed, external influences would eventually force National War Services to reorganise the branch.

Interestingly, Grierson's view of the state in society would have its corollary at the level of global relations. He believed that it was incumbent upon Canadians in the postwar era of international cooperation to recognise that within the new constellation of interstate relations, the ability to maintain the peace depended as much on understanding and compromise as it did on the use of might. In this regard Grierson advocated postwar accommodation with the Soviet Union, not on the basis of nostalgia for the wartime alliance, significant though it might have been, but as part of the new postwar geopolitical reality.[141] Soviet power and influence were here to stay and Western powers needed to reconcile themselves to the fact that the USSR was a global player that could no longer be treated as a pariah.

This view was not Grierson's alone. Officials in the Department of External Affairs had increasingly emphasised that some accommodation had to be made with the Soviet Union and that there was no better start than dealing with the Ukrainian question. Dana Wilgress, Canada's minister and, later, ambassador to the USSR, for instance, repeatedly called on Ottawa to deal with the problem of Ukrainian nationalist activities in Canada and even suggested that Canadian authorities abandon the Atlantic Charter, which legitimised their claims.[142] Indeed, the question of war aims was problematic, and Wilgress suggested independently of what was transpiring at the WIB that a new approach to propaganda should be adopted to redirect public attention from the more contentious issues of territorial claims and rights that were legitimised by the charter.

Wilgress, a long-time advocate of closer cooperation with the Soviet Union, was expressing a view that was widely shared among officials within External Affairs. Even those who were sceptical of Soviet postwar intentions believed there were advantages in dealing with the Ukrainian question once and for all, not least of which was that it would hasten the "assimilation" of the Ukrainian Canadian population. The extraordinary suggestion of granting diplomatic recognition to the Soviet Ukraine was even broached with the idea that recognition would finally drive from the minds of the nationalists "the mirage of absolute independence."[143] In the end, however, this option was rejected, principally because the Soviet leadership tied the issue of diplomatic recognition of Soviet Ukraine to the independent status of Canada in a political power bid to offset postwar Anglo-American influence. Recognition of Canadian sovereignty was to be reciprocated by recognition of the international status of the Ukrainian SSR. From the perspective of the Soviets, recognition was only a matter of fair exchange. For Canadian statesmen seeking to carve out Canada's niche in world affairs, however, the idea was unacceptable. Ukraine, arguably, was a colonial appendage of Moscow, while there was no such parallel, Ottawa insisted, in Canada's relations with London. Thinly masking Canadian insecurity, the objection would point both to Canada's overriding interest and to its need to consolidate its postwar position. Indeed, Canada was prepared to meet Soviet interests, but there had to be some demonstration that the USSR would welcome Canada as a genuine partner in the postwar system of international relations.

Canada's hope of resolving certain issues on its own terms – relations with the Soviet Union, Canada's postwar role, and the Ukrainian "problem" – vanished in the waning days of the European war with the defection of a little-known Soviet cipher clerk who had served as part of the USSR's mission in Ottawa. The evidence he produced of an espionage network that ranged from North America across the Atlantic to Europe had left the Canadian leadership dumbfounded. To their astonishment and dismay, External Affairs officials, hoping to advance Canadian interests through the Grand Alliance, would soon discover that USSR authorities were advancing their interests, but in their own way. With the Gouzenko affair – a rude introduction to the political power machinations of a quickly evolving international system – Canada had unexpectedly, yet inevitably, stumbled into the politics of the Cold War. The views of those who were strong advocates of the one-time Grand Alliance and had optimistic expectations for the future were instantly made unfashionable as the postwar struggle for power began to take shape. Others, although equally disappointed, would soon learn to adjust. They were, after all, and in the end, political realists.

6 Towards an Understanding of Canadian Statecraft

The year 1919 may well have marked a new beginning in the practice of international diplomacy. The signing of the Versailles Treaty, a hopeful, if not natural, reaction to the conflagration of the First World War, can be interpreted in part as a return to the constitutional tradition in international politics.[1] The Grotian doctrine regarding the enforcement of law on a delinquent state, for example, served as the cornerstone in the new covenant of the League of Nations, suggesting that law and not just power had now become a real factor in international diplomacy.[2] But arguably, the covenant also provided the legal framework for a new system of power relations that was to emerge after the war as a logical and necessary response to the perceived anarchy of both modern politics and the international system.[3]

In effect, what was institutionalised and given legal authority at this time was a new balance of power that would act against any state that threatened to defy the obligation to observe the covenant.[4] This was made possible because the legal order established at Versailles was understood to contain no substantial injustice when compared to what would challenge it.[5] Indeed, after 1919 the majority of European nations enjoyed political sovereignty. Those that did not could be explained either as anomalies – "nonhistoric" peoples – or as an unfortunate but necessary consequence of the European balance of power. In this sense, the legal order conceived at Versailles was considered synonymous with a just order, while the balance of power was consonant with both. Therefore, when the revisionism of Nazi Germany threatened the distribution of power in Europe, it was interpreted as being against the existing legal and moral order. Moreover, when the aggression that took place in 1939 was no longer tolerated, it was thought that simply returning to the preexisting status quo would be a sufficient response, because the weight of moral approval was with the states whose order had been violated.

Within this context the Grand Alliance of 1941 was also seen as a natural and moral response to Nazi aggression, but not because the international community consciously sought through this new arrangement to preserve the independence of its member states.[6] Nor was the alliance seen as doing battle with "evil." The new Soviet ally, in Churchill's opinion, was just as despicable as Nazi Germany. Rather, in aiming to repel and punish the principal power that sought to overturn Versailles, the alliance was understood to be acting in support of the old legal order. Moreover, since the old order was identified with a just order, the assumption was that political and moral right lay with the Allies.

The Soviet Union, of course, posed certain difficulties, having participated in the dismemberment of Poland in 1939. But 1941 was not 1939, and now that the Soviet Union was in the camp of the states that were preventing Germany from creating a universal empire, it was considered to be on the side of justice. In this regard, the USSR was recast as a reformed and respectable ally, a necessary move in view of the fact that the public in the West had long been led to suspect Soviet intentions. But there was also nothing to suggest, at least initially, that the Soviets sought any demonstrable change in the prewar balance of power. Even on the most contentious issue – Poland's eastern border – the Soviet Union, it appeared, was prepared to negotiate. Therefore, with the exception of some "minor" political adjustments, a return to the status quo ante was seen as both possible and desirable.

The status quo ante consequently became a recurring theme, at least until 1943, both in Western political thinking and in the Western strategic outlook. The Western position was reasonable, since the world was in flux and the pattern of prewar power relations offered some certainty, if not security, especially since the structure of prewar global relations favoured the Anglo-American powers. It was not surprising, therefore, that both Britain and the United States, in the aftermath of the German invasion of the Soviet Union, reaffirmed the validity of the legal order established at Versailles by giving credence to it through the Atlantic Charter – the joint declaration issued by Churchill and Roosevelt at sea, off the coast of Newfoundland.

The charter as it was originally conceived was no ordinary document. Rather, it sought to establish at the outset a vision for the postwar world that called for the return of freedom to nations that had been stripped of their independence. In doing so, however, it implied that the postwar order would not differ greatly from the prewar order. The importance of this implication was underscored by the fact that even when the charter became something of a liability and was interpreted by the politically dispossessed nations as having universal application, Britain and America did not retreat from the document. Rather, the tension between the publicly embraced liberal objectives of the war, on the one hand, and the restoration of an order based on a preexisting set of power relations, on the other, was neatly circumvented by emphasising that before justice could be achieved, the legal order had to be restored. Order preceded justice, and only those peoples who demonstrated a responsibility to the international community by assisting in the restoration of the legal order would be accepted within "the family of nations."

The initial reaction of the Soviet Union to the Atlantic Charter – silence – was mistaken for ambivalence, if not acceptance, a miscalculation that would become evident by 1943. Indeed, once the military situation on the Eastern front had stabilised in 1943 and the prospect of victory was no longer in doubt, Stalin made it clear that he viewed the charter, in the form it was being articulated, as an attack on Soviet interests.[7] The Soviet Union, he claimed, neither could nor would be bound by the rhetoric of a declaration that attempted to restore a political order that was inimical to its interests. For observers who were alert to such things, a new reality in international relations was taking shape.

For Ukrainian nationalists, on the other hand, especially in North America, the years 1939–41 marked a uniquely favourable period in the potential development of Ukrainian interests. Poland, a major obstacle in the drive toward achieving independence, had largely been removed from the political map. Moreover, the fact that the prewar legal order was being couched in terms of justice also meant that there was much to be hopeful about. Indeed, Ukrainians would not object to the restoration of the order originally established by Versailles, because it was expected, given the emphasis on the just nature of the war, that the terms conceived at Versailles would now be expanded to take into account the natural right of Ukrainians to self-determination.[8] They embraced the war with the firm belief not only that right was on their side but that fortune was as well.

The year 1941, however, would change all that as the Soviet Union became a valued partner in the Allied effort to contain Germany's global ambitions. It was an unwelcome development to which the nationalists were unwilling to reconcile themselves. Yet there was little they could do practically, except to press Ukraine's moral claim to independence within the framework of the Atlantic Charter. In part, the nationalists would accept the Anglo-American interpretation underpinning the charter, which said that the original legal order had to be restored first, because of the political constraints. But there was also the hope and belief that the stated objectives of the Western Allies were not false, since the legal order continued to be defined in terms of justice and the war was being waged on this very principle.[9] For Ukrainian nationalists in Canada, there was a clear sense not only that their claims were consonant with Allied objectives but that they were just under the terms of the charter as well. As to whether Ukraine had earned the right to assume a place among the community of nations, they would point to the sacrifices of their ethnic kindred participating in the struggle against the Axis and to the countless dead as irrefutable evidence.

To the extent that there was uncertainty in the direction of the conflict, the nationalists throughout 1941–43 were optimistic that the Ukrainian claim would be recognised. By mid-1943, however, the expectation was unrealistic. The Soviet Union had survived the worst years of its war with Germany and, having turned the invader back, was even less prepared to compromise on issues deemed vital to its interests, not least of which was the question of Poland's eastern frontiers. The Western Allies were initially slow to respond but would eventually accept this conclusion. As for the moral claim of Ukrainian self-determination, it became increasingly meaningless, if only because the postwar order was now being thought of not in terms of the status quo ante but rather in terms of the emerging global power structure.

Significantly, several Canadian officials recognised the shift in the balance of power, and in an effort to accommodate the new development they suggested that Canada distance itself from the Atlantic Charter as a policy statement governing Allied war aims. It was their view that the charter's abstract character and anachronistic references made it an inappropriate document, serving only as an unnecessary invitation to those who would promote territorial claims. They argued that this consequence complicated not only relations between the Allies but the normal diplomatic process as well, with potentially far-reaching consequences for Canada's postwar status and role.[10] Because it was perceived to be a political impediment and a liability, a recommendation was made to the prime minister that the charter be discarded as a statement guiding Canada's war aims and peace policy.

It was an extraordinary recommendation because it tended to ignore the political arguments upon which the previous four years of war had been based. Throughout 1940, 1941, and 1942, King, Coldwell, and Lapointe, as well as other Cabinet officers, had all described the war in various ways as a struggle for the preservation and defence of democratic freedoms and principles. Moreover, they had repeatedly made the case that Canada had accepted the necessity of war to restore what had been taken away from the peoples of Europe and to usher in "a new era of freedom."[11] The Atlantic Charter, in setting out the general goals of the war, echoed a simple message that was pressed home with the Canadian people: "Our aim," Prime Minister King declared, "must be social and international justice at home and abroad." It was strangely naive, if not dangerous, to assume that this statement could now be dismissed.

Indeed, at least until 1943 Canada's ability to conduct war was predicated on the legitimacy that flowed from its commitment and contribution to restoring the prewar legal order. That legitimacy was to be found in the notion that the legal order, the status quo ante, was a fundamentally just order and that Canada fully supported the restoration of that order. Much emphasis, for instance, was placed precisely on the point that Nazi Germany, in its drive for European and global hegemony, had stripped the nations of Europe of their sovereign rights. Britain and its allies, on the other hand, sought the restoration of those rights. Because it framed this distinction, the charter could not now be easily disregarded. Moreover, to the degree that a return to the order conceived at Versailles was impossible after 1943, the practical and symbolic importance of the charter as a legitimising feature of the war still needed to be maintained. Not surprisingly, to fit the new conditions, the argument of how international justice would be achieved was reworked; the notion of an order that would fulfil the promise of freedom and justice, a United Nations committed to peace and security, quickly replaced the idea of Versailles.

Ultimately, the Atlantic Charter, whether before or after 1943, emphasised as dual objectives winning the war and securing the peace. And yet the difficulty with this emphasis, as critics of the charter had pointed out, was that justice and security were not always compatible. Neither the argument used before 1943 (that the prewar balance of power as a security system was fundamentally just) nor the later argument that a United Nations was central to justice could mask sufficiently the essential incompatibility between the liberal premise upon which the struggle was said to be based and the reality of power politics that underpinned the search for security. The charter highlighted the contradiction between the two, and for this reason Prime Minister King was counselled that prudence dictated that Canada should distance itself from it.

It was, in short, unwise to draw attention to a statement that served only to excite an element of the population. But because of its legitimising role, the charter could not be abandoned. Consequently, given

the difficulties that could arise from the contradiction in terms both
of the war and of the peace, Canadian officials – who were increasingly
anxious – began to exercise the discretionary power of the state,
particularly in the case of the nationalist Ukrainians, a community that
insisted Canada and its allies adhere to the liberal promise of international justice. From an official perspective, of course, the position of
the nationalists as it pertained to Ukraine was impossible to satisfy,
and the unwillingness of state officials to respond positively was to be
expected. Less clear, and perhaps therefore more interesting, was the
manner in which the contradiction would condition the government's
dealings with the nationalist community during the war.

During 1939–41, continuing Allied support for Poland and the
caution demonstrated in dealing with the Soviet Union pointed to the
importance attached to the idea of containing German expansionism
while returning to the status quo ante. Ukrainian claims to independence could not have been realistically met within this context. But as
a problem, those claims could also not be ignored. At issue was not
the moral ambiguity in the Allied position but rather the effect of the
contradiction on the large numbers of Ukrainians engaged in agriculture and the war industries of North America, especially in Canada,
the so-called Arsenal of the Empire. Because disillusionment would
have had potentially untold political consequences in Canada, practical
measures were deemed necessary. These measures included an extensive
surveillance operation initiated at the time and support for the formation of the Ukrainian Canadian Committee, a coordinating body that,
it was thought, could prove useful in channelling information while
helping to shape community attitudes in support of the war effort.

After the alliance with the Soviet Union was concluded in June 1941,
the contradiction in the Western Allied position became more conspic-
uous. Indeed, the Soviet Union had participated in the dismemberment
of Poland in 1939 and had annexed its territory in 1940. Although
the sweeping German advance in 1941 made the issue academic, it
was nevertheless imperative that the Soviet Union acknowledge the
legitimacy and validity of the prewar order. The Atlantic Charter,
consequently, was issued as a subtle reminder that justice would be
served only when freedom was returned to those who had been
deprived of that right. It was apparent, however, that disagreement
could arise on this point and that the Ukrainian question, if introduced
into the equation, would have only complicated matters.

In Canada, considerable anxiety was expressed over the possibility
that statements emanating from the nationalist community might add
to the dispute and reflect poorly on the country as an ally, undercutting

its international position. It was therefore imperative that the Ukrainian question should not become a matter of public discussion, since it was sure to provoke controversy. Not only was the government forced, consequently, to increase its monitoring of the community and its leadership, but it also found itself in a position where it had to begin to manage potentially volatile situations while distancing itself from statements and events that could be misinterpreted abroad.

By August 1943, with the military situation finally favouring the Soviets, a new pattern of postwar relations began to take shape. The emerging political power structure, however, meant that the contradiction between the publicly embraced goals informing the character of the struggle in the West and the competing national interest could no longer be masked. It was evident that Canada, preoccupied with its postwar status, would have to deal in a more circumspect manner with the Ukrainian "problem" that threatened this interest. Suspicious and hostile, senior officials at first entertained the idea of using security measures to prevent the situation from further escalating. They stopped short, however, of taking such precipitous action because, as even the author of the plan admitted, such measures would have been difficult to defend.[12] Government officials, consequently, employed more discreet measures to contain the situation and make certain that the claims of the nationalists did not find their way onto the wider public agenda. As for Canada's wartime partners, they would be nervously reassured that everything was under control.

In the autumn of 1944 Canadian officials would take a more hardened stand with respect to the appeals of the nationalists. This stand was possible because the power structure in Europe, which had considerable bearing on the prospects for Ukrainian independence, had effectively changed. The clear dominance of the Soviet Union in Eastern Europe meant that an independent Ukraine was not simply improbable but impossible. Since the political map had been cast and was unlikely to change, Ukrainian nationalist claims could now be legitimately ignored without fear of the consequences. With the fate of Ukraine finally settled, there was also, however, the expectation that Ukrainian Canadians would get on with the task of being Canadians. Indeed, when the issue of extending diplomatic recognition to Soviet Ukraine was discussed among the Allies in July 1944, Canadian officials favoured the idea because it was felt that recognition would assist in driving "the mirage of absolute independence" from the minds of the nationalists, hastening their assimilation.[13] There was, to be sure, some concern that the move might excite the nationalists unnecessarily. But Canadian officials also believed they could insulate themselves from political criticism by invoking the principle of national interest and pointing to the complexity of issues associated with higher politics, arguments that were successfully repeated at San Francisco.[14]

Importantly, the idea that granting diplomatic recognition to Soviet Ukraine would serve to hasten the assimilation of Ukrainians in Canada pointed to the nature of the official understanding of ethnicity in Canada. Reinforced by anecdotal evidence, it was thought that the Ukrainian ethnic minority in Canada would be quickly absorbed into the mainstream and that the problem would disappear of its own accord. Not especially resilient in the face of assimilatory pressures, ethnic identity was seen as a transitory phenomenon. Ottawa officials consequently concluded that the problem would be resolved by simply waiting it out. This conclusion, however, was seen as wishful and false thinking by some, notably officials in the Nationalities Branch. As they would argue, identity was subject to a host of dynamics – social, cultural, and political – that conditioned ethnic consciousness in a profound, yet unpredictable, way. The point, therefore, was not to ignore ethnic groups and hope for their disappearance but to try to channel ethnic identity in a way that would lend itself to the creation of a more complete nation.

The contradiction between the publicly embraced principles governing Canada's war policy and the need to ensure that state interests would be met highlighted the difficulty in both promoting the political culture of the nation and furthering the nation-building process. The belief that ethnic identity was a transitional phenomenon that would eventually and inevitably melt away under the pressures of assimilation was as much a function of the need to view ethnic identification this way as it was the result of any serious analysis of the issue. As Norman Robertson would relay to the Soviet minister after the latter had protested against the activities of the Ukrainian Canadian nationalists, he, Robertson, wanted very much for this group "to see the world through Canadian eyes." The nationalists were making the affairs of state difficult to manage, and it was to assimilation that officials would look expectantly, in the hope of seeing an end to the "problem." As for the importance Canadian officials attached to assimilation as a way of resolving the problem, it was revealed in several ways. Canadian authorities signalled to their Soviet counterparts that they only hindered their cause by bringing attention to the activities of the nationalists and explained that it was in the mutual interest of Canada and the Soviet Union to ensure that nothing be done to retard the process of their assimilation.[15] The tendency to see ethnicity as a puzzle to be avoided rather than dealt with constructively would point both to the opportunity that was lost in providing the political foundation for ethnic integration and the difficulty in reconciling the contradiction.

Nowhere was this better demonstrated than in the differences in views between the European adviser to the Department of National War Services, Tracy Philipps, and the officials at the Department of External Affairs. Philipps would argue that the contradiction in the government's position undermined its authority and legitimacy among this element of the population and that ultimately the nation-building process was in this way being jeopardised. It was necessary to reconcile the contradiction between the liberal principles guiding the war and actual policy, he argued, because in the final analysis the long-term security of Canada depended on it. On the question of immigrants, genuine security would occur only by nurturing their sense of trust and connecting that trust to the government. This could be done, in Philipps' opinion, only by using their ethnic identity as a reference point in bringing them into the body politic. Canada consisted of diverse peoples. The point was not to ignore this fact or expect that differences would simply melt away but to draw these diverse peoples closer to the government by addressing their concerns, especially if they meshed with the basic values of the country. Admittedly, it was a dangerous strategy requiring careful planning and close attention. But it would also require political will, without which the various communities, in the ideologically charged atmosphere, would fall prey to demagogues on the right and on the left.

It was in this context that Philipps began to define the role and purpose of the Nationalities Branch in the Department of National War Services. The function of the branch was to promote Canadianization by drawing ethnic Canadians out of their largely insular communities. To do so, it had to address and filter their concerns so that they would both see themselves as a part of the nation and recognise the importance of their participation and contribution to the country. This strategy implied in the case of Ukrainian Canadians, for instance, some acknowledgment of the legitimacy of their claim that the Ukrainian nation had a right to self-determination, a claim that fell squarely within the liberal parameters defining Canada's public stand on the war.

This course of action was not a matter of choice in Philipps' view; it was a matter of necessity, not only from the perspective of nation-building but also from the point of view of the very security of the state. It was false to believe Ukrainian Canadians were not prepared to take the government of Canada at its word when it said that the war was being fought for "social and international justice." Moreover, having publicly embraced these aims, it was dangerous now for the government to suggest that they did not apply or that they applied in some cases but not in others. Instead of avoiding the issue, according to Philipps, it was important to recognise the hidden opportunity that was presented here, to make it work in such a way that it would lend itself to reinforcing the democratic character of the country while consolidating the nation.

Senior officials at External Affairs rejected Philipps' views on the strategic role of the Nationalities Branch because they were convinced that they would not lead to the integration of Canada's foreign-born but, on the contrary, simply deepen the "ethnic particularism" of these groups. More importantly, the strategy would have conflicted with other interests. In the case of the Ukrainian question, as was often repeated, no matter how just the claim, any endorsement of the Ukrainian nationalist position, even as a matter of principle, would be misconstrued as an attack on a valued ally and postwar partner, the Soviet Union. The envisioned role of the Nationalities Branch as seen by officials in the Department of External Affairs – the agency most concerned with the potential repercussions of a public discussion of the Ukrainian question – was, therefore, not to encourage unrealistic expectations but to collect information and conduct propaganda work among this element of the population. As External Affairs officials observed, the group needed to be brought into line with mainstream opinion, not given a forum.

The difficulties posed by the Nationalities Branch and its European adviser prompted External Affairs to manœuvre with the hope of bringing the agency under its direction. This was no easy task, and the inability of External Affairs to assume control over the branch – a matter of jurisdiction – meant, in the end, that the role prescribed for it would not be realised. Nevertheless, in the course of the struggle for control over the branch, an understanding was reached between External Affairs and the Wartime Information Board, an agency thought capable of providing the necessary policy direction in the area. The vision of John Grierson, who headed the WIB, complemented very much the desired objectives of senior officials in External Affairs, and it was to Grierson that they would look as the person who could deal effectively with Philipps and the predicament posed by the "foreign-born." It was an extraordinary situation in which the conflict between Philipps and career officials not only was coloured by great bitterness and acrimony but also pointed to fundamental differences in philosophical orientation.[16]

The antagonism shown toward Philipps at the most senior levels of the public service was the result of conflicting worldviews. Philipps was interested in promoting public opinion both with the view to integrating the ethnic element and increasing their participation on the basis of a new relationship with the state. Among senior officials there was no quarrel with the underlying sentiment or the objectives. But there was concern that they not take precedence over other political goals, namely, Canada's status, role, and function as an international player with certain responsibilities.

This difference in emphasis highlighted contrasting assumptions about politics. Whereas Philipps' policy prescriptions flowed from an open-ended image and understanding of politics, official concerns, shaped by the constraints of office, were more narrowly defined and conceived. In Philipps' case, political strategy was predicated on the idea that politics was a process that involved the articulation and accommodation of interests within the framework of widely shared values. The modus operandi of officials, on the other hand, followed from the premise that politics involved a hierarchy of practical require-ments that needed to be addressed, the most elemental of which was the survival of the state. This paradigm, political realism, was informed by both the role of the official as a stakeholder in the political process and the public authority granted the official by virtue of the office. Professionally and psychologically bound, the function of the official was to ensure that the interests of state were met. In the context of uncertainty brought on by war, these interests necessarily were victory, security, stability, and peace. All else was secondary.

From this vantage point it was thought that the prescriptions offered up by Philipps served only to complicate the affairs of state, detracting as they did from more immediate and pressing political tasks. Unwilling to examine more closely the underlying assumptions of their arguments, senior officials simply explained Philipps' views away as ideologically motivated. The ease with which his views were dismissed, however, pointed to a profound inability among officials to understand the prob-lematic nature of their own strategic outlook. This was understandable.

The realist image of politics, with its emphasis on the role of the state as a rational actor seeking to maximise its interests, not only demands political sobriety but also imputes similar motives to others. Innovation, consequently, does not naturally constitute part of the official repertoire, while politics is never a matter of hypotheticals, only imperatives. In this sense, there was no room for Philipps, with his unorthodox views. By way of contrast, Norman Robertson, in a disarmingly honest conversation with a Soviet official in 1943, con-veyed his satisfaction with what he observed as the new "moderate tone" of Soviet politics.[17] For Robertson, the Soviet Union was a strategic partner whose leadership not only was now committed to similar broad political goals but also shared a common political vocabulary and a framework within which future cooperation could take place.

Not surprisingly, the certainty that led senior officials to reject Philipps' arguments and characterise his views as ideologically driven also persuaded officials both to ignore the complexities associated with the issue of Ukrainian independence and to treat the politics of the community in terms that fit a recognisable pattern. The conflict within the community was portrayed as ideological, despite the fact it was widely recognised – by the RCMP and the Soviet foreign ministry, among others, ironically – that the essential difference between the two major factions was not ideology per se but their respective positions on the national question in the Soviet Union. One group claimed that the political, social, and national aspirations of the Ukrainian people had been achieved within the framework of the Soviet constitution. The other group argued otherwise.[18] By dichotomizing the conflict as a communist/anticommunist struggle – a category error, if only because some individuals in the "nationalist" camp were committed to the idea of an independent *Soviet*, and later socialist, Ukraine – the dilemma posed by the legitimacy of the Ukrainian independence claim could be ignored.

The debate over Ukrainian independence was seen as a community squabble that, although awkward and complicating, had little to do with Canada and its foreign policy goals. As an internal dispute fed by the uncertainty of the historical moment, it was felt that it would disappear shortly. For Canadian officials, the point was not to be drawn into the fracas but to keep "an eye on the prize" – Canada's role and place in the postwar order.

By its very nature, conflict produces uncertainty, and the war of 1939–45 was no exception. During this time, there was much anxiety among officials about how best to cope with the shifting political landscape. For instance, during the critical summer of 1941, Justice Davis, a deputy minister at National War Services, spoke of the need for clear and decisive leadership. In this respect, Davis was confident about the judgment of officials and their ability to advance and protect Canada's interests. He was not alone. Like many of his colleagues, he was convinced that they could do so because he worked from the premise that the world of politics was both knowable and manageable if read accurately and without sentiment. All would be right if decisions and policy were crafted with this appreciation in mind. It was a realist's prescription, one that officials fully expected would serve Canada and its interests well. Ironically, however, what the Gouzenko affair would show was that, although versed in the tenets of realism, those who would lead Canada still had much to learn in terms of praxis.

Notes

ABBREVIATIONS

ASSSR-MID Arkhiv vneshnei politiki SSSR, Ministerstvo Inostrannykh Del
           (Archives of the Union of Soviet Socialist Republics,
           Ministry of Foreign Affairs)
     CIPO Canadian Institute of Public Opinion
      DEA Department of External Affairs Records, History Division (Canada)
      NAC National Archives (Canada)
      PRO Public Records Office (United Kingdom)
      SAB Saskatchewan Archives Board
      UAA University of Alberta Archives
      USA University of Saskatchewan Archives
     USNA National Archives and Records Service (United States)

CHAPTER ONE

1 J.W. Pickersgill, *The Mackenzie King Record*, vol. 1 (Toronto: University of Toronto Press, 1960), 21.
2 National Archives of Canada (hereafter NAC), RG2 F6, vol. 102, file 139, "Memorandum to the Canadian Delegation at the United Nations Conference on International Organisation from the Ukrainian Canadian Committee," n.d. [18 May 1945].
3 Ibid., CN Telegram, Ukrainian Canadian Committee to the Department of External Affairs, 19 May 1945.

4 Ibid., D. Wilgress, Canadian ambassador to the USSR, to Norman Robertson, under-secretary of state for external affairs, 25 May 1945.

5 NAC, RG25 G1, vol. 1896, file 165-39c, part 4, J.E. Read, secret memorandum to Prime Minister Mackenzie King, "Re: Ukrainian Refugees in Europe," 4 June 1945.

6 Ibid., R.G. Riddell to the associate under-secretary of state for external affairs, H. Wrong, "Re: Memorandum from Ukrainian Canadian Committee Concerning Ukrainian Refugees," 8 September 1945. A reply was drafted but never sent to the UCC. The draft letter stated that the government of Canada was assisting the United Nations Relief and Rehabilitation Administration in its work with refugees but that as for repatriation, the government was unaware "that any decision has been made to force any particular group of refugees to accept repatriation to territory to which they do not wish to return." Noting that the response was "really an evasion," Riddell thought that perhaps "it would be more satisfactory to make no reply." Hume Wrong, the associate under-secretary of state for external affairs, would agree to the strategy after consulting with Lester Pearson – another senior Department of External Affairs colleague. Ibid., draft copy, under-secretary of state for external affairs to J.W. Arsenych, Ukrainian Canadian Committee, 23 August 1945, together with attached hand written note, R.G. Riddell to H. Wrong, n.d.

7 NAC, William Lyon Mackenzie King Papers, MG26 J4, vol. 336, file 3650, N. Robertson, "Memorandum to the Prime Minister," 12 December 1945.

8 University of Saskatchewan Archives (hereafter USA), George Simpson Papers, box 1, file "Ukrainian Files, 1930–57," copy of letter, Ukrainian Canadian Committee to Rt Hon. W.L. Mackenzie King, 19 December 1945.

9 T. Skocpol, *States and Social Revolutions: A Comparative Analysis of France, Russia, and China* (Cambridge: Cambridge University Press, 1979), 31–2. See also T. Skocpol, "Bringing the State Back In: Strategies of Analysis in Current Research," in P. Evans, D. Rueschemeyer, and T. Skocpol, eds., *Bringing the State Back In* (Cambridge: Cambridge University Press, 1985).

10 The tradition has its origins in a number of classical works, notably Thucydides' *History of the Peloponnesian War*, Machiavelli's *The Prince*, Hobbes' *Leviathan*, and Clausewitz's *On War*. The theory of political realism is also represented in the following important works, among others: H. Morgenthau, *Politics among Nations: The Struggle for Power and Peace*, 6th ed. (New York: Knopf, 1961); H. Bull, *The Anarchical Society: A Study of Order in World Politics* (London: Macmillan, 1977); G. Kennan, *Realities of American Foreign Policy*

(Princeton: Princeton University Press, 1954); H. Kissinger, *A World Restored* (New York: Grosset and Dunlap, 1964); and K. Waltz, *Man, the State and War: A Theoretical Analysis* (New York: Columbia University Press, 1969). See also the debate on realism in the special issue "Symposium in Honor of Hans J. Morgenthau," *International Studies Quarterly*, 25, no. 2 (June 1981).

11 The political character of bureaucracy is carefully detailed in the work of Max Weber. See, for instance, his "Bureaucracy," in H.H. Gerth and C.W. Mills, eds., *From Max Weber: Essays in Sociology* (New York: Oxford University Press, 1978), 196–204. The influence of the realist paradigm on the political behaviour of officials, especially foreign-policy makers, is expertly explored in Robert Rothstein, "On the Costs of Realism," *Political Science Quarterly*, 87, no. 3 (1972): 347–62.

12 Morgenthau, *Politics among Nations*, 539–45.

13 The argument made here is that foreign policy concerns take precedence within the larger public policy arena. This precedence does not preclude the possibility of "unevenness" in policy implementation. But this unevenness has more to do with competition between the official ranks than lack of resolve.

14 See E. Nordlinger, *On the Autonomy of the Democratic State* (Cambridge: Harvard University Press, 1981).

CHAPTER TWO

1 United States National Archives and Records Service (hereafter USNA), State Department Records, M1286 reel 3, Division of European Affairs, "Summary of Dispatch, no. 844," 7 January 1939.

2 National Archives of Canada (NAC), RG25 G1, vol. 1896, file 165, part 1, Dr O.D. Skelton, under-secretary of state for external affairs, to Hon. N.A. McLarty, postmaster general, 25 January 1939.

3 Ibid., Dr O.D. Skelton, under-secretary of state for external affairs, to RCMP Commissioner S.T. Wood, 27 January 1939.

4 Ibid., Wood to Skelton, secret letter, ref. no. 175/4476, 4 February 1939, and Wood to Skelton, secret letter, ref. no. 175/6088, 23 February 1939. In the same file, see also Dr O.D. Skelton, to Hon. N.A. McLarty, 28 February 1939.

5 Ibid., Skelton to Wood, 31 January 1939. This document includes a copy of a letter from Dr G.E. Dragan to the prime minister of Canada, Rt Hon. W.L. Mackenzie King, 23 January 1939.

6 The memorial was entitled "Declaration of Ukrainian Canadians and Friends Regarding Ukraine," issued by the Representative Committee of Ukrainian Canadians, Saskatoon, Saskatchewan, 1939. USNA, State Department Records, M1286 reel 3.

7 For a brief discussion of the formation of the Representative Committee of Ukrainian Canadians, see O. Gerus, "The Ukrainian Canadian Committee," in M. Lupul, ed., *A Heritage in Transition: Essays in the History of Ukrainians in Canada* (Toronto: McClelland and Stewart, 1982), 196–7; and Thomas M. Prymak, *Maple Leaf and Trident: The Ukrainian Canadians during the Second World War* (Toronto: Multicultural History Society of Ontario, 1988), 27–8.

8 For an account of the political and military developments affecting the Carpatho-Ukraine, see P. Stercho, *Diplomacy of Double Morality: Europe's Crossroads in Carpatho-Ukraine, 1919–39* (New York: Carpathian Research Centre, 1971). See also V. Shandor, *Carpatho-Ukraine in the Twentieth Century: A Political and Legal History* (Cambridge, MA: Distributed by Harvard University Press for the Harvard Ukrainian Research Institute, 1997).

9 USNA, State Department Records, M1286 reel 3, "Declaration of Ukrainian Canadians and Friends Regarding Ukraine."

10 Appeals came from dozens of Ukrainian Canadian organisations. An especially moving but simple appeal directed to the prime minister was from the Ukrainian community in the small Ontario town of Espanola. See NAC, RG25 G1, vol. 1896, file 165, part 1, "Resolution," 11 April 1939. Acknowledgments from the Department of External Affairs (DEA) are also contained in the file.

11 NAC, O. Woycenko Papers, MG30 D2/2, vol. 3, file "Humeniuk," Ukrainian Press Bureau to T. Humeniuk, 19 April 1939.

12 NAC, RG25 G1, vol. 1896, file 165, part 1, W. Burianyk to Hon. W. Tucker, member of parliament, 28 March 1939, and Burianyk to Tucker, 25 April 1939.

13 Ibid., Dr O.D. Skelton to the prime minister, 27 April 1939.

14 Ibid., Skelton to the prime minister, 2 May 1939.

15 For a discussion of the origins, politics, and activities of the USRL before 1940, see O. Gerus, "Consolidating the Community: The Ukrainian Self Reliance League," in L. Luciuk and S. Hryniuk, *Canada's Ukrainians: Negotiating an Identity* (Toronto: University of Toronto Press, 1991), 158–72.

16 See NAC, RG25 G1, vol. 1896, file 165, part 1, Dr O.D. Skelton to W. Tucker, 14 April 1939.

17 A record of this and other conversations with officials in Ottawa can be found in W. Burianyk, "My Recollections Regarding the Founding of the Ukrainian Canadian Committee" (mimeographed, [1981]). During the course of three days, Burianyk would meet with Skelton on several occasions, sometimes in the company of Rev. Wasyl Giegychuk, a Ukrainian Catholic cleric who was also a delegate. A copy of the manuscript is in the possession of the author.

18 Robertson was well informed, obtaining information from even the
   most unlikely of sources. At a much later date, Robertson would
   acknowledge that in 1939 he had received information from Fred
   Rose, a Canadian communist implicated after the war in the Gouzenko
   affair: "I told Fred Rose that I would be glad to receive information he
   could furnish me about Fascist and Nazi activities, and passed on
   to [Superintendent] Bavin, who was then in charge of RCMP
   Intelligence, information of this kind which was unlikely to reach the
   RCMP direct." As quoted in J.L. Granatstein, *A Man of Influence:
   Norman A. Robertson and Canadian Statecraft, 1929–68* (Ottawa:
   Deneau, 1981), 85.
19 United Kingdom Public Record Office (hereafter PRO), Foreign Office
   Records, FO 371 23138/08019, S. Holmes, office of the high commissioner to C.W. Dixon, British Foreign Office, 13 July 1939.
20 Ibid., FO 7379/123/55, Sir H. Kennard, British ambassador to Poland,
   to Viscount Halifax, British foreign secretary, 20 May 1939.
21 NAC, RG25 GI, vol. 1896, file 165, part 1, T. Pavlychenko to Hon.
   W.J. Patterson, premier of Saskatchewan, 6 June 1939.
22 Ibid., W. Kossar to Dr O.D. Skelton, under-secretary of state for external affairs, 8 June 1939.
23 Ibid., Dr O.D. Skelton, "Note for the File," 12 June 1939.
24 NAC, RG25 A12, vol. 2095, file 39/1, Dr O.D. Skelton to the Canadian
   high commissioner to Great Britain, Vincent Massey, 15 June 1939.
25 Soon after, the Canadian high commissioner in London relayed to
   Ottawa that Kossar had in fact made an appearance at the British Foreign Office. The high commissioner informed Ottawa that in keeping
   with its wishes, the Foreign Office had been told "the Canadian Government did not wish to take any responsibility in the views which
   Mr Kossar might express." NAC, RG25 A12, vol. 2095, file 39/1,
   Canadian high commissioner (London) to the secretary of state for
   external affairs and prime minister, Rt Hon. W.L. Mackenzie King,
   18 July 1939.
26 For a copy of the statement, see NAC, Norman Robertson Papers,
   MG30 E163, vol. 12, file 133, "Draft Statement to be made by the
   Acting Prime Minister," 29 May 1939.
27 Ibid. The effect of foreign propaganda and influence was a matter of
   some concern to the deputy minister of justice, J.F. MacNeill, who
   advocated the use of public information as an antidote. N.F. Dreisziger, "The Rise of a Bureaucracy for Multiculturalism: The Origins
   of the Nationalities Branch, 1939–41," in N. Hillmer, B. Kordan, and
   L. Luciuk, eds., *On Guard for Thee: War, Ethnicity and the Canadian
   State, 1939–45* (Ottawa: Canadian Committee for the History of the
   Second World War, 1988), 4–5.

28 NAC, MG30 E163, vol. 12, file 138, letter to the prime minister, 7 June 1939. For a description of the Alliance's activities, see P. Krawchuk, *Na novii zemli: Storinky z zhyttia, borotby, tvorchoi pratsi kanadskykh ukraintsiv* [In the New Land: Pages from the Life, Struggle, and Work of the Canadian Ukrainians], (Toronto: Obiednanykh Ukrainskykh Kanadtsiv, 1958), 292–7.

29 NAC, RG25 G1, vol. 1896, file 165, part 1, letter to the prime minister, 7 July 1939. Representatives of the Brotherhood of Ukrainian Catholics, the Ukrainian Greek Orthodox Church, and the Ukrainian Self Reliance League signed the petition.

30 Ibid., Dr O.D. Skelton to RCMP Commissioner S.T. Wood, 21 June 1939.

31 Kossar's trip to Europe included Britain, which he had spoken to Skelton about, Italy, Yugoslavia, Hungary, newly independent Slovakia, German-occupied Prague, and Khust, the former capital of the Carpatho-Ukrainian Republic. The trip is detailed in Prymak, *Maple Leaf and Trident*, 31–2.

32 NAC, MG30 E163, vol. 12, file 138, W. Burianyk to W. Tucker, 7 August 1939, and W. Tucker to Dr O.D. Skelton, 15 August 1939. A great number of rumours circulated about the purpose of Kossar's trip and his activities while in Europe. The allegations, which became more fanciful and speculative with time, forced Kossar to place on record with the RCMP, at their request , a formal statement denying the rumours. Kossar's statement, made in 1943, is reproduced in Prymak, *Maple Leaf and Trident*, appendix D, 138–43.

33 For Burianyk's views on the UNF, see NAC, RG25 G1, vol. 1896, file 165, part 2, "Confidential Report on the Ukrainian Situation in Canada," n.d. His views are also recorded in his unpublished manuscript "My Recollections regarding the Founding of the Ukrainian Canadian Committee." For an assessment of Burianyk's report and especially his opinion of the UNF, see ibid., Professor W. Kirkconnell to N. Robertson, 14 December 1940.

34 NAC, E. Lapointe Papers, MG27 III B10, vol. 50, file 41, confidential memo, ref. no. 449, RCMP Commissioner S.T. Wood to the minister of justice, Hon. E. Lapointe, 25 August 1939; and RG25 G1, vol. 1964, file 855E, part 1, RCMP commissioner to the minister of justice, 26 August 1939. Norman Robertson, of the Department of External Affairs, who served as liason between the deparment and the RCMP, was opposed to the recommendation. For a description of his reaction, see J. Hilliker, *Canada's Department of External Affairs: The Early Years, 1909–1946*, vol. 1 (Montreal and Kingston: McGill-Queen's University Press, 1990), 224.

35 See I. Avakumovic, *The Communist Party in Canada: A History* (Toronto: McClelland and Stewart, 1975), 139–41; and J.L. Black,

Canada in the Soviet Mirror: Ideology and Perception in Soviet Foreign Affairs, 1917–91 (Ottawa: Carleton University Press, 1998), 122–4.

36 See, for example, the protest resolution of the Toronto Branch of the Ukrainian National Federation (UNF), 27 November 1939 in NAC, MG30 E163, vol. 12, file 138. For protest resolutions signed by Ukrainian Canadian organisations in Oshawa, Ontario, see NAC, RG25 G1, vol. 1896, file 165, part 1.

37 NAC, MG30 E163, vol. 12, file 138, UNF submission to Prime Minister W.L. Mackenzie King, "Ukrainian Canadians in the Present European War," 17 October 1939.

38 For a discussion of the proposal in the context of other efforts to organise Ukrainian units in the Canadian military, see Prymak, *Maple Leaf and Trident*, 35–7.

39 The Ukrainian Flying School of Oshawa, the so-called Ukrainian Air Force, had in fact been under surveillance by the RCMP since early 1939 because of its association with the UNF.

40 NAC, MG30 E163, vol. 12, file 138, Dr O.D. Skelton to H. Keenleyside and N. Robertson, 6 December 1939.

41 NAC, V.J. Kaye-Kisilevsky Papers, MG31 D69, vol. 9, file 26, V. Kisilevsky to P. Lazarovich, Ukrainian Self Reliance League, 25 October 1939.

42 For a brief description of the Ukrainian Press Bureau and a biographical sketch of V.J. Kaye-Kisilevsky, see Prymak, *Maple Leaf and Trident*, 23–4.

43 NAC, MG31 D69, vol. 9, file 26, V. Kisilevsky to W. Kossar, Ukrainian National Federation, 2 November 1939.

44 Ibid., P. Lazarovich to V. Kisilevsky, 29 November 1939. See also Gerus, "Consolidating the Community," 177.

45 PRO, Foreign Office Records, FO 371/23138, "Note to Mr Makins" from R.A. Leeper, British Foreign Office (Political Intelligence Department), with accompanying minutes by F. Roberts and L. Collier, 20 October 1939.

46 The broadcast was entitled "Canadian Ukrainians and the Crisis." A transcript of the broadcast is found in NAC, MG31 D69, vol. 9, file 26.

47 Ibid., file 27, Kisilevsky to Lazarovich, 1 January 1940.

48 Kaye, however, was also a pragmatist. "It has to be borne in mind that Poland is a member of the Alliance and that the Allies would like to have full accord between the nations threatened or attacked by eastern aggressors. It is imperative to take a line in these matters and to show our understanding of the situation. If we do not show enough foresight, the question may be settled over our heads, unilaterally, as it was settled once before. Policy is one thing and sentiment is quite a different thing. I must say, as much as I regret, Ukrainians are more often

obeying the impulse of sentiment than measur[ing] facts by sound fore-sight." Ibid., V. Kisilevsky to I. Danylchuk, Ukrainian Self Reliance League, 16 February 1940.

49 See NAC, MG30 D2/2, vol. 3, file "Danylchuk," T. Pavlychenko to the Ukrainian Self Reliance League Executive, 17 February 1940.

50 For a discussion of the political division within the nationalist commu-nity during this period, a division that centred primarily around the UNF, on the one hand, and the USRL, on the other, see Prymak, *Maple Leaf and Trident*, 44–5, and Gerus, "Consolidating the Community," 177–81. The relevant press articles are identified in Gerus, "The Ukrai-nian Canadian Committee," 212n5.

51 Secret intelligence reports on the situation in Western Ukraine were made available to Canada's Department of External Affairs in 1943. Fearing the consequences should the contents of the "top secret" reports become widely known, they were circulated only among a select few in the department: "The aim of the present report is not to contribute to any further dispute in the camps of the United Nations. We are fully aware that it is in the interest both of Poland and the Soviet Union to re-establish friendly relations based on solid founda-tions. Nevertheless, it seems advisable that a few persons, especially selected for this purpose, be confidentially informed of the fate of Polish citizens under Soviet rule, and this to avoid any misunderstand-ing which may arise and to refute certain false statements emanating from specific sources." Department of External Affairs Records (hereaf-ter DEA), file 266-40-C, "Soviet Deportation of the Inhabitants of East-ern Poland in 1939–41," December 1943. For the American analysis of population loss during the Soviet annexation of Western Ukrainian ter-ritories of 1939–41, see USNA, Micro. Pub. M1221, OSS Research and Analysis Report no. 2325, "Wartime Population Changes in Areas Incorporated into the Soviet Union, 1939–40."

52 NAC, RG25 G1, vol. 1896, file 165, part 2, "Communiqué," Press Bureau of the Ukrainian Democratic Republic, 25 March 1940.

53 Ibid., W. Sywstun to N. Robertson, Department of External Affairs, 15 May 1940.

54 Censorship's views tended to reflect the widely held view in govern-ment circles that "ethnic Canadians with sentimental ties outside the country continually faced 'exploitation' by foreign governments." W.R. Young, "Chauvinism and Canadianism: Canadian Ethnic Groups and the Failure of Wartime Information," in *On Guard for Thee*, 33.

55 NAC, RG25 G1, vol. 1896, file 165, part 2, Dr O.D. Skelton, "Memo-randum," 23 April 1940.

56 Ibid.

57 Ibid., Dr O.D. Skelton to N. Robertson, 24 April 1940.

58 Ibid., Skelton to Robertson, 5 May 1940, and Robertson to Skelton, 29 May 1940.

59 Prymak, *Maple Leaf and Trident*, 46.

60 NAC, RG25 G1, vol. 1896, file 165, part 2, Dr O.D. Skelton to N. Robertson, 20 May 1940.

61 Ibid.

62 Ibid., Dr O.D. Skelton to RCMP Commissioner S.T. Wood, 20 May 1940. Skelton's concern with the political orientation of *Kanadiiskyi farmer* revived his interest in the "political tendencies" of other Ukrainian Canadian newspapers. See ibid., Skelton to Wood, 23 May 1940.

63 Ibid., Wood to Skelton, reference no. D. 935-2333, 27 May 1940.

64 NAC, MG30 E163, vol. 12, file 152, Charles Bland, chairman, Civil Service Commission of Canada, to N. Robertson, 18 June 1940, including separate report entitled "Organisation for Internal Defence," 17 April 1940.

65 In their 1940 *Annual Report* of 1940, the RCMP noted with some exasperation that the force had been "inundated with complaints of the activities of alleged enemy aliens, causing our work to increase out of all proportion to the results obtained." As quoted in H. Palmer, "Ethnic Relations in Wartime: Nationalism and European Minorities in Alberta during the Second World War," *Canadian Ethnic Studies*, 14, no. 3 (1982): 7.

66 See I. Avakumovic, *The Communist Party in Canada*, 142; Reg Whitaker, "Official Repression of Communism during World War II," *Labour/Le Travail*, 17 (spring 1986): 136–9; and J. Stanton, "Government Internment Policy," *Labour/Le Travail*, 31 (spring 1993): 212–19.

67 See NAC, RG14, vol. 1, file 10, "Ukrainian Labour Farmer Temple Association," brief submitted by L. Cohen, Civil Liberties Association, to the Special Parliamentary Committee on Defence of Canada Regulations, 11 July 1942. See also P. Krawchuk, *Na Novii zemli*, 299–302, and Whitaker, "Official Repression of Communism," 157.

68 NAC, RG14, vol. 3, file 96, "A Political Letter on Our Present Tasks," September 1940. An example of a particularly articulate petition calling for the release of the internees can be found ibid., vol. 1, file 5, "Brief on Section 21 and Labour Cases Involved under Same," 2 April 1941.

On the internment of communists, see Krawchuk, *Na novii zemli*, 304–9. For first-hand accounts, see W. Repka and K. Repka, *Dangerous Patriots: Canada's Unknown Prisoners of War* (Vancouver: New Star Books, 1982), and Ben Swankey, "Reflections of a Communist: Canadian Internment Camps," *Alberta History* (spring 1982): 11–21.

69 NAC, RG25 G1, vol. 1896, file 165, part 2, "Note on Certain Ukrainian Organisations and Hemispheres," n.d. The quality of intelligence

and the level of analysis were less than reliable. Of the five organisations referred to in this report, three references were to the same organisation; the other two were to one other organisation. The church-affiliated *Ukrainskyi holos* [Ukrainian Voice] of Winnipeg and *Ukrainski visti* [Ukrainian News] of Edmonton were among the newspapers described as having "fascist leanings." Equally revealing was the intelligence report from the British Consulate General in Chicago. The report said that the Ukrainian acronym BUK – used to designate the lay organisation *Bratstvo Ukrainskykh Katolykiv* [Brotherhood of Ukrainian Catholics] – meant *Boh, Ukraina, Kanada* [God, Ukraine, Canada], "indicating an appeal to the childlike religious feelings of this Slav people, [and that it] may disguise a form of anti-democratic political influence." Ibid., British Consulate General to the Chancery, Canadian Legation, Washington, DC, 26 August 1940.

70 Ibid., British Consulate General to Chancery, Canadian Legation, Washington, DC, "Additional Ukrainian Notes," 16 September 1940.

71 NAC, RG25 A12, vol. 2095, file 39/1, ciphered telegram from Canadian high commissioner, London, to External Affairs, 20 June 1940.

72 NAC, RG25 G1, vol. 1896, file 165, part 2, Dr O.D. Skelton to Commissioner S.T. Wood, 6 September 1940, Skelton to L. Christie, Canadian minister to the United States, 23 September 1940, and Skelton to Wood, 23 September.

73 Ibid., Skelton to Wood, 6 September 1940.

74 Ibid., W. Eggleston, Censorship Co-ordination Committee, to Dr O.D. Skelton, 28 October 1940, and Skelton to Eggleston, 30 October 1940. For Censorship's analysis of the British reports, see the document in the same file entitled "Memorandum for Mr J. Roe," 16 October 1940.

75 Ibid., W. Burianyk, "Confidential Report on the Ukrainian Situation in Canada," n.d.

76 See *The Trident*, 4, no. 6 (July–August 1940).

77 USA, George Simpson Papers, box 1, file "Citizenship Division, 1941–46," G. Simpson to Rt Rev. Bishop I. Buchko, 17 October 1940.

78 Ibid., file "Ukrainian Files, 1930–57," Buchko to Simpson, 14 November 1940.

79 The growing public resentment is described in Gerus, "Consolidating the Community," 181.

80 An interesting first-hand account of the fractious and tendentious nature of the debates is provided in T. Kobzey, *Na ternystykh ta khreshchatykh dorohakh* [On a Thorny Crossroads], vol. 2 (Winnipeg: n.p., 1973), 76–85. See also in this regard, W. Burianyk's unpublished manuscript "My Recollections regarding the Founding of the Ukrainian Canadian Committee."

81 NAC, Tracy Philipps Papers, MG30 E350, vol. 2, file "Kaye Correspondence with T. Philipps, 1940," V.J. Kaye-Kisilevsky to T. Philipps, 11 August 1940.

82 An adventurer-soldier, Philipps was described in the *Financial Post* as "one of the world's most colorful characters." In 1915 Philipps, MC, FRAI, Doctor of Civil Law *honoris causa*, etc., was chief political officer for the Western Military Area of formerly German East Africa; intelligence officer in the Arab Bureau (HQ, Cairo); British Red Cross Commissioner under F. Nansen for Ukraine and Caspian region in 1920–23; deputy director of intelligence, Khartoum 1924–25; chief administrator of Tembura Military District, 1925–26; political administrator, British East Africa, 1933–35; and foreign correspondent in Morocco, Syria, Yugoslavia, Greece, Romania, and Bulgaria, 1936–38. He was also the principal character, under the thinly veiled disguise of Philip Tracy, of F.A.M. Webster's historical romance, *The Man Who Knew*. Ibid., vol. 1, file 1. More generally on Philipps as well as his relationship with Kaye, see N.F. Dreisziger, "Tracy Philipps and the Achievement of Ukrainian-Canadian Unity," in *Canada's Ukrainians: Negotiating an Identity*, 334–6.

83 NAC, MG30 E350, vol. 2, file "Kaye Correspondence with T. Philipps, 1940," V.J. Kaye, "The Ukrainian Canadian Committee," 11 August 1940.

84 See, for example, *Edmonton Bulletin*, 25 September 1940, "Empire Loyalty Is Voiced Here by Ukrainians: 600 Display Enthusiasm in Support of War Effort, Hear Address by Expert on Problems of Europe."

85 NAC, MG30 E350, vol. 2, file "Kaye Correspondence with T. Philipps, 1940," Rt Rev. Bishop V. Ladyka to T. Philipps, 18 September 1940.

86 Dreisziger, "The Rise of a Bureaucracy," 8–9.

87 NAC, MG30 E350, vol. 2, file "Kaye Correspondence with T. Philipps, 1940," Philipps to Kaye, 21 September 1940.

88 Ibid., Philipps to Kaye, 26 September 1940.

89 Ibid., T. Philipps to J.N. Macalister, CNR commissioner of colonisation, 19 October 1940.

90 NAC, MG30 D2/2, vol. 3, file "Danylchuk," Ukrainian Self Reliance League to the Ukrainian Central Committee, 29 October 1940, and W. Swystun to J. Arsenych, 31 October 1940.

91 NAC, RG25 G1, vol. 1896, file 165, part 2, T. Philipps to Colonel J. Mess, president of the Association of Canadian Clubs, 14 November 1940. See also Dreisziger, "The Achievement of Ukrainian-Canadian Unity," 338.

92 Ibid.; and NAC, MG30 E350, vol. 2, file "Kaye Correspondence with T. Philipps, 1940," CN telegram, n d [November 7].

93 NAC, RG25 G1, vol. 1896, file 165, part 2, T. Philipps to Colonel J. Mess, 14 November 1940.

94 NAC, Ukrainian Canadian Congress Papers, MG28, vol. 9, reel M2778, "Protokoly zasidan Ekzekutyvy Komitetu Ukraintsiv Kanady" [Minutes of the Executive Meeting of the Ukrainian Canadian Committee], 6–7 November 1940. See also NAC, RG25 G1, vol. 1896, file 165, part 2, Philipps to Mess, 14 November 1940.

95 NAC, MG30 E350, vol. 1, file 15, secret RCMP report, ref. no. D 945-1-Q-39 (10), 21 October 1941.

96 NAC, MG28, vol. 9, reel M2778, "Protokoly zasidan Ekzekutyvy Komitetu Ukraintsiv Kanady" [Minutes of the Executive Meeting of the Ukrainian Canadian Committee], 21 January 1941.

97 NAC, RG25 G1, vol. 1896, file 165, part 2, Justice T.C. Davis to N. Robertson, "Re: Ukrainian Problem," 18 November 1940, together with Davis to Robertson, "Re: Ukrainian Problem," 2 December 1940; and NAC, RG44, vol. 36, file "Foreign Section – Ukrainians," Robertson to Davis, 26 December 1940.

98 NAC, RG25 G1, vol. 1896, file 165, part 2, W. Burianyk to Hon. W. Patterson, 17 November 1940, Burianyk to Patterson, 20 November 1940, W. Burianyk to W. Tucker, 22 November 1940, O. Zerebko to W. Patterson, 23 November 1940, and W. Tucker to Dr O.D. Skelton, 25 November 1940. See also NAC, RG44, vol. 36, file "Foreign Section – Ukrainians," W.C. Barrie to Hon. J. MacKinnon, minister of trade and commerce, 14 December 1940.

For press coverage of Philipps' tour and lectures, see *Edmonton Journal*, 20 November 1940, "Distinguished Soldier Is Sure Britain Will Remain Supreme in Mediterranean"; and *Edmonton Journal*, 23 November 1940, "Tracy Philipps Speaks Wednesday."

99 NAC, MG30 E350, vol. 2, file "Kaye Correspondence with T. Philipps, 1940," Davis to Robertson, 27 November 1940.

100 NAC, RG25 G1, vol. 1896, file 165, part 2, Davis to Robertson, "Re: Ukrainian Problem," 18 November 1940. See also NAC, RG44, vol. 35, file "Bureau of Public Information," Justice T.C. Davis, associate deputy minister to Hon. J.G. Gardiner, minister of national war services, 13 November 1940.

101 "The first job we asked you to undertake, in conjunction with the Association of Canadian Clubs, was a speaking tour through Western Canada and we asked you to particularly direct your efforts towards harmonising the viewpoint of those citizens of that section of Canada who came to this country from other lands, particularly from central Europe, and the descendants of these people. You did a very excellent job for us and you were largely instrumental in having a Canadian

Ukrainian Committee created in Winnipeg. This Committee is representative of every element in the Ukrainian population of Canada ... This action on your part contributed materially toward increasing the support given by these people to the National War Effort of this Nation ... I am writing this note to let you note that your services have not gone unnoticed nor have we failed in appreciation of them." NAC, MG30 E350, vol. 1, file 19, Justice T.C. Davis to T. Philipps, 15 April 1941.

102 Philipps was among the original number of propagandists sent across North America under the auspices of the nongovernmental body the National Council of Education, which worked closely in Canada with the Association of Canadian Clubs. The initiative was undertaken by the Ministry of Information and authorised by the foreign secretary, Rt Hon. Viscount Halifax, with whom Philipps was in contact and from whom he carried letters of introduction. The purpose of the Ministry of Information project was to strengthen North American opinion in support of British war objectives. Philipps was operating in a semiofficial capacity, and it is in this sense that his views would seem out of keeping with British policy. See ibid., file 5, T. Philipps to Dr S.P. Duggan, 15 June 1940, T. Philipps to Rt Hon. Viscount Halifax, foreign office secretary, 25 June 1940, and Philipps to Halifax, 9 July 1940.

103 The letters in question were those from W. Burianyk to the premier of Saskatchewan and W. Tucker, member of parliament. NAC, RG25 G1, vol. 1896, file 165, part 2, W. Burianyk to Hon. W. Patterson, 17 November 1940, Burianyk to Patterson, 20 November 1940, and W. Burianyk to W. Tucker, 22 November 1940.

104 Ibid., Dr O.D. Skelton to Justice T.C. Davis, 13 December 1940.

105 Ibid., Justice T.C. Davis to N. Robertson, 13 December 1940.

106 Ibid.

107 Ibid., T. Philipps, "Dear Colonel [Mess]," with attachment marked "Strictly Confidential," 6 December 1940.

108 Philipps repeated similar views to W. Burianyk. Ibid., W. Burianyk to Hon. W. Patterson, 17 November 1940, and Burianyk to Patterson, 20 November 1940. See Dreisziger, "The Achievement of Ukrainian-Canadian Unity," 337–8.

109 NAC, RG25 G1, vol. 1896, file 165, part 2, T. Philipps, "Dear Colonel [Mess]," with attachment marked "Strictly Confidential," 6 December 1940.

110 Ibid.

111 Ibid., Justice T.C. Davis to N. Robertson, 13 December 1940.

112 NAC, RG44, vol. 36, file "Foreign Section – Ukrainians," Dr O.D. Skelton, "Ukrainian Organisation," 17 December 1940.

113 The following is taken from Philipps' report of his Western tour, NAC, MG30 E350, vol. 1, file 16, T. Philipps, "Tour in Western Canada, part 1," 8 January 1941.

114 The Ukrainian Worker's League, or "Lobayists," was a splinter group that was formed by several Ukrainian dissidents of the Communist Party of Canada and the ULFTA. The group broke with the party in 1935, after drawing no satisfaction from enquiries regarding the disappearance of Ukrainian Canadian comrades who had left Canada for the Soviet Union and after having received disturbing reports on conditions in Ukraine. In 1939 the leadership of the group continued to call for the creation of a "free and independent Soviet Ukraine," modifying its position in 1940 as a condition of its acceptance into a number of representative committees. For an early statement on the group's political concerns, see D. Lobay, *Za diisne vyiasnennia polozhennia na Radianskii Ukraini* [For a Truthful Explanation of the Situation in Soviet Ukraine] (Winnipeg and New York: n.p., 1935).

The RCMP described the Ukrainian Worker's League (later reconstituted as the League of Ukrainian Organisations) as "trotskyist" in orientation. Philipps considered the group the most important and valuable of all the Ukrainian Canadian organisations. Philipps insisted on their inclusion in the Ukrainian Canadian Committee despite the objection of the other constituent organisations, notably the UNF, which feared that the league was a communist-front organisation. See NAC, MG30 E350, vol. 2, file "Kaye Correspondence with T. Philipps, 1940," CN Telegram, n.d. [November 7]; Kobzey, *Na ternystykh ta khreshchatykh dorohakh*, 87; and Gerus, "Consolidating the Community," 179.

115 NAC, MG30 E350, vol. 1, file 16, T. Philipps, "Tour in Western Canada, Part II," 13 January 1941.

116 NAC, RG25 G1, vol. 1896, file 165, part 2, T. Philipps, "Dear Colonel [Mess]," with attachment marked "Strictly Confidential," 6 December 1940.

117 NAC, MG30 E350, vol. 2, file "Kaye Correspondence with T. Philipps, 1941," T. Philipps to Justice T.C. Davis, 25 February 1941.

118 NAC, RG25 G1, vol. 1896, file 165, part 2, T. Philipps to Colonel Mess, 7 December 1940. Others also offered suggestions concerning the disposition of the halls. See University of Alberta Archives (hereafter, UAA), Donald Cameron Papers, acc. no. 75–112, box 1, file 6, D. Cameron, "Submission to the Custodian of Enemy Property with Respect to the Use of Sundry Halls and the Proceeds Thereof," 27 September 1940.

119 See NAC, MG30 E350, vol. 2, file "Kaye Correspondence with T. Philipps, 1941"; T. Philipps, "Sequestered Halls, no. 1 in Series,"

13 January 1941, together with "Sequestered Halls, no. 2 in Series," 22 March 1941; and ibid., file "Committee on Co-operation – October 1942," T. Philipps, "Sequestered Halls, no. 3 in Series," 23 October 1942.

120 NAC, RG25 G1, vol. 1896, file 165, part 2, N. Robertson to Justice T.C. Davis, 10 December 1940, and Robertson to Davis, 13 December 1940.

121 NAC, MG30 E350, vol. 1, file 21, T. Philipps, "Canadian Unity and Use of the ex-Communistic Halls," 22 March 1941, and T. Philipps, "Memorandum for the Commissioner," 31 May 1941.

122 See *Globe and Mail*, 17 January 1941, "Probe Ordered of Ukrainian Nationalists"; and *Toronto Star*, 17 January 1941, "Further Probe Is Ordered of Ukrainian Nationalists." See also Prymak, *Maple Leaf and Trident*, 51.

123 NAC RG44, vol. 36, file "Foreign Section – Ukrainians," T. Philipps to W. Kirkconnell, CN telegram, 28 January 1941. See also NAC, RG25 G1, vol. 1896, file 165, part 2, W. Swystun to N. Robertson, 4 February 1941. The *Globe and Mail* editorial was published 28 January 1941.

124 NAC, RG44, vol. 36, file "Foreign Section – Ukrainians," T. Philipps to Justice T.C. Davis, 5 February 1941

125 NAC, MG30 E350, vol. 1, file 17, T. Philipps to unidentified correspondent, 17 February 1941, and T. Philipps, "Personal, no. 8," 17 February 1941. See also ibid., vol. 2, file "Kaye Correspondence with T. Philipps, 1940," V.J. Kaye to T. Philipps, 7 April 1941. Professor Dreiszger notes that the "temporising" on the part of officials was the result of the drawn-out search for a suitable candidate to lead a proposed government foreign-languages section that was to work with the ethnic communities. See Dreisziger, "The Rise of a Bureaucracy," 15.

126 NAC, RG44, vol. 36, file "Foreign Section – Ukrainians," Justice T.C. Davis to G.H. Lash, director of public information, CP telegram, 24 February 1941.

127 NAC, MG30 E350, vol. 1, file 6, Commissioner S.T. Wood to T. Philipps, ref. no. 41 D 1-Q-3, 8 May 1941, Philipps to Wood, 17 May 1941, and T. Philipps, "Memorandum for the Commissioner," 28 May 1941.

128 Ibid., Philipps to Wood, 11 April 1941; NAC, RG44, vol. 36, file "Foreign Section – Ukrainians," Philipps to Wood, 13 April 1941; and NAC, MG30 E350, vol. 1, file 6, "Memorandum for the Commissioner," 28 May 1941.

129 NAC, RG44, vol. 36, file "Foreign Section – Ukrainians," Philipps to Wood, 13 April 1941. Philipps, however, was not especially hopeful for the future: "Ukrainians are confused about the issue in Eastern Europe.

Most of us are too. We still can not tell their 40 million kindred in Europe what we will do for them when we win. By caution, we do not even tell them that we should like them too to be able to throw off dictatorship, tyranny and enslavement. Our sauce is for the geese but not for the ganders. But Hitler is promising them something quite definite. Whatever the Germans offer Ukrainians, it will be better than what they suffer now. So the months pass, until one day something will 'surprise' us."

130 See NAC, MG30 E350, vol. 1, file 21, T. Philipps, "My Today's Confidential Comment on Two Ukrainian Reports by H.B.M. Consul in Chicago," 4 June 1941, and "Reports, Dated Chicago, 1st and 7th May, by H.B.M. Consul General on Ukrainian Organisations in the United States with Their Links throughout the Americas," 4 June 1941.

131 NAC, RG25 G1, vol. 1896, file 165, part 3, N. Robertson to Commissioner Wood, 10 May 1941.

132 The notion of sacrifice was a recurring theme often used by Ukrainian Canadians to legitimise their claims. It was a theme reiterated in G. Simpson's radio address "The Ukrainian Question and the Present Crisis," delivered on the CBC program *Frankly Speaking*: "If liberty in the final analysis is guaranteed by willingness to make the supreme sacrifice, then Ukrainians ... [have] paid the first instalment for the re-establishment of European freedom." For a transcript of the radio broadcast, see ibid., file 165, part 1.

133 Ibid., Dr O.D. Skelton, under-secretary of state for external affairs, to Rt Hon. W.L. Mackenzie King, 27 April 1939.

134 See remarks by Dr O.D. Skelton, ibid., file 165, part 2, "Memorandum," 23 April 1940, and Justice T.C. Davis to N. Robertson, 13 December 1940.

135 G. de T. Glazebrook, *Canadian External Relations* (Toronto: Oxford University Press, 1950), 415.

136 See H. Morgenthau, *Politics among Nations: The Struggle for Power and Peace* (New York: Knopf, 1961), 90–1. See also his chapter 4, "The Struggle for Power: Policy of the *Status Quo*," 38–43.

137 NAC, MG30 E350, vol. 1, file 16, T. Philipps, "Tour in Western Canada, Part II," 13 January 1941.

138 NAC, MG27 III B10, vol. 50, file 41, confidential memo, ref. no. 449, RCMP Commissioner S.T. Wood to the minister of justice, Hon. E. Lapointe, 25 August 1939.

139 Within the leadership it was recognised that the UCC was being used by the government. But there was also a sense that because of this "relationship," the committee could influence the government in a way that had not been possible before.

140 NAC, MG30 E163, vol. 12, file 152, C. Bland, chairman, Civil Service Commission of Canada to N. Robertson, 18 June 1940, and attached report entitled "Organisation for Internal Defence," 17 April 1940.

141 NAC, MG30 E350, vol. 1, file 16, T. Philipps, "Tour in Western Canada, Part I," 8 January 1941.

CHAPTER THREE

1 The appeal was made 23 June 1941. On 5 July a Polish-Soviet agreement was concluded between the Polish president, General W. Sikorski, and the deputy commissar for Soviet foreign affairs, A. Zaleski. For the Polish position and conditions regarding the Polish-Soviet agreement, see United States National Archives and Records Service (USNA), State Department Records, M982 reel 69, Ambassador J. Ciechanowski to Cordell Hull, U.S. secretary of state, 24 July 1941.

2 The legal basis for Ukrainian claims in the Polish-Ukrainian dispute was contained in the decision of March 1919 of the Supreme Council of the Allied Powers, which provided for Polish governance over Ukrainian East Galicia for twenty five years, under an Allied mandate. A special statute was to guarantee full autonomy to Eastern Galicia until 1944, when a referendum was to take place on the question of national independence. In February 1923 the council of the League of Nations confirmed the statute. It was repeated at the time that the Poles were to hold only a provisional mandate on behalf of the Allied and Associated Powers. Shortly thereafter, Poland unilaterally declared in Geneva that it would not be bound by the Minorities Treaty. As the UCC would argue, Poland's abrogation of the treaty and violation of international law did not release the Associated Powers from their original commitment to the indigenous Ukrainian population in that region.

3 National Archives of Canada (NAC), Tracy Philipps Papers, MG30 E350, vol. 1, file 21, "Office of the United Committee of Ukrainian Canadians to Tracy Philipps," 24 June 1941.

4 NAC, RG25 G1, vol. 1896, file 165, part 3, ciphered dispatch, secretary of state for external affairs to the Canadian high commissioner, London, n.d. See also Public Records Office of the United Kingdom (PRO), Foreign Office Records, FO 371/29532, minutes of L. Collier, 9 July 1941.

5 NAC, RG44, vol. 36, file "Foreign Section-Ukrainians," CN telegram, T. Philipps to Justice T.C. Davis, 25 June 1941.

6 NAC, RG25 G1, vol. 1896, file 165, part 3, RCMP Commissioner S.T. Wood to Norman Robertson, 26 June 1941.

7 The official Polish view of the Ukrainian community in Canada is described in A. Reczyńska, "Ukrainians and the 'Ukrainian Question' as Seen by Poles in Canada during the Second World War," *Journal of Ukrainian Studies*, 16, nos.1–2 (summer–winter 1991): 195–8.

8 PRO, Foreign Office Records, FO 371/29532, minutes of L. Collier, 9 July 1941, and minutes of B.H. Sumner, 17 July 1941.

9 N.F. Dreisziger, "The Rise of a Bureaucracy for Multiculturalism: The Origins of the Nationalities Branch, 1939–41," in N. Hillmer, B. Kordan, L. Luciuk, eds., *On Guard for Thee: War, Ethnicity and the Canadian State, 1939–45* (Ottawa: Canadian Committee for the History of the Second World War, 1988), 17–18.

10 NAC, RG44, vol. 35, file "Bureau of Public Information," Justice T.C. Davis to Hon. J. T. Thorson, minister of national war services, 27 June 1941.

11 The press censors would in fact issue a warning to the paper that articles such as these, which were harmful to the war effort, were in contravention of the Defence of Canada Regulations. Thomas M. Prymak, *Maple Leaf and Trident: The Ukrainian Canadians during the Second World War* (Toronto: Multicultural History Society of Ontario, 1988), 56–7.

12 NAC, RG44, vol. 35, file "Foreign Section-Ukrainians," Justice T.C. Davis to Prof. Simpson, 28 July 1941.

13 University of Saskatchewan Archives (hereafter USA), George Simpson Papers, box 1, file "Citizenship Division, 1941–46," Prof. Simpson to Justice T.C. Davis, 31 July 1941.

14 R.A. Davies, "Ukrainian-Canadians and the War's New Phase," *Saturday Night*, 12 July 1941. Rudolph Shohan (Raymond Arthur Davies, Roy Davies) wrote extensively on matters pertaining to the Soviet war effort. He was the first Canadian and one of the few Western journalists allowed entry into the Soviet Union to cover developments on the Eastern front in 1944. Ever suspicious of his activities, External Affairs was kept abreast of his movements in the Soviet Union by way of regular information from embassy staff in Moscow. See Department of External Affairs Records (DEA), file 5616-40. The file also contains a departmental assessment of Davies and his published work.

15 NAC, RG25 G1, vol. 1896, file 165, part 3, B.K. Sandwell to W. Swystun, 23 July 1941.

16 W. Swystun, "Ukrainian-Canadians and the Russo-German War," *Saturday Night*, 26 July 1941.

17 NAC, MG30 E350, vol. 1, file 11, "RCMP Report on the First National Eucharistic Congress of Eastern Rites," ref. no. D 945-2-M-2, 29 July 1941.

18 For a description of the resolutions, see Prymak, *Maple Leaf and Trident*, 57.

19 NAC, MG30 E350, vol. 1, file 12, "RCMP Report on the Eighth National Convention of the Ukrainian National Federation," ref. no. D 945-1-Q-39, 30 September 1941. Reproduced in B. Kordan and L.Y. Luciuk, *A Delicate and Difficult Question: Documents in the History of Ukrainians in Canada*, (Kingston, ON: Limestone Press, 1986), 80–90.

20 For a brief but good sketch of the UHO, see Prymak, *Maple Leaf and Trident*, 22–3.

21 NAC, MG30 E350, vol. 1, file 13, "RCMP Report on the United Hetman Organisation," ref. no. D 945-1-Q-39, 6 October 1941. For Philipps' assessment of the Hetman organisation, see NAC, RG25 G1, vol. 1896, file 165, part 3, notes labelled "Strictly Confidential," 30 June 1941.

22 NAC, MG30 E350, vol. 1, file 15, RCMP Reports captioned "Prominent Ukrainians on the UNF and its Leaders" and "Ukrainian Canadian Committee," ref. no. D 945-1-Q-39, 21 October 1941.

23 NAC, RG44, vol. 35, file "Bureau of Public Information," Justice T.C. Davis to G.H. Lash, director, Bureau of Public Information, 23 October 1941; and ibid., vol. 36, file "Committee on Co-operation," Justice T.C. Davis to Dr E.H. Coleman, under-secretary of state for Canada, 28 October 1941. See also Dreisziger, "The Rise of a Bureaucracy," 19.

24 NAC, MG30 E350, vol. 2, file "Committee on Co-operation," T. Philipps, "Proposed European Section for War Services and Canadianization of Immigrant Europeans," 22 October 1941.

25 USA, Simpson Papers, box 1, file "Citizenship Division, 1941–46," "Minutes of Interdepartmental Meeting of Proposed Committee on Cultural Group Co-operation under Ministry of National War Services," 1 November 1941.

26 The general investigations were supplemented by police interrogations of both leaders and activists. For an interesting account, see Prymak, *Maple Leaf and Trident*, 60–1.

27 Denis Smith, *Diplomacy of Fear: Canada and the Cold War 1941–48* (Toronto: University of Toronto Press, 1988), 28.

28 NAC, RG25, acc. 83/84/259, box 154, file 2462-40, S.F. Rae, "Canadian Comment on Recent Developments in Canadian-Russian Relationships," 30 July 1941.

29 For a description of some of the logistical arrangements, see J.L. Black, *Canada and the Soviet Mirror: Ideology and Perception in Soviet Foreign Affairs, 1917–91* (Ottawa: Carleton University Press, 1998), 132–3.

30 NAC, RG25, acc. 83/84/259, box 154, file 2462-40, S.F. Rae, "Relations between Canada and the USSR," 6 December 1941.

31 Although a Gallup poll showed some indication that public opinion was beginning to favour closer relations with the Soviet Union, the regional differences in the poll were most pronounced, with overwhelming opposition registered in Quebec and mixed reaction on the Canadian Prairies. Canadian Institute of Public Opinion (hereafter CIPO), "Tremendous Majorities in Every Province Approve Aid to Russia," 6 December 1941.

32 NAC, RG25, acc. 83/84/259, box 154, file 2462-40, S.F. Rae, "Relations between Canada and the USSR," 6 December 1941.

33 Ibid., J.E. Read, "Relations between Canada and the USSR," 16 December 1941.

34 Saskatchewan Archives Board (SAB), George Simpson Papers, RGA26, file 25, J.A. Arsenych to G. Simpson, 13 October 1942, and Simpson to Arsenych, 19 October 1942. See also ibid., "Protokoly zasidan Ekzekutyvy Komitetu Ukraintsiv Kanady" [Minutes of the Executive of the Ukrainian Canadian Committee], 13 October 1942, "Protokoly zasidan Ekzekutyvy Komitetu Ukraintsiv Kanady" [Minutes of the Executive of the Ukrainian Canadian Committee], 27 October 1942, and A. Yaremovich to G. Simpson, 20 October 1942.

35 NAC, RG2 7C, vol. 5, reel C-4652, minutes of the Cabinet War Committee, 29 October 1941. See also Lawrence Aronsen and Martin Kitchen, *The Origins of the Cold War in Comparative Perspective: American, British and Canadian Relations with the Soviet Union, 1941–48* (London: Macmillan Press, 1988), 152.

36 Canada would eventually declare war on Finland, Romania, and Hungary. Significantly, so as not to alienate the domestic constituencies that could trace their origins to these lands, a policy was adopted exempting persons of Finnish, Romanian, and Hungarian nationality from being treated as enemy aliens. See N.F. Dreisziger, "7 December 1941: A Turning Point in Canadian Wartime Policy toward Enemy Ethnic Groups?" *Journal of Canadian Studies*, 32, no. 1 (spring 1997): 100–1.

37 USNA, State Department Records, M982 reel 68, Ambassador Drexel Biddle Jr to the U.S. secretary of state, Cordell Hull, 27 July 1941.

38 It was a point that was not lost on the Soviet leadership. When discussion between the British foreign secretary, Anthony Eden, and Marshall Stalin turned to the issue of Polish-Soviet frontiers, Stalin quipped, "I thought that the Atlantic Charter was directed against those people who were trying to establish world dominion. It now looks as though the Charter was directed against the USSR." As quoted in Smith, *Diplomacy of Fear*, 29.

39 See USNA, Micro. Pub. M1221, OSS Research and Analysis Report no. 1972, "British and American Views on the Applicability of the Atlantic Charter."

40 See, for example, USNA, State Department Records, M982 reel 69, dispatch from Ambassador Brady to the U.S. secretary of state, 16 August 1941, commenting on the reaction of the Burmese government to the Atlantic Charter.

41 See, for example, NAC, Ukrainian Canadian Congress Papers, MG28, vol. 9, reel M2278, "Protokoly zasidan Ekzekutyvy Komitetu Ukraintsiv Kanady" [Minutes of the Ukrainian Canadian Committee], 6 October 1942; and in SAB, RGA26, file 25, "Protokoly zasidan Ekzekutyvy Komitetu Ukraintsiv Kanady" [Minutes of the Ukrainian Canadian Committee], 17 October 1942, "Protokoly zasidan Ekzekutyvy Komitetu Ukraintsiv Kanady" [Minutes of the Ukrainian Canadian Committee], 9 March 23 1943, "Protokoly zasidan Ekzekutyvy Komitetu Ukraintsiv Kanady" [Minutes of the Ukrainian Canadian Committee], 16 March 23 1943.

In the March 23 memorial of the Ukrainian Canadian Committee to the Prime Minister of Canada, several "indisputable" principles were identified that governed the position of their community on the war, among which it was stated, "The Atlantic Charter clearly and unmistakably lays down as a principle the right of a people to determine their political destiny. The allied Nations have made this the basis of the present war objective." See NAC, RG25 G1, vol. 1896, file 165, part 4, "Memorandum of the Ukrainian Canadian Committee to Rt Hon. W.L. Mackenzie King, Prime Minister and Minister for External Affairs, Canada," 23 March 1943.

42 Inter alia, NAC, RG25 G1, vol. 1896, file 165, part 3, UK Report "Efforts to carry on Ukrainian Nationalist Propaganda amongst Ukrainians Serving in Canadian Forces," 4 June 1943, A.J. Halpern, British Security Co-ordination, to T.A. Stone, Department of External Affairs, 22 February 1943, G. de T. Glazebrook, Department of External Affairs, to A.J. Halpern, 19 March 1943, Glazebrook to Halpern, 30 March 1943, Halpern to Glazebrook, 5 April and 19 May 1943, Glazebrook to Halpern, 14 June 1943, Halpern to Glazebrook, 19 June 1943, G. de T. Glazebrook to H. Allard, Canadian Legation in Washington, 25 June 1943, Allard to Glazebrook, 13 July and 31 July 1943, J. Garner, Office of the High Commissioner for the UK, to S.F. Rae, Department of External Affairs, 19 July 1943, and R.G. Riddell, Department of External Affairs, to J. Garner, 27 July 1943. See also PRO, Foreign Office Records, FO 371/36974, "The Ukrainian Canadian Committee," 13 May 1943.

43 Officially, service records would show an enlistment of approximately 24,700 who were "fluent Ukrainian speakers." Taking into account ethnic Ukrainians whose home language or mother tongue was not Ukrainian, the number is estimated to be upwards of 30,000 to 40,000. Prymak, *Maple Leaf and Trident*, 107.

44 For a statement outlining the Ukrainian nationalist claim in the context of the Atlantic Charter and the obligations of ethnic Ukrainians as citizens of Canada, see Myroslaw Stechishin, *Samostiinist, Sobornist, Federatsiia* [Independence, Unity, Federation], (Winnipeg: Soiuz Ukrainskykh Samostiinykiv, 1942), 17–24.

45 NAC, RG25 G1, vol. 1896, file 165, part 3, N. Robertson to RCMP Commissioner S.T. Wood, 1 October 1941.

46 Editorial, *Ukrainskyi holos* [Ukrainian Voice], 28 January 1942.

47 Canada, Parliament, *House of Commons Debates*, 2 February 1942, 234–5.

48 NAC, RG25 G1, vol. 1896, file 165, part 3, G. Simpson to N. Robertson, 4 April 1942.

49 See, for example, a letter from M. Chornohus to Rt Hon. W.L. Mackenzie King, 20 March 1942, which includes an appeal endorsed by sixty electors from the Vegreville riding, ibid. See also NAC, RG26, vol. 6, file 34-L-2, D.J. Prystash to G. Lash, director, Bureau of Public Information, 15 March 1942.

50 As quoted in J. Kolasky, *The Shattered Illusion: The History of Pro-Communist Ukrainian Organisations in Canada* (Toronto: PMA Books, 1979), 68.

51 Editorial, *Toronto Star*, 7 February 1942. The Ukrainian reaction to the *Star* editorial is described in Prymak, *Maple Leaf and Trident*, 66–7.

52 NAC, RG26, vol. 9, file 50-1, copy of editorial, "Time for Revision of Canada's Immigration Laws," *Canadian Grocer*, n.d.

53 Ibid., vol. 6, file 34-L-2, copy of letter to the editor, "Only Two Sides," *Edmonton Bulletin*, 6 March 1942.

54 Ibid., copy of P. Lazarovich, letter to the editor, *Edmonton Bulletin*, 9 March 1942. See also NAC, RG26, vol. 9, file 46-1, "New Attacks on 'Foreigners,'" n.d.

55 On the anniversary date commemorating the independence of the Ukrainian Democratic Republic (January 22), the pro-Soviet Ukrainian Canadian newspaper *Ukrainske zhyttia* [Ukrainian Life] published a critical but tongue-in-cheek account of the UCC and the nationalists. Norman Robertson, the under-secretary of state for external affairs, found it "not without humour." NAC, RG26, vol. 9, file 46-1, editorial, *Ukrainske zhyttia*, 22 January 1942, and N. Robertson to G. Simpson, 12 February 1942.

56 W.A. Kardash, *Hitler's Agents in Canada*, (Toronto: Morris Printing, 1942). The pamphlet's stated intention was to disclose the alleged subversive activities of the Ukrainian National Federation – an organisation described as sowing "fascist ideology among the Ukrainian population in this country, whose leaders looked forward to the aid of Hitler to achieve their aims of a fascist Ukraine, and who today under the cloak of anti-Soviet slander are giving praise to the gang of Nazi-murderers." *Novyi shliakh* (New Pathway), the press organ of the Ukrainian National Federation, also came under attack, accused of fabricating news of Soviet atrocities in Western Ukraine and "of propagating a line which even Gobbels – the Nazi Minister of Propaganda – could not even have better concocted." On William Kardash, see chap. 4, n52.

57 NAC, O. Woycenko Papers, MG30 D2/2, vol. 4, file "J. Stechishin," 'Dorohyi brate' [Dear Brother], Julian Stechishin to Myroslav Stechishin, 9 April 1942.

58 NAC, MG30 E350, vol. 1, file 32, W. Burianyk to G. Simpson, 3 June 1942.

59 NAC, RG26, vol. 1, file 22-2, part 1, Simpson to Burianyk, 19 March 1942.

60 CIPO, "Public Thinks Russia behind Ideals of Atlantic Charter," 1 August 1942.

61 NAC, RG2, series 18, vol. 43, file U-5, N. Robertson to W.L. Mackenzie King, 13 April 1942; and USNA, State Department Records, M982 reel 69, report entitled "General Attitude in Sweden to the War in the East and to the Finnish Cause," 24 July 1941.

62 NAC, RG2, series 18, vol. 43, file U-5, N. Robertson to W.L. Mackenzie King, 13 April 1942. There may have been an indirect benefit as well. Norman Robertson relayed to J. Pierrepoint Moffat, the United States ambassador to Canada, that "nobody worried about Finland [while] Estonia, Latvia, and Lithuania was a small price to pay to convince Russia of Britain's trust and earnestness." In light of Russia's persistent demand for supplies which it could not justify, Robertson concluded that if British and Canadian acceptance of annexation were to "re-establish a relationship of mutual trust with Russia, it may mean a great saving of supplies for the common good." As quoted in J.L. Granatstein, *A Man of Influence: Norman A. Robertson and Canadian Statecraft 1929–68* (Ottawa: Deneau, 1981), 170.

63 NAC, RG2, series 18, vol. 43, file U-5, G. de T. Glazebrook, memo to the prime minister, "Proposed Anglo-Russian Treaty," 14 April 1942. Reproduced in L.Y. Luciuk and B. Kordan, *Anglo-American Perspectives on the Ukrainian Question, 1938–51: A Documentary Collection* (Kingston, ON: Limestone Press, 1987), 100–9.

64 Ibid.
65 Ibid.
66 Ibid.
67 Smith, *Diplomacy of Fear*, 34–6.
68 NAC, RG25 G1, vol. 1896, file 165, part 3, G. de T. Glazebrook, "Policy toward Foreign Groups," 2 July 1942. Reproduced in Luciuk and Kordan, *Anglo-American Perspectives*, 110–13. For purposes of classification, nationals of states whose governments or provisional governments were recognised by Canada were distinguished from "enemy aliens." Persons from nonrecognised states – with the exception of those associated with the Free French – were identified as enemy aliens. However, since the question of enemy aliens was already being dealt with through the Defence of Canada Regulations, the real issue was the relationship of Canada to those who were in the unenviable role of having no status or, as External Affairs officials described it, who were affiliated with "non-recognised movements."
69 The government's relatively benign attitude toward Germans, Italians, Hungarians, and other "foreign-born" is described in R. Keyserlingk, "The Canadian Government's Attitude toward Germans and German Canadians in World War II," *Canadian Ethnic Studies*, 16, no. 1 (1984): 16–28; H. Palmer, "Ethnic Relations in Wartime: Nationalism and European Minorities in Alberta during the Second World War," *Canadian Ethnic Studies*, 14, no. 3 (1982): 1–23; and N.F. Dreisziger, "7 December: A Turning Point." By comparison, for Canada's official treatment of Japanese Canadians, see Ann Gomer Sunahara, *The Politics of Racism: The Uprooting of Japanese Canadians during the Second World War* (Toronto: Lorimer, 1981); Ken Adachi, *The Enemy That Never Was: A History of the Japanese Canadians* (Toronto: McClelland and Stewart, 1976); and E. Roy, J.L. Granatstein, M. Iimo, and H. Takamura, *Mutual Hostages: Canadians and Japanese during the Second World War* (Toronto: University of Toronto Press, 1990).
The "relative freedom" enjoyed by certain groups did not preclude the selective use of state security measures. For a critical assessment of government policy and the abridgment of civil liberties, see R. Keyserlingk, "'Agents within the Gates': The Search for Nazi Subversives in Canada during World War II," *Canadian Historical Review*, 66, no. 2 (1985): 211–39; and R. Keyserlingk, "Breaking the Nazi Plot: Canadian Government Attitudes towards German Canadians, 1939–45," and B. Ramirez, "Ethnicity on Trial: The Italians of Montreal and the Second World War," in *On Guard for Thee*, 53–69, 71–84.
70 NAC, RG25 G1, vol. 1896, file 165, part 3, G. de T. Glazebrook, "Policy toward Foreign Groups," 2 July 1942.
71 Ibid.

72 The OSS reports include USNA, Records of the Office of Strategic Services, RG226, entry 100, box 98, UK-371–380, FNB report no. 247, "Ukrainian-American Organisations in the United States"; and ibid., box 119, FNB-Int-33, FNB report no. 178, "The Ukrainian Language Press in the United States"; FNB report no. 184, "Ukrainians in Latin America"; and FNB report no. 205, "The Ukrainians in Canada."

73 USNA, RG226, entry 100, box 95, UK-11–20, "Ukrainians in the United States of America." The other three copies were sent to the State Department (Division of European Affairs and Department of Political Intelligence) and to the FBI.

74 See NAC, RG25 G1, vol. 1896, file 165, part 3, Overseas Security Bulletin, "Ukrainian Nationalists and the Germans," n.d.

75 USNA, RG226, entry 100, box 95, UK-1-10, memorandum of H. Regan on Ukrainian Americans, 27 February 1942.

76 NAC, RG25 G1, vol. 1896, file 165, part 3, A.J. Halpern to T.A. Stone, 22 February 1943.

77 USNA, State Department Records, M1286 reel 5, L. Henderson, comment on British Overseas Security Bulletin "Ukrainian Nationalists and the Germans," 20 May 1943.

78 Ibid., unidentified memorandum to London, 17 August 1943.

79 NAC, RG25 G1, vol. 1896, file 165, part 3, RCMP Commissioner S.T. Wood to N. Robertson, 4 June 1943.

80 Ibid., G. de T. Glazebrook to H. Allard, 25 June 1943; ibid., file 165, part 4, Allard to Glazebrook, 31 July 1943. Interestingly, the Ukrainian problem in North America was to provide the first occasion for extensive collaboration between the OSS and Canadian security officials: "Until recently I don't suppose we had anything to communicate to them." Ibid., file 165, part 3, Allard to Glazebrook, 13 July 1943.

81 See discussion in SAB, RGA26, file 25, "Protokoly zasidan Ekzekutyvy Komitetu Ukraintsiv Kanady" (Minutes of the Ukrainian Canadian Committee), 9 March 1943.

82 NAC, RG25 G1, vol. 1896, file 165, part 4, N. Robertson, "Memorandum of the Ukrainian Canadian Committee to Rt Hon. W.L. Mackenzie King," 23 March 1943. The original draft of the memorial excluded any reference to the Soviet Union. Only after considerable debate did the UCC executive feel that it was imperative that the statement should also be directed against the Soviet Union. Point 4 in the memorial was amended to include a more embracing statement that had in mind both Poland and the USSR: "They [the Ukrainian people] believe that in the postwar settlement their claims to an independent free state in a free Europe should not be disregarded and that the Ukrainian question should be included in any just and permanent settlement of Europe." See SAB, RGA26, file 25, "Protokoly zasidan

Ekzekutyvy Komitetu Ukraintsiv Kanady" [Minutes of the Ukrainian Canadian Committee], 16 March 1943.

83 SAB, RGA26, file 25, letter to G. Simpson from the Ukrainian Canadians, Alberta Division, 25 February 1943.

84 Editorial, *Vancouver News Herald*, 3 April 1943; and editorial, *Windsor Star*, 1 April 1943.

85 NAC, RG25 G1, vol. 1896, file 165-A, Department of National War Services, "TASS Bureau Report on the Ukrainian Canadian Committee," 1 April 1943.

86 Ibid., file 165, part 3, R.G. Riddell, "Memorandum Re: Ukrainian Canadians," 10 April 1943.

87 Ibid., A.J. Halpern to G. de T. Glazebrook, 19 May 1943.

88 Ibid., ciphered telegram from D. Wilgress to Rt Hon. W.L. Mackenzie King, 15 May 1943, and ciphered telegram, King to Wilgress, 15 May 1943.

89 For transcripts of the radio broadcasts, see PRO, Foreign Office Records, FO 371/36974, "Soviet Monitor: Radio Bulletins from the USSR. no. 2690," 15 May 1943. See also J.L. Black, *Canada and the Soviet Mirror*, 150. Excerpts from the Bogomolets article were also published under the title "A Hitlerite Agency in Canada," *Canadian Tribune*, 22 May 1943.

90 A. Bogomolets, *Soviet Ukraine and Ukraino-German Nationalists in Canada*, (Toronto: NEC-Ukrainian Canadian Association, n.d.).

91 The *Toronto Star* would editorialise, asking "What would be said in Canada if representatives of a little group of Canadian separatists who wish to set up an independent nation on the St. Lawrence were recognised in some allied country as the group entitled to favour as being representative of Canada." The *Vancouver Sun*, meanwhile, cautioned the government that the nationalists were threatening to embroil Canada and its Western allies in a war with the USSR. Editorial, *Toronto Star*, 15 May 1943; and *Vancouver Sun*, 25 June 1943.

92 Arkhiv vneshnei politiki SSSR, MID (hereafter ASSSR, MID), Fond 06 – Sekretariat Molotova, opis 5, papka 24, delo 265, F. Gusev, USSR minister plenipotentiary to Canada, "Zapis besedy s Robertsonom vo vremia zavtraka s nim 6 maia 1943 g." [Record of conversation with (N.) Robertson during breakfast, 6 May 1943], 14 May 1943.

93 NAC, RG25 G1, vol. 1896, file 165, part 3, N. Robertson, "Memorandum to the Prime Minister," 6 May 1943. When Robertson repeated his views to G. Tunkin, USSR chargé d'affaires, the Soviet official reported that the government was "embarrassed" and that "they were hoping the problem would disappear with time in Canada." See ASSSR, MID, Fond 06 – Sekretariat Molotova, opis 5, papka 24, delo 265, G. Tunkin, USSR chargé d'affaires, "Zapis besedy Poverennogo v Delakh

tov. Tunkina s Zam. Gosudarstvennogo Sekretaria po Inostrannym Delam g-nom Robertsonom 8 iiuliia 1943 g." [Record of conversation of Comrade Tunkin, chargé d'affaires, with the under-secretary of state for external affairs, Mr Robertson, 8 July 1943], 12 July 1943.

94 By way of contrast, the injudicious Wilgress would condemn the United States for its "tendency to support lost causes" and the U.S. State Department, in particular, for "[having] favoured reactionary rather than progressive elements in certain European countries." He noted that "the vested interests of Polish landowners, Latvian ship owners or Estonian politicians seem very insignificant in comparison with the major issues at stake, but the danger is that these vested interests can evoke the natural sympathy for the small country and the main issues can become blurred in the haze of endless debate to which such controversies give rise." NAC, W.L. Mackenzie King Papers, MG26, J1, vol. 353, reel C7047, D. Wilgress, Canadian minister to the USSR to the secretary of state for external affairs and prime minister, W.L. Mackenzie King, 6 May 1943.

For a brief discussion of Wilgress' views on Poland, especially in relation to the Soviet Union and the Western allies, see D. Page, "Getting to Know the Russians – 1943–48," in A. Balawyder, ed., *Canadian-Soviet Relations 1939–80* (Oakville: Mosaic Press, 1981), 21–2; and J.L. Granatstein, *The Ottawa Men: The Civil Service Mandarins 1935–57* (Toronto: Oxford University Press, 1982), 233.

95 NAC, RG25 G1, vol. 1896, file 165, part 3, ciphered telegram from D. Wilgress to W.L. Mackenzie King, 17 May 1943. See also J.L. Black, *Canada in the Soviet Mirror*, 159.

96 NAC, RG25 G1, vol. 1896, file 165, part 3, Wilgress to King, 17 May 1943.

97 Ibid., Wilgress to King, 19 May 1943.

98 Ibid., King to Wilgress, 15 May 1943, and N. Robertson to D. Wilgress, 28 May 1943.

99 Ibid., G. de T. Glazebrook, "Memorandum for the Under-Secretary," 12 September 1942.

100 Ibid.

101 Ibid., S.F. Rae to N. Robertson, 24 September 1942.

102 NAC, RG44, vol. 36, file "Committee on Co-operation," Justice T.C. Davis to N. Robertson, 25 September 1942.

103 Ibid.

104 Ibid., vol. 35, file "Bureau of Public Information," Justice T.C. Davis to G. Simpson, 28 September 1942. Justice Davis sent the following telegram: "Have consulted with External affairs and they expressed somewhat same fears I expressed yesterday but feel that you can keep meeting in control and restrict resolutions to one proposed by you

which seems to be satisfactory to all stop Under these circumstances can see no reason why you should not proceed Stop." See also NAC, RG25 G1, vol. 1896, file 165, part 3, Justice T.C. Davis to N. Robertson, 6 October 1942.

105 NAC, RG44, vol. 35, file "Bureau of Public Information," Justice T.C. Davis to G. Simpson, 1 October 1942.

106 Ibid.

107 Ibid., Davis to Simpson, 5 October 1942.

108 Ibid., N. Robertson to Justice T.C. Davis, 7 October 1942.

109 NAC, MG30 D2/2, vol. 4, file "J. Stechishin," 'Dorohyi brate' [Dear Brother], Julian Stechishin to Myroslav Stechishin, 12 October 1942.

110 NAC, RG44, vol. 36, file "Foreign Section-Ukrainians," G. Simpson to Justice T.C. Davis, 23 October 1942.

111 NAC, MG28, vol. 9, reel M2278, "Protokoly zasidan Ekzekutyvy Komitetu Ukraintsiv Kanady" [Minutes of the Ukrainian Canadian Committee], 6 October 1942; and SAB, RGA26, file 25, "Protokoly zasidan Ekzekutyvy Komitetu Ukraintsiv Kanady" [Minutes of the Ukrainian Canadian Committee], 13 October 1942, "Protokoly zasidan Ekzekutyvy Komitetu Ukraintsiv Kanady" [Minutes of the Ukrainian Canadian Committee], 17 October 1942, "Protokoly zasidan Ekzekutyvy Komitetu Ukraintsiv Kanady" [Minutes of the Ukrainian Canadian Committee], 27 October 1942, and "Protokoly zasidan Ekzekutyvy Komitetu Ukraintsiv Kanady" [Minutes of the Ukrainian Canadian Committee], 10 November 1942.

112 SAB, RGA26, file 25, A. Yaremovich to G. Simpson, 30 October 1942.

113 Significantly, Simpson commented that committee members had reservations about adopting a compromise position. The belief was that a political price would have to be paid in terms of the their own standing within the community, especially if the pro-Soviet Ukrainians discovered and publicised the fact "that the Canadian government ... advised the Committee to devote its attention to Canadian affairs exclusively." Ibid., Yaremovich to Simpson, 10 February 1943.

114 NAC, RG25 G1, vol. 1896, file 165, part 3, RCMP Intelligence Report, ref. no. D 945–1-Q-39 (10), "Ukrainian National Federation, 1943 Annual Convention, Winnipeg," together with N. Robertson, undersecretary of state for external affairs, to RCMP Commissioner S.T. Wood, 27 February 1943, and Wood to Robertson, 12 March 1943. See also Prymak, *Maple Leaf and Trident*, 89–90.

115 SAB, RGA26, file 25, "Protokoly zasidan Ekzekutyvy Komitetu Ukraintsiv Kanady" [Minutes of the Ukrainian Canadian Committee], 9 March 1943, "Protokoly zasidan Ekzekutyvy Komitetu Ukraintsiv Kanady" [Minutes of the Ukrainian Canadian Committee], 16 March 1943, "Protokoly zasidan Ekzekutyvy Komitetu Ukraintsiv Kanady"

[Minutes of the Ukrainian Canadian Committee], 23 March 1943; and NAC, MG28, vol. 9, reel M2278, "Protokoly zasidan Ekzekutyvy Komitetu Ukraintsiv Kanady" [Minutes of the Ukrainian Canadian Committee], 11 May 1943.

116 NAC, MG28, vol. 9, reel M2278, "Protokoly zasidan Ekzekutyvy Komitetu Ukraintsiv Kanady" [Minutes of the Ukrainian Canadian Committee], 11 May 1943.

117 NAC, RG25 G1, vol. 1896, file 165, part 3, L. Malania, "Note for File," 11 June 1943. On W. Swystun's resignation, see ibid., R.G. Riddell, "Note for the Under-Secretary, Re: W. Swystun," 11 June 1943. See also Prymak, Maple Leaf and Trident, 93.

118 NAC, RG25 G1, vol. 1896, file 165, part 3, R.G. Riddell, "Note, Re: All-Canadian Ukrainian Congress," 28 May 1943.

119 Prymak, Maple Leaf and Trident, 92.

120 NAC, RG2, series 18, vol. 43, file U-15-2, N. Robertson, "Note for the Prime Minister," 1 June 1943. A number of senior Cabinet ministers had by this time expressed an interest and a willingness to attend.

121 NAC, RG25 G1, vol. 1896, file 165, part 3, CN telegram from H.R. Henry, prime minister's office, to J.W. Arsenych, 14 June 1943. It was probably noticed among the UCC executive that the prime minister, having declined the offer to appear at the congress on the pretext of not being able to get away, did attend a Salute to Russia rally held at the same time as the UCC congress. See Kolasky, The Shattered Illusion, 44.

122 NAC, RG25 G1, vol. 1896, file 165, part 4, RCMP report, "The First Ukrainian Canadian Congress," n.d. The Department of External Affairs and the RCMP were not alone in their interest in the UCC Congress. The Americans obtained accurate information from their consular representative in Winnipeg and the British from intelligence sources. For their respective appraisals of the congress, see USNA, State Department Records, M1286 reel 5, American consul general, A. Kleinforth, to the U.S. secretary of state, 25 June 1943; and NAC, RG25 G1, vol. 1896, file 165, part 4, BSC report no. 426, "Canada: Ukrainian Groups and Mr Tracy Philipps," 12 October 1943.

The UCC Congress was also of interest to the Soviets, whose embassy officials compiled their own extensive report based primarily on press materials. See ASSSR, MID, Fond 06 – Sekretariat Molotova, opis 5, papka 24, delo 262, V. Pavlov, second secretary, USSR mission, "Sekretno. Kongress Profashistkikh Ukrainskikh Natsionalistov KUK" [Secret. Congress of the pro-fascist Ukrainian nationalists – UCC], 4 August 1943.

123 Pershyi vse-kanadiiskyi kongres ukraintsiv v Kanadi [First All-Canadian Congress of Ukrainians in Canada] (Winnipeg: Ukrainian Canadian

Committee, 1943). For a comprehensive account of the Congress, see Prymak, *Maple Leaf and Trident*, 94–6.

124 NAC, RG25 G1, vol. 1896, file 165, part 4, RCMP Report, "The First Ukrainian Canadian Congress," n.d. See also Prymak, *Maple Leaf and Trident*, 95.

125 "There is evidence ... that the conference leaders were concerned to avoid statements or discussions of a kind which would cause embarrassment to the Government or give ammunition to their Communist opponents, and on the whole they appear to have been very successful in this regard." In fact, it was pointed out that only one of the resolutions discussed and passed at the conference referred to the Ukrainian question and that this resolution was found to be unobjectionable since its wording was very general and guarded in nature. NAC, RG25 G1, vol. 1896, file 165, part 3, R.G. Riddell, "First All Canadian Ukrainian Congress: Winnipeg, June 22–24, 1943," n.d.

126 Ibid., H. Wrong to N. Robertson, 22 May 1943.

127 Ibid., G. de T. Glazebrook, "Meeting on Ukrainian Farmer Labour Temples," n.d.

128 On the campaign for the return of the seized Labour-Farmer Temples, see Petro Kravchuk, *Na novii zemli: Storinky z zhyttia, borotby i tvorchoi pratsi kanadskykh ukraintsiv* [In the New Land: Pages from the Life, Struggle and Work of Canadian Ukrainians] (Toronto: Tovarystva Obiednanykh Ukrainskykh Kanadtsiv, 1958), 320–1; and J. Kolasky, ed., *Prophets and Proletarians: Documents on the History of the Rise and Decline of Ukrainian Communism in Canada* (Edmonton: CIUS Press, 1990), 270–8.

129 NAC, RG25 G1, vol. 1896, file 165, part 3, N. Robertson to J. Grierson, director, Wartime Information Board, 17 May 1943.

130 German estimates of Soviet losses in the first two months of the war were 14,000 tanks, 14,000 pieces of artillery, 11,000 planes and 5 million men, of whom more than 1 million were said to be prisoners of war. Soviet figures for the same period were 5,500 tanks, 7,500 pieces of artillery, 4,500 planes and 700,000 soldiers. Unofficial sources indicated that as of November 1941, 3.6 million Soviet combatants had been taken as prisoners of war. Of this number 1.3 million were Ukrainians. USNA, State Department Records, M982, reel 69, "The Soviet Front from August 22–24," *Information Bulletin*, Soviet Information Bureau, Moscow, 24 August 1941. See also B. Krawchenko, *Social Change and National Consciousness in Twentieth Century Ukraine* (London: Macmillan Press, 1985), 154.

131 See, for example, PRO, Foreign Office Records, FO 371/22461, "Ukrainian Question," 10 January 1939; and FO 371/23056, "Ukraine," 2 February 1939. Reproduced in Luciuk and Kordan, *Anglo-American Perspectives*, 45–50.

132 USNA, State Department Records, M1286, reel 4, "Political Conditions in the Ukraine in October 1942," 16 December 1942, "General Conditions in the Ukraine in the Third Quarter of 1943 as Reflected in the German Controlled Press," 10 February 1944, "Conditions in the German-Occupied Ukraine in the Last Quarter of 1943," 19 April 1944; and ibid., M1286, reel 6, "Ukrainian Nationalist Movements," 29 May 1946. See also Y. Boshyk, ed., *Ukraine during World War II: History and its Aftermath* (Edmonton: CIUS Press, 1986).

133 PRO, Foreign Office Records, FO 371/43314, "Liberated Ukraine," 29 March 1944. On the character of the resistance in Soviet Ukraine, see Krawchenko, *Twentieth Century Ukraine*, 168–9.

134 British support for the idea of modified Ukrainian autonomy in Poland and possible independence is detailed in PRO, Foreign Office Records, FO 371/23138, "Note to Mr Makins from Mr Leeper," Foreign Office (Department of Political Intelligence), 20 October 1939; FO 371/23138, F. Savery, H.M.G. ambassador to the Polish Government-in-Exile to W. Strang, Foreign Office, 6 November 1939; FO 371/24473, "Memo of Conversation regarding Polish-Ukrainian rapprochement," 22 January 1940; and FO 371/24473, memo of E.S. Carlton, Department of Political Intelligence, Foreign Office, 5 March 1940. Reproduced in Luciuk and Kordan, *Anglo-American Perspectives*, 64–79.

135 NAC, RG2, series 18, vol. 43, file U-5, G. de T. Glazebrook, "Proposed Anglo-Russian Treaty," 14 April 1942. That Britain would resist any political change to pre-1939 Eastern Europe was also made clear by Anthony Eden in a private conversation with Marshall Stalin in December 1942, when the latter pressed for territorial concessions. See PRO, FO 181/963, "Transcript of Conversation between the British Foreign Secretary, the USSR Commissar for Foreign Affairs and Marshall Stalin," 17 December 1942. Reproduced in Luciuk and Kordan, *Anglo-American Perspectives*, 123–31.

136 For a transcript of the discussion between Churchill and Roosevelt on the Atlantic Charter, see USNA, State Department Records, M982, reel 69, "British American Co-operation," 11 August 1941.

137 USNA, Micro. Pub. M1221, OSS Research and Analysis Report no. 1972, "British and American Views on the Applicability of the Atlantic Charter," 2.

138 USNA, State Department Records, M982, reel 69, Berlin despatch, 15 August 1941, Tokyo despatch, 15 August 1941, Helsinki despatch, 19 August 1941; and Stockholm despatch, 15 August 1941.

139 USNA, Micro. Pub. M1221, OSS Research and Analysis Report no. 1972, "British and American Views on the Applicability of the Atlantic Charter," 7–8.

140 USNA, State Department Records, M982, reel 69, Ambassador Biddle to U.S. secretary of state, 7 August 1941.

141 NAC, MG30 E350, vol. 1, file 12, RCMP report, "Eighth National Convention of the Ukrainian National Federation of Canada and the Affiliated Sections," ref. no. D 945-1-Q-39, 30 September 1941. See also Stechishin, *Samostiinist, Sobornist, Federatsiia.*

142 NAC, RG25 G1, vol. 1896, file 165, part 3, Canadian minister to the USSR, D. Wilgress, to Rt Hon. W.L. Mackenzie King, prime minister and secretary of state for external affairs, 19 May 1943.

143 The moral imperative in maintaining a principled position in the war was not an abstraction but a profoundly important political consideration that weighed heavily on senior External Affairs officials. See, for example, the description in J. Hilliker, *Canada's Department of External Affairs: The Early Years, 1909–1946*, vol. 1 (Montreal and Kingston: McGill-Queen's University Press, 1990), 253.

144 Daniel Robinson notes the official distinction made between European and Japanese enemy aliens in 1938–39 and outlines the social and political factors that would influence the difference in the treatment of German and Italian Canadians, on one hand, and Japanese Canadians, on the other. The relatively benign attitude the government adopted with respect to Ukrainian Canadians follows this argument. See D. Robinson, "Planning for the 'Most Serious Contingency': Alien Internment, Arbitrary Detention and the Canadian State, 1938–39," *Journal of Canadian Studies*, 28, no. 2 (summer 1993): 8–11.

CHAPTER FOUR

1 National Archives of Canada (NAC), Tracy Philipps Papers, MG30 E350, vol. 1, file 21, Ukrainian Canadian Committee (Toronto Branch) to T. Philipps, 24 June 1941.

2 Ibid., file 6, T. Philipps to unidentified correspondent, 25 June 1941.

3 Ibid.

4 Ibid., file 21, T. Philipps to External Affairs, 24 June 1941; NAC, RG44, vol. 36, file "Foreign Section – Ukrainians," CN telegram from T. Philipps to Justice T.C. Davis, 26 June 1941; and NAC, RG25 G1, vol. 1896, file 165, part 3, RCMP Commissioner S.T. Wood to the under-secretary of state for external affairs, Norman Robertson, 26 June 1941.

5 NAC, RG44, vol. 36, file "Foreign Section – Ukrainians," Philipps to Davis, 28 June 1941.

6 Ibid.

7 NAC, RG25 G1, vol. 1896, file 165, part 3, ciphered telegram from the secretary of state for external affairs to the Canadian high commissioner (London), n.d.. See also Public Records Office of the United Kingdom (PRO), Foreign Office Records, FO 29332, "Pro-Ally Ukrainians in France," 9 July 1941.

8 NAC, RG44, vol. 35, file "Bureau of Public Information," Justice T.C. Davis to the Hon. J.T. Thorson, 27 June 1941.

9 The proposal appears to have paralleled a discussion in the Department of National War Services about creating a committee that would deal with the "foreign-born" issue, the deputy minister raising the subject with the minister, J. Gardiner. See Dreisziger, "The Rise of a Bureaucracy for Multiculturalism: The Origins of the Nationalities Branch, 1939–41," in N. Hillmer, B. Kordan, and L. Luciuk, eds., *On Guard for Thee: War, Ethnicity and the Canadian State, 1939–45* (Ottawa: Canadian Committee for the History of the Second World War, 1988), 13.

10 NAC, MG30 E350, vol. 1, file 16, T. Philipps, "Tour of Western Canada: November-December 1940," 8 January 1941.

11 Ibid., file "Kaye Correspondence with T. Philipps, 1941," T. Philipps, "Hemisphere Defence. Foreign-born Population. Positive Co-operation. Part II. Canada." 13 May 1941.

12 Ibid.

13 Ibid., file 16, T. Philipps, "Tour of Western Canada: November-December 1940," 8 January 1941.

14 Ibid., vol. 2, file "Kaye Correspondence with T. Philipps, 1941," T. Philipps, "Hemisphere Defence. Foreign-Born European Populations in the Americas," 1 May 1941.

15 See Dreisziger, "The Rise of a Bureaucracy," 16.

16 NAC, MG30 E350, vol. 1, file 24, T. Philipps to Rt Hon. Malcolm MacDonald, British High Commission, 4 September 1941.

17 Ibid., Philipps to MacDonald, 27 September 1941.

18 Dreisziger, "The Rise of a Bureaucracy," 18; and Leslie Pal, "Identity, Citizenship and Mobilization: The Nationalities Branch and World War Two," *Canadian Public Administration,* 32, no. 3 (fall 1989): 415.

19 NAC, RG44, vol. 35, file "Bureau of Public Information," Justice T.C. Davis to Professor G. Simpson, 18 October 1941.

20 Ibid., vol. 36, file "Committee on Co-operation," T. Philipps, "Memorandum on the Establishment of a Committee on Cultural Group Co-operation to Advise the Minister of National War Services," n.d.; and NAC, MG30 E350, vol. 1, file 16, T. Philipps, "Tour of Western Canada: November-December 1940," 8 January 1941.

21 NAC, RG44, vol. 36, file "Committee on Co-operation," T. Philipps, "Memorandum on the Establishment of a Committee on Cultural Group Co-operation to Advise the Minister of National War Services," n.d.

22 NAC, MG30 E350, vol. 2, file "Kaye Correspondence with T. Philipps, 1941," T. Philipps, "Proposed European Section for War Services, and Canadianization of Immigrant Europeans," 22 October 1941.

23 University of Saskatchewan Archives (USA), George Simpson Papers, box 1, file "Citizenship Division, 1940–46," "Interdepartmental Meeting on Organisation of Proposed Committee on Cultural Group Co-operation under Ministry of National War Services," 1 November 1941.

24 NAC, RG44, vol. 36, file "Committee on Co-operation," Justice T.C. Davis to the under-secretary of state for Canada, Dr E.H. Coleman, 28 October 1941. See also ibid., vol. 35, file "Bureau of Public Information," Justice T.C. Davis, "Memorandum for Mr G.H. Lash," 23 October 1941.

25 The organisational and administrative structure of the Committee on Co-operation in Canadian Citizenship is outlined in the report "Advisory Committee on Co-operation in Canadian Citizenship (Nationalities Branch), Part I," n.d. USA, Simpson Papers, box 1, file "Citizenship Division, 1940–46." See also Leslie Pal, "Identity, Citizenship, and Mobilization: The Nationalities Branch and World War Two," 415–16.

26 Philipps had hoped to secure the position of Director of the Nationalities Branch but apparently was passed over, since Robertson "was not in favour of giving him an 'administrative' position, as opposed to the 'roving commission' he held at the time." Dreisziger, "The Rise of a Bureaucracy," 19.

27 NAC, RG26, vol. 1, file 22-2, part 1, T. Philipps, "Communist Labour Halls and Other Closed Community Centres," 13 January 1941. Philipps revised the report in August 1941, and the extract dealing with halls was resubmitted in October.

28 Ibid.

29 Ibid., vol. 4, file 33-s-1, C. Smith to G. Simpson, 30 December 1941.

30 Ibid., Simpson to Smith, 9 January 1942.

31 Ibid.

32 See for example, NAC, RG26, vol. 9, file 46-1, editorial, *Ukrainske zhyttia* [Ukrainian Life], 22 January 1942.

33 Ibid., vol. 1, file 22-2, part 1, G. Simpson to W. Burianyk, 19 March 1942.

34 See J. Kolasky, *The Shattered Illusion: The History of Ukrainian Pro-Communist Organizations in Canada* (Toronto: PMA Books, 1979), 34–5.

35 Canada, Parliament, *House of Commons Debates*, 6 March 1942, 1094; and *House of Commons Debates*, 9 March 1942, 1117.

36 NAC, RG26, vol. 6, file 34-L-2, D.J. Prystash to G.H. Lash, director of public information, 15 March 1942. See also NAC, RG14, vol. 2, file 56, letter of Mrs M.P. Prokopchak, 30 May 1942. The campaign is described in I. Avakumovic, *The Communist Party of Canada: A History* (Toronto: McClelland and Stewart, 1975), 150–1.

37 NAC, RG26, vol. 6, file 34-K-2, W. Kossar to G. Simpson, 10 February 1942. See also NAC, RG25 G1, vol. 1896, file 165, part 3, "Memorandum: Re Enclosed Letter from W. Kossar," n.d., together with instructions to district commanding officers, "New Opportunities for Recruits," n.d.

38 NAC, O. Woycenko Papers, MG30 D2/2, vol. 4, file "J. Stechishin, 'Dorohyi brate'" [Dear Brother], Julian Stechishin to Myroslav Stechishin, 9 April 1942.

39 NAC, RG25 G1, vol. 1896, file 165, part 3, G. Simpson, "Mr Hlynka's Speech on the Ukrainian Question," 4 April 1942. See also Kolasky, *The Shattered Illusion*, 68–9.

40 See the discussion in J.L. Granatstein, *Conscription in the Second World War* (Toronto: Ryerson Press, 1969), 41–4.

41 NAC, RG44, vol. 35, file "Bureau of Public Information," Justice T.C. Davis to G. Simpson, 19 March 1942.

42 Department of External Affairs Records (DEA), file 3846-40c, "The Ukrainian Canadian Committee: Communiqué on Plebiscite," n.d.

43 See Thomas M. Prymak, *Maple Leaf and Trident: The Ukrainian Canadians during the Second World War* (Toronto: Multicultural History Society of Ontario, 1988), 70–1.

44 For a statistical survey of the voting patterns of the various groups, see DEA, file 3182-40, Gallup Poll Report, 4 March 1943. See also Prymak, *Maple Leaf and Trident*, 71–2; and L. Luciuk and B. Kordan, *Creating a Landscape: A Geography of Ukrainians in Canada* (Toronto: University of Toronto Press, 1989), map 22 "Conscription Plebiscite, 1942."

45 NAC, RG26, vol. 6, file 34-K-2, W. Kossar to G. Simpson, 10 May 1942. See also NAC, MG30 E350, vol. 1, file 32, I. Hanchard, "The Ukrainians and the Plebiscite," copy of letter to the editor, *Yorkton Enterprise*, 14 May 1942. Simpson would describe Hanchard's letter as "the best single comment on the plebiscite from a Ukrainian point of view."

46 In response to criticism from the *Winnipeg Free Press*, members of the UCC executive privately met with the editor of the paper, J. Dafoe. Outlining their assessment of the results, the *Free Press* would later issue a retraction. Several arguments were made that they claimed explained the confusion among the Ukrainians and/or their rejection of the government position, including the "close co-operation between the Canadian government and the Left elements"; the government's "silence ... with respect to the Ukrainian Question in Europe"; the counterproductive activity of the opposition parties, which "claimed that a 'Yes' vote was a vote for the Liberal Party"; and the prospect of "economic ruin" on the farm as a result of the conscription of the

young men. See NAC, Ukrainian Canadian Congress Papers, MG28, vol. 9, reel 2778, "Protokoly zasidan Ekzekutyvy Komitetu Ukraintsiv Kanady" [Minutes of the Executive of the Ukrainian Canadian Committee], 30 April 1942. For a comprehensive discussion of the reaction to the plebiscite, see Prymak, *Maple Leaf and Trident*, 73–6.

47 NAC, MG30 E350, vol. 1, file 32, G. Simpson to J.W. Estey, office of the Saskatchewan attorney general, 2 June 1942.

48 Ibid., file 30, T. Philipps, "Brief Report, as Asked, for the Personal Information of General LaFleche, Minister of National War Services, on the (a) Origin, (b) Aim and (c) Functions of the Nationalities Branch," 26 December 1942.

49 Ibid., file 32, Justice T.C. Davis to G. Simpson, 2 June 1942.

50 NAC, RG26, vol. 6, file 24-K-2, transcript of CKPR (Fort William) broadcast, 13 May 1942.

51 See Prymak, *Maple Leaf and Trident*, 77–8.

52 W. Kardash, *Hitler's Agents in Canada*, (Toronto: Morris Printing, 1942). A veteran of the Spanish Civil War and a member of both the banned Communist Party of Canada and the Ukrainian Labour Farmer Temple Association, William Arthur Kardash was elected 22 April 1941 to the Manitoba legislature as a Labour Progressive Party candidate. He would represent the heavily populated ethnic Ukrainian constituency of Winnipeg-North. In June 1942, Kardash became president of the national association The Communist Total War Committee.

53 NAC, MG30 E350, vol. 1, file 32, W. Burianyk to G. Simpson, 3 June 1942.

54 NAC, RG26, vol. 6, file 34-U-1, T. Philipps to I. Maclennan, Office of the High Commissioner for the United Kingdom, 27 March 1942.

55 Ibid., Philipps to Maclennan, 25 April 1942.

56 NAC, RG44, vol. 36, file "Committee on Co-operation," "Summary of Conference between the Hon. J.T. Thorson, the Hon. Justice T.C. Davis, G. Simpson and T. Philipps," 9 June 1942.

57 NAC, MG30 E350, vol. 2, file "Committee on Co-operation, June 1942," T. Philipps, "Memorandum on Broadcasting to Canadian Communities of Recent European Origin," 12 June 1942.

58 Ibid.

59 Ibid., T. Philipps, "External Broadcasting for Canada," 14 June 1942.

60 NAC, RG26, vol. 1, file 22-2, part 1, T. Philipps to Mr Lash, 27 June 1942.

61 NAC, MG30 E350, vol. 2, file "Committee on Co-operation, January 1942," T. Philipps, "Nationalities Branch: Canadian Communities of Recent European Origin. Survey and Construction Period, 1941–42," n.d.

62   NAC, RG26, vol. 1, file 22-2, part 1, T. Philipps memorandum to the under-secretary of state for external affairs, "Subject: The General Attack by Communist Ukrainians on the United Ukrainian Canadian Committee and on the Nationalist Ukrainian Group within the Committee," 17 July 1942.

63   Ibid.

64   NAC, MG30 E350, vol. 2, file "Committee on Co-operation, July 1942," T. Philipps, "The Meaning of the 1ST of May Manifesto by the Communist Party of Canada to the Canadian People, 1941," n.d.

65   NAC, RG25, acc. no. 83/84–259, box 223, file 4174-40, T. Philipps to Justice T.C. Davis, 21 July 1942.

66   The under-secretary of state, Norman Robertson, was of the same view. At a dinner, in conversation with G. Tunkin, the Soviet chargé d'affaires, Robertson, reportedly in an intoxicated state, voiced his opinion that Stalin's Russia represented Thermidor, that the experiment of the October Revolution had ended, and that the Soviet Union "was falling back on old traditions." Robertson, however, went further, claiming, rather extraordinarily, that the USSR "was evolving toward Western democracy." As a senior government official, Robertson stated that he welcomed the "change" as did the Canadian government but also added that personally, as a "liberal," he "regretted that which has transpired." Arkhiv vneshnei politiki SSSR, MID (ASSSR, MID), Fond 06 – Sekretariat Molotova, opis 5, papka 24, delo 267, G. Tunkin, USSR chargé d'affaires, "Zapis razgovor na obede 15 sentabria 1943 g." [Record of Dinner Conversation, 15 September 1943], 23 October 1943; and ibid., S. Kudriatsev, first secretary, USSR mission, "Zapis besedy c pomoshchnikom Gosudarstvennogo Sekretaria po Inostrannym Delam Kanady Norman Robertsonom" [Record of Conversation with the Under-Secretary of State for Canadian External Affairs, Norman Robertson], 23 October 1943.

67   NAC, RG36/31, vol. 13, file 8-9-1A, T. Philipps, "The All-Slavic Movement in North America," 25 June 1942.

68   Ibid.

69   Ibid.

70   Ibid.

71   NAC, RG25, acc. no. 83/84–259, box 223, file 4174-40, Justice T.C. Davis to N. Robertson, 1 September 1942.

72   Ibid., S.F. Rae, "The Pan Slavic Movement in Canada," 31 July 1942.

73   Ibid.

74   The position of External Affairs, as elaborated by Rae, was formally repeated to Philipps on two separate occasions by Norman Robertson and the assistant under secretary of state for external affairs, Hume Wrong. Nothing, however, was said to Philipps indicating that his

usefulness was being questioned. See ibid., N. Robertson to T. Philipps, 10 September 1942, and H. Wrong, assistant under-secretary of state for external affairs, to T. Philipps, 12 September 1942.

75 Ibid., G. de T. Glazebrook, "Memorandum to the Under-Secretary," 4 September 1942.

76 NAC, MG30 E350, vol. 2, file "Committee on Co-operation, September 1942," T. Philipps, "Note for the File," 4 September 1942.

77 NAC, RG14, vol. 2, file 36, secret report prepared for the Defence of Canada Regulations Committee, "The Communists," n.d.

78 Kolasky, *The Shattered Illusion*, 36; Avakumovic, *The Communist Party of Canada*, 151. For copies of literature used in the mail campaign by the Saskatoon Council for Democratic Rights, see NAC, RG14, vol. 2, file 40, "Lift the Ban from the Communist Party," n.d. For copies of literature used in the public campaign by the *Canadian Tribune*, Civil Liberties Bureau, see ibid., file 39, "Re: The Lifting of the Ban on the Communist Party of Canada, et al." The Civil Liberties Association, on behalf of the ULFTA, also submitted a formal brief before the special parliamentary committee "with a request to the Committee that it recommend the amendment of Section 39c by striking out the name of, and thus restoring legality to, the above named Association." See ibid, vol. 1, file 10, "Re: Ukrainian Labour Farmer Temple Association," brief of L. Cohen, counsel, 11 July 1942.

Ontario Premier Mitchell Hepburn, Liberal MP Arthur Roebuck, and the Very Reverend Peter Bryce, Moderator of the United Church, were among the more prominent personalities calling for a lift on the ban. A host of other politicians at the municipal level also protested. See, for example, ibid., vol. 2, file 39, F.N. Clarke, alderman, City of Saskatoon, to the Hon. J. Michaud, DCR Committee, 15 July 1942.

79 Canadian Institute of Public Opinion (CIPO), "Opinion Splits Fairly Evenly on Issue of Releasing 'Reds,'" 17 October 1942. Overall Canadian public opinion was moderately in favour of release (44 percent for, 39 percent against, 17 percent undecided). Regional differences, however, were pronounced. In Ontario, 38 percent were opposed to release. By way of contrast 80 percent in Catholic Quebec supported the policy of continuing internment, reflecting a widespread and deep antipathy to the notion of any accommodation with the CPC.

80 After twenty-six meetings, the final decision of the Special Commons Committee on the Defence of Canada Regulations recommending amendment to the DCR was ignored. See NAC, RG14, vol. 3, file 91, House of Commons [Commons Committee on DCR], "Second and Final Report," n.d.

81 NAC, RG25, acc. no. 83/84–259, box 223, file 4174-40, L.B. Pearson, minister counsellor (Washington) to N. Robertson, under-secretary of

state for external affairs, 3 October 1942. According to the State Department official, U.S. authorities were favourably disposed toward the movement and would work quietly behind the scenes insofar as it was thought "[the] movement had a chance of uniting the various Slavic groups, at least to the extent of preventing open conflicts." Berle, however, conceded that "there were so many conflicting elements in the movement that an eventual breakup seemed likely."

82 Ibid., Robertson to Pearson, 6 October 1942.

83 NAC, MG30 E350, vol. 2, file "Committee on Co-operation, October 1942," Ukrainian National Federation (Provincial Executive for Eastern Canada) to the Minister of Justice, 19 October 1942; and NAC, RG25 G1, vol. 1896, file 165, part 3, Association of Canadian Ukrainians (National Executive Committee) to N. Robertson, 7 November 1942.

84 See NAC, RG25, acc. no. 83–84/259, box 213, file 3866-F-40, excerpts with notes, *Ukrainske zhyttia*, 3 September 1942.

85 NAC, RG25 G1, vol. 1896, file 165, part 3, G. de T. Glazebrook, "Policy toward Foreign Groups," 2 July 1942. Reproduced in L.Y. Luciuk and B. Kordan, *Anglo-American Perspectives on the Ukrainian Question: A Documentary Collection* (Kingston, ON: Limestone Press, 1987), 110–13.

86 NAC, RG44, vol. 36, file "Committee on Co-operation," Justice T.C. Davis to N. Robertson, 25 September 1942.

87 See W.R. Young, "Chauvinism and Canadianism: Canadian Ethnic Groups and the Failure of Wartime Information," in Hillmer et al. (eds.), *On Guard for Thee: War, Ethnicity and the Canadian State, 1939–45*, 38–9; W.R. Young, "'A Highly Intelligent and Unselfish Approach': Public Information and the Canadian West, 1939–45," in *Canadian Historical Review*, 62, no. 4 (1981): 502–3; and Pal, "Identity, Citizenship, and Mobilization: The Nationalities Branch and World War Two," 417.

88 NAC, RG44, vol. 36, file "Committee on Co-operation," "Memorandum of Conference," 24 September 1942.

89 Ibid., vol. 35, file "Bureau of Public Information," Justice T.C. Davis to G. Simpson, 5 October 1942; and ibid., vol. 36, file "Committee on Co-operation," Justice T.C. Davis to T. Philipps, "Re: Functions and Administrative Place, Nationalities Branch," 2 November 1942.

90 NAC, MG30 E350, vol. 2, file "Committee on Co-operation – Correspondence, August 1942," T. Philipps to Hon. A. Knatchbull-Hugesson, 15 August 1942.

91 Ibid., vol. 1, file 30, T. Philipps, "Memorandum for the Deputy Minister and for the Committee," 25 September 1942.

92 Ibid.

93 NAC, RG36/31, vol. 13, file 8-9-1A, T. Philipps, "Political Controversies Reflected in the Press of Canada," 7 October 1942.

94 NAC, RG25, acc. no. 83/84–259, box 223, file 4174-40, T. Philipps, "The Pan-Slavic Movement in the Americas. Report on Conditions," 13 October 1942.

95 Ibid.

96 NAC, RG44, vol. 36, file "Committee on Co-operation, T. Philipps," T. Philipps, "Memorandum: Functions and Administrative Place of the Virtual Nationalities Branch of the Department of National War Services," 24 October 1942.

97 Ibid.

98 "It is becoming increasingly evident that the Wartime Information Board and the Department of External Affairs will and must co-operate in the closest possible way, and in my opinion, this ever-growing co-operation in functioning between the Wartime Information Board and External Affairs is going to make it much more satisfactory for you to be part and parcel of the Wartime Information Board." Ibid., Justice T.C. Davis to T. Philipps, "Re: Functions and Administrative Place, Nationalities Branch," 2 November 1942.

99 Ibid., vol. 26, file "Foreign Section – Ukrainians," G. Simpson to Justice T.C. Davis, 23 October 1942.

100 Ibid., Justice T.C. Davis to N. Robertson, 26 October 1942.

101 NAC, RG36/31, vol. 13, file 8-9-1, "Mr Philipps Goes to Washington," The Hour, 26 September 1942. Rather extraordinarily, Philipps' trip to Washington caught the attention of President Roosevelt, who, personally concerned about the allegations, asked the U.S. secretary of state to make enquiries about Philipps' mission. See USNA, RG59, Department of State Decimal File, 1940–44: 800.20211/1030, Secretary Sumner Welles to President Roosevelt, "My dear Mr President," 6 October 1942.

102 NAC, RG36/31, vol. 13, file 8-9-1, R. Gordon, Canadian Tribune, to Major General L.R. LaFleche, minister of national war services, 29 October 1942.

103 See ibid., Major General LaFleche to N. Robertson, 2 November 1942; T. Philipps, "Response to invitation by the Globe and Mail," 1 November 1942; and Justice T.C. Davis to Major General LaFleche, 7 November 1942.

104 NAC, MG30 E350, vol. 2, file "Committee on Co-operation, November 1942," T. Philipps, note for the file marked "Secret," n.d.

105 Ibid., vol. 1, file 29, R.A. Davies to C. Vining, Public Information Bureau, 21 December 1942.

106 Ibid., vol. 2, file "Committee on Co-operation, November 1942," T. Philipps to Justice T.C. Davis, 9 November 1942.

107 NAC, RG36/31, vol. 13, file 8-9-1, D.B. Rogers to A. Dunton, Wartime Information Board, 13 November 1942. See also Young, "Chauvinism and Canadianism," 40.

108 NAC, RG44, vol. 35, file "Bureau of Public Information," Justice T.C. Davis to General LaFleche, "Memorandum: Re Committee on Co-operation in Canadian Citizenship," 13 November 1942.

109 NAC, RG36/31, vol. 13, file 8-9-1, G. Simpson to Justice T.C. Davis, 17 November 1942.

110 Ibid., Davis to Simpson, n.d.

111 Ibid., D. Cameron to Justice T.C. Davis, 21 November 1942.

112 NAC, MG30 E350, vol. 2, file "Committee on Co-operation, November 1942," T. Philipps to J.W. Dafoe, 16 November 1942.

113 Ibid., T. Philipps, "Note: The Committee on Co-operation in Canadian Citizenship," 25 November 1942.

114 By November 1942 the Department of National War Services had undergone massive reorganisation due to the frequent changes at the level of the minister and the deputy minister as responsibility for various functions shifted in and out of the department because of a poorly defined mandate. See Pal, "Identity, Citizenship, and Mobilization," 412–14.

115 NAC, MG30 E350, vol. 1, file 30, T. Philipps, "Brief Report, as Asked, for the Personal Information of General LaFleche, Minister of National War Services, on the (a) Origin, (b) Aim and (c) Functions of the Nationalities Branch," 26 December 1942.

116 Ibid., vol. 2, file "Committee on Co-operation, January 1942," T. Philipps, "Note on Field Work," 13 January 1943.

117 Saskatchewan Archives Board (SAB), George Simpson Papers, RGA26, box 1, file 26, G. Simpson to A. Yaremovich, Executive Secretary, Ukrainian Canadian Committee, 28 December 1942. For text of resolution see ibid., file 25, "Protokoly zasidan Ekzekutyvy Komitetu Ukraintsiv Kanady" [Minutes of the Executive of the Ukrainian Canadian Committee], 15 December 1942. The Aid to Russia campaign was sponsored by the charitable organisation Canadian Aid to Russia Fund (CARF), which sought to coordinate relief efforts to the USSR. The pro-Soviet Ukrainian Association to Aid the Fatherland, which had been organising Soviet relief since 1941, agreed to participate in the campaign.

118 NAC, RG25 G1, vol. 1896, file 165, part 3, N. Robertson to J. Horbatiuk, chairman, Association of Canadian Ukrainians, 28 December 1942.

119 Ibid., file 165-A, Department of National War Services – Cable Telegraph Telephone Censorship, "TASS Cablegrams."

120 Raymond Arthur Davies, *This Is Our Land. Ukrainian Canadians against Hitler* (Toronto: Progress Books, 1943).

121 NAC, RG25 G1, vol. 1896, file 165, part 3, Secret RCMP Report, Division D, Intelligence Section, ref. no. D 945-1-Q-39 (10), "Ukrainian National Federation 1943 Annual Convention," 18 January 1943. Although unsure of which of the two "poisons" was worse, the Intelligence Section of the RCMP felt obliged to offer the suggestion that "with proper supervision and immediate action, when and if necessary, this organisation [UNF] might yet be made to serve a useful purpose."

122 Ibid., G. de T. Glazebrook, Department of External Affairs, to A.J. Halpern, British Security Co-ordination, 30 March 1943.

123 Although Philipps refrained from commenting publicly, Watson Kirkconnell, a member of the Advisory Committee on Canadian Co-operation and Citizenship and a right-wing ideologue, gladly took up the "challenge." He responded to the allegations in the Davies book by publishing his own equally inflammatory account, *Seven Pillars of Freedom* (London and Toronto: Oxford University Press, 1944). See Prymak, *Maple Leaf and Trident*, 103–4.

124 NAC, MG30 E350, vol. 1, file 33, T. Philipps to G. Simpson, 14 May 1943.

125 See Young, "Chauvinism and Canadianism," 43.

126 NAC, RG2, series 18, vol. 20, file W-34-5, Wartime Information Board, "Joint Memorandum," 25 March 1943.

127 NAC, RG36/31, vol. 13, file 9-9-3, General Manager, Canadian Broadcasting Corporation, to J. Grierson, Wartime Information Board, 11 May 1943, and J. Grierson to G. de T. Glazebrook, 15 May 1943.

128 NAC, RG2, series 18, vol. 43, file U-15-2, N. Robertson to J. Grierson, 17 May 1943. Reproduced in Luciuk and Kordan, *Anglo-American Perspectives*, 134–6.

129 NAC, RG44, vol. 35, file "Bureau of Public Information," Justice T.C Davis to the Hon. J.T. Thorson, minister of national war services, 27 June 1941. Davis' recommendation echoed similar remarks made by the under-secretary, Norman Robertson. See J.L. Granatstein, "Changing Alliances: Canada and the Soviet Union, 1939–45," in David Davies, ed., *Canada and the Soviet Experiment: Essays on Canadian Encounters with Russia and the Soviet Union, 1900–91* (Toronto and Waterloo: Centre for Russian and East European Studies/Centre on Foreign Policy and Federalism, n.d.), 77.

130 See B. Kordan, "Soviet-Canadian Relations and the Ukrainian Ethnic Problem," *Journal of Ethnic Studies*, 13, no. 2 (summer 1985): 1–3.

131 Saul Rae of the Department of External Affairs, for example, thought Philipps was motivated by a strong anti-Soviet bias. NAC, RG25 acc. no. 83/84-259, box 223, file 4174-40, S.F. Rae, "The Pan-Slavic Movement in Canada," 31 July 1942.

132 This is not to suggest that Philipps was without a strong sense of public service. He was deeply committed, which perhaps explains why he was originally brought into the ranks of government service as a specialist-adviser. But as a largely unpaid adviser, he also did not have the same responsibilities or allegiance to "office" as did his peers.

133 NAC, MG30 MGE 350, vol. 2, file "Kaye Correspondence with T. Philipps, 1941," T. Philipps, "Hemisphere Defence, Foreign-Born Population, Positive Co-operation. Part 2. Canada," 13 May 1941.

134 Ibid., passim; NAC, RG44, vol. 36, file "Committee on Co-operation," T. Philipps, "Memorandum on the Establishment of a Committee on Cultural Group Co-operation to Advise the Minister of National War Services," n.d.; NAC, MG30 E350, vol. 1, file 16, T. Philipps, "Tour of Western Canada: November-December 1940," 8 January 1941; ibid., vol. 2, file "Committee on Co-operation, June 1942," T. Philipps, "Memorandum on Broadcasting to Canadian Communities of Recent European Origin," 12 June 1942; NAC, RG36/31, vol. 13, file 98-9-1a, T. Philipps, "The All-Slavic Movement in North America," 25 June 1942; NAC, MG30 E350, vol. 1, file 30, T. Philipps, "Memorandum for the Deputy Minister and for the Committee," 25 September 1942; and NAC, RG44, vol. 36, file "Committee on Co-operation," T. Philipps, "Memorandum: Functions and Administrative Place of the Virtual Nationalities Branch of the Department of National War Services," 24 October 1942.

135 NAC, MG30 E350, vol. 1, file 16, T. Philipps, "Tour of Western Canada: November-December 1940," 8 January 1941.

136 On the department's efforts at acquiring an intelligence capacity, see J. Hilliker, *Canada's Department of External Affairs: The Early Years, 1909–1946*, vol. 1 (Montreal and Kingston: McGill-Queen's University Press, 1990), 268–9.

137 NAC, RG25 G1, vol. 1896, file 165, part 3, G. de T. Glazebrook, "Policy toward Foreign Groups," 2 July 1942.

CHAPTER FIVE

1 For an extensive discussion of the Wartime Information Board, see W.R. Young, "Making the Truth Graphic: The Canadian Government's Home Front Information Structure and Programs during World War Two." Unpublished PHD dissertation, University of British Columbia, 1978.

2 G. Evans, *John Grierson and the National Film Board: The Politics of Wartime Propaganda* (Toronto: University of Toronto Press, 1984); and Young, "Making the Truth Graphic."

3 See W.R. Young, "'A Highly Intelligent and Unselfish Approach': Public Information and the Canadian West, 1939–45," *Canadian Historical Review* 62, no. 4 (1981): 503.

4 Commenting on Grierson's NFB documentary war films, the film historian Peter Morris notes that they were decidedly didactic and infused with a "stridency that seems calculated more to bludgeon the viewer into mute submission than to stimulate reasoned reflection." Grierson made no apology about the approach or its intent, claiming that "You can't sell the war as you would cornflakes. You may have at times to make people believe what they ought to believe rather than what they want to believe." Peter Morris, "After Grierson: The National Film Board, 1945–53," *Journal of Canadian Studies*, 16, no. 1 (spring 1981): 4; and Evans, *John Grierson and the National Film Board*, 124.

5 National Archives of Canada (NAC), RG2, series 18, vol. 53, file W-34, J. Grierson, "The Necessity and Nature of Public Information," 3 June 1943. See also W.R. Young, "Building Citizenship: English Canada and Propaganda during the Second War," *Journal of Canadian Studies*, 16, no. 3–4 (autumn 1981): 125–6.

6 NAC, RG2, series 18, vol. 53, file W-34, J. Grierson, "The Necessity and Nature of Public Information," 3 June 1943.

7 NAC, RG36/31, vol. 13, file 8-9-1, T. Philipps, "Tentative Draft for a Circular Letter for Issue by Censorship or Wartime Information Board," 5 December 1942, and "Confidential Note Covering the Draft," 7 December 1942, T. Philipps to D.B. Rogers, Wartime Information Board, 4 January 1943, and Philipps to Rogers, 29 January 1943.

8 Ibid., A.D. Dunton, Wartime Information Board, to T. Philipps, 1 March 1943.

9 Ibid., Philipps to Dunton, 4 March 1943.

10 Ibid., Dunton to Philipps, 12 March 1943.

11 W.R. Young, "Chauvinism and Canadianism: Canadian Ethnic Groups and the Failure of Wartime Information," in N. Hillmer, B. Kordan, and L. Luciuk, eds., *On Guard for Thee: War, Ethnicity and the Canadian State, 1939–45* (Ottawa: Canadian Committee for the Study of the Second World War, 1988), 42–3.

12 NAC, RG36/31, vol. 13, file 8-9-1, J. Grierson to H.R.L. Henry, office of the prime minister, 5 March 1943. There was some evidence to suggest that this hostility was occurring, although Grierson was definitely overstating the case. The overwhelming tendency, given the irreconcilable differences over the future of East Galicia/Western Ukraine, was for Poles and Ukrainian nationalists in Canada to regard each other with suspicion and hostility. See A. Reczyńska, "Ukrainians and the 'Ukrainian Question' As Seen by Poles during the Second World War," *Journal of Ukrainian Studies*, 16, no. 1–2 (summer-winter 1990): 195–210.

13 NAC, RG2, series 18, vol. 20, file W-34-5, "Joint Memorandum," 25 March 1943.

14 NAC, RG36/31, vol. 13, file 8-9-1, CBC General Manager to J. Grierson, 11 May 1943.

15 More generally, however, the department showed a keen interest in the board because of its external activites. J. Hilliker, *Canada's Department of External Affairs: The Early Years, 1909–1946*, vol. 1 (Montreal and Kingston: McGill-Queen's University Press, 1990), 274.

16 After conducting a public opinion survey in April 1943 and detecting "ambivalent and conflicting" attitudes toward the Soviet Union among certain Canadian groups, the WIB recommended an approach to public information that would improve the image of the Soviet Union among Canadians. The approach would stress that the Soviet Union had retreated from its ideological origins and that it was now a trusted ally of the liberal democracies. Moreover, the Soviets were portrayed as a people not unlike Canadians, and it was implied that the tolerance and respect for minorities mirrored a nonaggressive foreign policy. See J.L. Granatstein, "Changing Alliances: Canada and the Soviet Union, 1939–45," in David Davies, ed., *Canada and the Soviet Experiment: Essays on Canadian Encounters with Russia and the Soviet Union, 1900–91* (Toronto and Waterloo: Centre for Russian and East European Studies/ Centre of Foreign Policy and Federalism, n.d.), 80. The work of the NFB in promoting a sympathetic image of the USSR in 1943–44 – especially in its *World in Action* and *Canada Carries On* series – is discussed in Evans, *John Grierson and the National Film Board*, 200–10.

17 NAC, RG2, series 18, vol. 43, file U-15-2, N. Robertson, under-secretary of state for external affairs to J. Grierson, WIB, 17 May 1943. See also ibid., N. Robertson, "Memorandum for the Prime Minister," 1 June 1943. "The position of the Ukrainian Nationalist organisations in Canada is becoming more delicate and more difficult as the war develops. Their historic feud with the Poles is in danger of becoming a row with the Russians, which is a more serious question ... If you have read my letter to Grierson of the 16th, you will see that the Government's contacts with the foreign language press and the foreign language groups generally are pretty confused and unsatisfactory. I hope to get the Wartime Information Board to straighten out the press side of the picture, but I am more worried about the possible mischief which may develop from the activities of the Foreign Groups Division [Nationalities Branch] of the Department of National War Services."

18 NAC, RG36/31, vol. 13, file 8-9-2, "Ukrainian Question," 4 June 1943. Reproduced in B. Kordan and L.Y. Luciuk, *A Delicate and Difficult Question: Documents in the History of Ukrainians in Canada, 1899–1962* (Kingston, ON: Limestone Press, 1986), 100–3.

19 NAC, RG36/31, vol. 13, file 8-9-1, M. Ross to D. Buchanan, 7 June 1943.

20 Ibid., file 8-9-2, "Minutes of WIB Meeting no. 15," 14 June 1943.

21 NAC, RG25 GI, vol. 1896, file 165, part 3, N. Robertson, under-secretary of state for external affairs to Justice T.C. Davis, Canadian high commissioner to Australia, 25 June 1943.

22 NAC, RG2, series 18, vol. 12, file w-34-7, J. Grierson to A.D.P. Heeney, clerk of the privy council and secretary to the cabinet, 28 June 1943. See also ibid., vol. 53, file w-34, J. Grierson, "Observations on the Co-ordination of Information," 23 June 1943.

23 Ibid., vol. 12, file w-34-7, A.D.P. Heeney to N. Robertson, 30 June 1943.

24 Ibid., vol. 53, file w-34, A.D.P. Heeney to D. Gordon, chairman, Wartime Prices and Trade Board, 28 June 1943.

25 Ibid., vol. 12, file w-34-7, Heeney to Robertson, 30 June 1943.

26 Ibid., vol. 53, file w-34, Heeney to Gordon, 2 July 1943.

27 NAC, RG25 GI, vol. 1896, file 165, part 3, G. de T. Glazebrook, Department of External Affairs, to A.J. Halpern, British Security Co-ordination, 30 March 1943.

28 NAC, RG25, acc. no. 83/84–259, box 234, file 4595-L-40, D. Wilgress, Canadian minister to the USSR, to W.L. Mackenzie King, secretary of state for external affairs and prime minister, 14 April 1943.

29 NAC, RG25 GI, vol. 1896, file 165, part 3, N. Robertson to Prime Minister W.L. Mackenzie King, 6 May 1943, D. Wilgress to W.L. Mackenzie King, 15 May 1943, and King to Wilgress, 15 May 1943.

30 Ibid., Wilgress to King, 17 May 1943.

31 Ibid., Wilgress to King, 19 May 1943.

32 NAC, RG25, acc. no. 83/84–268, box 274, file 5496-40, A. Smith, "Prosperity is Indivisible," 18 May 1943.

33 Ibid.

34 Smith's preoccupation with Canada's postwar position and his hawk-ish ideas on the Soviet Union would later earn him considerable notori-ety. See Denis Smith, *Diplomacy of Fear: Canada and the Cold War 1941–48* (Toronto: University of Toronto Press, 1988), 75–82; Lawrence Aronsen and Martin Kitchen, *The Origins of the Cold War in Comparative Perspective: American, British, and Canadian Relations with the Soviet Union, 1941–48* (London: Macmillan Press, 1988), 169–70; and Reg Whitaker and Gary Marcuse, *Cold War Canada: The Making of a National Insecurity State, 1945–57* (Toronto: University of Toronto Press, 1994), 118–19.

35 King's assessment was correct. Soviet officials noted that the Ukrainian nationalists relied on the Atlantic Charter to legitimise Ukraine's inde-pendence claim. See, for example, Arkhiv vneshnei politiki SSSR, MID (ASSSR, MID), Fond 06 – Sekretariat Molotova, opis 5, papka 24, delo 269, K. Novikov, USSR Commissariat for Foreign Affairs,

2d European Department, "Sekretno. Spravka vrazhdebnye SSSR ukrainskie natsionalisticheskie organizatsii v Kanade" [Secret. Information on Ukrainian Nationalist Organisations in Canada Hostile to the USSR], 11 May 1943.

36 For an autobiographical account, see *Dana Wilgress: Memoirs* (Toronto: Ryerson Press, 1967); and "From Siberia to Kuibyshev: Reflections on Russia, 1919–43," *International Journal*, 22 (summer 1967): 364–75.

37 D. Page "Getting to Know the Russians – 1943–48," in A. Balawyder, ed., *Canadian-Soviet Relations, 1939–80* (Oakville, ON: Mosaic Press, 1981), 15–28; J.L. Granatstein, *The Ottawa Men: The Civil Service Mandarins 1935–57* (Toronto: Oxford University Press, 1982), 232–4; and Smith, *Diplomacy of Fear*, 45–9, 58–60.

38 In April 1945, at the San Francisco conference on postwar security where he participated, Wilgress would privately confide to a colleague after negotiations with the Soviets had failed that he felt he had "misled the government in his prophecies about the moderate line which [the Soviet Union] were likely to adopt after the war." Smith, *Diplomacy of Fear*, 85.

39 NAC, RG2, series 18, vol. 43, file U-15-2, N. Robertson, "Note for the Prime Minister," 1 June 1943.

40 "The chances of Soviet co-operation are endangered if we do not give to them the active help they think they need in driving the Germans from Soviet territory and if we do not pay due regard to their vital interests in eastern Europe. The delay in opening the second front, the dispute over Poland, or a clash with the Soviet Union over the Baltic states may spoil the chances of Soviet co-operation and turn this country into an aggressor state." NAC, W.L. Mackenzie King Papers, MG26, J1, reel C7047, D. Wilgress to Prime Minister W.L. Mackenzie King, 23 September 1943.

41 NAC, MG26 J4, vol. 336, file 3650, "Restoration of Property of Ukrainian Farmer Labour Temples," 7 June 1943.

42 NAC, RG25 G1, vol. 1896, file 165, part 3, G. de T. Glazebrook to N. Robertson, 15 June 1943, and N. Robertson to Justice T.C. Davis, 25 June 1943.

43 Ibid., L. Malania, "Note for File," 11 June 1943. See also ibid., R.G. Riddell to N. Robertson, 11 June 1943.

44 "In these centres the authority of leaders of European origin is still effective, and the younger generation are being held to old ways of living. This situation is aggravated by the unwillingness of the few young people who do leave the community for higher education to return to an environment which they wish to reject. It is thought in Winnipeg that the hard core of Ukrainian nationalism may be found in isolated

rural communities of this nature." Ibid., R.G. Riddell, "Memorandum re: Canadian Ukrainians," 6 July 1943.

45 *A Program and Record* (Winnipeg and Saskatoon: Ukrainian National Federation, 1943).

46 NAC, RG25 G1, vol. 1896, file 165-39c, part 4, copy of letter "Dear Mr Kossar," n.d. See also ibid., G. de T. Glazebrook to N. Robertson, 14 June 1943.

47 United States National Archives and Records Service (USNA), State Department Records, M1286, reel 5, A.W. Klieforth, American consul general to the U.S. secretary of state, 1 April 1943.

48 USNA, State Department Records, M1286, reel 5, Klieforth to the U.S. secretary of state, 25 June 1943.

49 Ibid., S. Welles, U.S. under-secretary of state, "Possibility of Increased Co-operation between Ukrainian Nationalists and Nazis in the Other American Republics," 23 August 1941. Reproduced in Luciuk and Kordan, *Anglo-American Perspectives on the Ukrainian Question: A Documentary Collection, 1938–51* (Kingston, ON: Limestone Press, 1987), 98–9.

50 NAC, RG25 G1, vol. 1896, file 165-39c, part 3, G. de T. Glazebrook to H. Allard, Canadian Legation, Washington, 25 June 1943; ibid., file 165, part 4, Allard to Glazebrook, 13 July 1943, and Allard to Glazebrook, 31 July 1943.

51 See ibid., file 165-39c, part 4, J. Garner, Office of the High Commissioner, to S.F. Rae, Department of External Affairs, 19 July 1943, N. Robertson to A.J. Halpern, British Security Co-ordination, 2 August 1943, G. de T. Glazebrook to H. Sichel, British Security Co-ordination, 16 September 1943; ibid., file 165-A, BSC report no. 428, "Ukrainian Activities in the Argentine," 12 October 1943, and BSC report no. 426, "Canada: Ukrainian Groups and Mr Philipps," 12 October 1943.

52 Ibid.

53 NAC, RG25, acc. no. 83/84–259, box 234, file 4595-L-40, D. Wilgress to Prime Minister W.L. Mackenzie King, 7 July 1943. See also J.L. Black, *Canada in the Soviet Mirror: Ideology and Perception in Soviet Foreign Affairs, 1917–91* (Ottawa: Carleton University Press, 1998), 152.

54 ASSSR, MID, Fond 06 – Sekretariat Molotova, opis 5, papka 24, delo 262, V. Pavlov, 2d secretary, USSR mission to Canada, "Sekretno. Kongress Profashistkikh Ukrainskikh Natsionalistov KUK" [Secret. Congress of Pro-Fascist Ukrainian Nationalists – UCC], 4 August 1943, and ibid., delo 269, K. Novikov, USSR Commissariat for Foreign Affairs, 2d European Department, "Sekretno. Spravka vrazh- debnye SSSR ukrainskie natsionalisticheskie organizatsii v Kanade"

[Secret. Information on Ukrainian nationalist organisations in Canada hostile to the USSR], 11 May 1943. Head of the Second European Department, Mr Novikov was the chief Soviet foreign ministry official responsible for Soviet-Canadian affairs.

55 NAC, RG2, series 18, vol. 12, file W-41, secretary of state for dominion affairs (London) to the secretary of state for external affairs (Ottawa), "Secret Circular D. 544," 14 August 1943, and "Secret Circular D. 545," 14 August 1943.

56 Ibid., "Secret Circular D. 714," 29 September 1943: "Apart from constitutional difficulties, acceptance of this separate representation would imply recognition by all participants in the Commission of Soviet Union's claims to the Baltic States, Eastern Poland, etc. and would prejudge the whole frontier question. Russians must know that their suggestion is impracticable for this reason alone until all Governments represented on the Commission recognise these claims."

57 Ibid., N. Robertson to the assistant under-secretary of state, H. Wrong, "Most Secret Cipher no. H-43," 15 August 1943, and Wrong to Robertson, "Most Secret Cipher no. H-46," 16 August 1943.

58 In April 1943, for example, Wilgress, in conversation with the Soviet foreign ministry official S. Lozovskii, lamented the fact that Canada was unable to secure representation on key postwar planning committees, to which Lozowskii responded that Canada's interests were already well represented by Britain. Wilgress would reply that Canada and Britain shared only their allegiance to the Crown and that Canada was following and would continue to follow an independent foreign policy. See J.L. Black, "Canada and the Soviet Union in 1945: The View from Moscow," in G. Donaghy, ed., *Uncertain Horizons: Canadians and Their World in 1945* (Ottawa: Canadian Committee for the History of the Second World War, 1997), 292–3.

59 NAC, RG25, acc. no. 83/84–259, box 234, file 4595-L-40, D. Wilgress to the secretary of state for external affairs, 7 July 1943. Wilgress would attribute the Soviet attitude to an inability "to understand the subtleties of the constitution of the British Commonwealth." He would remark, "Being clever and conscientious men they will have read all the documents, but being brought up on the German conception of government they are incapable psychologically of comprehending the fine distinction between allegiance to an English sovereign and independence of English rule." NAC, MG26, J1, reel C7060, D. Wilgress, Canadian minister to the USSR to the secretary of state for external affairs, W.L. Mackenzie King, 10 February 1944.

60 NAC, RG2, series 18, vol. 12, file W-41, King to Wilgress, 28 August 1943.

61 Since the issue was also of concern to Australia, the Australian chargé d'affaires, Keith Officer, accompanied Wilgress to the meeting with Molotov. The conversation with Molotov is reproduced in ASSSR, MID, Fond 06 – Sekretariat Molotova, opis 5, papka 24, delo 268, V. Molotov, "Sekretno. Priem Poverennogo v Delakh Avstralii Offisera i Poslannika Kanady Uilgressa, 9 sentiabria 1943 g. v 18 chas" [Secret. Reception of the Australian chargé d'Affaires [Keith] Officer and the Canadian envoy [Dana] Wilgress, 9 September, 6 o'clock], 9 September 1943. Canada's formal position was outlined and delivered in an aide-mémoire. See ibid., "Pamiatnaia zapiska" [aide-mémoire], 9 September 1943. See also NAC, RG2, series 18, vol. 12, file W-41, H. Wrong, "Memorandum for the Prime Minister," 11 November 1943.

62 Ibid., copy of Soviet aide-mémoire to United Kingdom government, 18 October 1943.

63 Ibid., secretary of state for dominion affairs (London) to the secretary of state for external affairs (Ottawa), "Secret Circular D. 1077," 8 December 1943.

64 Ibid., secretary of state for external affairs to the secretary of state for dominion affairs, 10 December 1943.

65 NAC, MG26, J1, reel C7060, D. Wilgress to Prime Minister W.L. Mackenzie King, 18 January 1944. "Crisis calls for statesmanship of high order. United Kingdom Government should make clear to Polish Government that they can no longer count on Allied support in their quarrel with the Soviet Union. Reorganisation of Polish Government is first prerequisite to situation of problem. United Kingdom Government should offer to consult with Soviet Government about reorganisation of Polish Government so as to make it more representative of the ideals for which they will be fighting. This may be unwarranted interference in Polish Affairs but it is better than waiting until another Government is set up with Soviet support. It is also in the best interests of Polish Government and Poland. Recommend you urge these views on London since Foreign Office have shown little understanding of Soviet point of view in their handling of the Polish problem."

66 ASSSR, MID, Fond 06 – Sekretariat Molotova, opis 6, papka 39, delo 494, Molotov, "Sekretno. Priem kanadskogo posla Uilgressa," [Secret. Reception of the Canadian envoy Wilgress], 28 February 1944.

67 NAC, RG25 G1, vol. 1896, file 165, part 4, N. Robertson to the Prime Minister, 4 July 1944. Reproduced in Kordan and Luciuk, *A Delicate and Difficult Question*, 113–15.

68 Arguably, the Teheran Conference, held December 1943, proved to be the first occasion where some indication was given that Britain was prepared to meet the Soviet Union on the issue of Poland's eastern borders. In British governing circles, there was a growing sense that

precious little could be done to help the Poles on the frontiers question. From now on, the Polish frontier question – the Curzon Line or some variation thereof – was to serve as leverage in Anglo-Soviet diplomacy. The point was no longer how to restore but how to maintain Britain's political role in Eastern Europe before the USSR had consolidated its position in the region, a matter that would become central to British negotiations with the Soviet leadership in October 1944. For a brief discussion of the evolving character of the British position on Poland's eastern frontiers, see Aronsen and Kitchen, *The Origins of the Cold War in Comparative Perspective*, 91–9.

69 NAC, RG25 G1, vol. 1896, file 165, part 4, N. Robertson to the Prime Minister, 4 July 1944.

70 Ibid.

71 ASSSR, MID, Fond 06 – Sekretariat Molotova, opis 5, papka 24, delo 266, V. Pavlov, second secretary, USSR mission to Canada, "Sekretno. Zapis besedy s Dzhon Rid, Iuridicheskim Sovetnikom Ministerstva Inostrannykh Del Kanady" [Secret. Record of Conversation with John Read, Legal Counsellor, Canada's Department of External Affairs], 14 May 1943.

72 NAC, RG25 G1, vol. 1896, file 165, part 3, G. de T. Glazebrook to N. Robertson, 23 June 1943.

73 NAC, Tracy Philips Papers, MG30 E350, vol. 1, file 29, C.H. Payne, deputy minister, to General LaFleche, minister of national war services, 11 August 1943. See also ibid., vol. 2, file "Committee on Co-operation – Correspondence, September 1943," T. Philipps, "The Matter Comes to a Head," 14 September 1943.

74 Ibid., vol. 2, file "Committee on Co-operation – Correspondence, August 1943," T. Philipps, "Nunc Dimittis Domine ...," 27 August 1943.

75 Ibid., vol. 2, file "Committee on Co-operation – Correspondence, September 1943," T. Philipps, "Off the Record Notes," 15 September 1943: "It is a platitude to state that a senior official who bears the responsibility for executing difficult work in the field has a right to expect *positive and constructive* guidance from his Minister. So far, for nearly a year, we have received only warnings and criticisms which constitute only a *negative and destructive* attitude. It does not need either intelligence or anyone of the calibre of a Cabinet Minister to criticise. Any man on the street can do that."

76 Ibid., T. Philipps, "The Position," 13 September 1943; and Saskatchewan Archives Board (SAB), George Simpson Papers, RGA26, file 25, T. Philipps to G. Simpson, n.d. "External Affairs, to whom I had hoped to look for understanding and support, have always been very jealous. In fact, but not in manner, they have always been hostile.

When our then Minister (Thorson) and I came, as was natural, under fire and slander from the Communists ... External Affairs seemed to wish to confuse Communist Canadians with Soviet Russians 'whom you must not offend.' That department prepared to appease the wolves, if they attacked and howled loud enough, by throwing them the heads of a few cheap government servants on a charger." See also NAC, MG30 E350, vol. 1, file 33, T. Philipps to G. Simpson, 1 October 1943.

77 NAC, MG30 E350, vol. 2, file "Committee on Co-operation – Correspondence, September 1943," V.J. Kaye to T. Philipps, 21 September 1943, and G. Simpson to T. Philipps, 22 September 1943. Simpson's letter of resignation to the minister read in part: "My reason for resigning is the conviction reluctantly reached that your department has no plan or policy with respect to the above Committee or the Nationalities Branch with which it has been connected ... the Nationalities Branch was left without adequate help or direction to the very great discouragement of those in charge, and to the obvious detriment of the work already begun. I believe the work for which the Committee was originally set up ... is no less important now than at the time of establishment. Indeed I believe the need is even more urgent. It is therefore with great regret that I find it necessary to submit my resignation."

78 Ibid., vol. 1, file 29, C.H. Payne to the minister of national war services, 24 September 1943.

79 NAC, MG26 J4, vol. 376, file 3944, J. Grierson to General L.R. LaFleche, minister of national war services, 28 October 1943. After meeting with Grierson, the executive head of the Canadian Unity Council, R. Fletcher, submitted a memorandum repeating the council's discontent with the Nationalities Branch. Mr Fletcher, however, may have exceeded his authority in making a representation on behalf of the council to the government. The council claimed to represent thirty-four member organisations, the largest of which was the Ukrainian Canadian Committee. However, the UCC, in its submission to the minister of national war services, expressed strong support for the branch. See NAC, RG36/31, vol. 13, file 8-9-1A, R. Fletcher, Canadian Unity Council, to J. Grierson, WIB, 13 November 1943; and NAC, MG30 E350, vol. 1, file 29, Ukrainian Canadian Committee to General LaFleche, 15 November 1943. See also W.R. Young, "'A Highly Intelligent and Unselfish Approach': Public Information and the Canadian West, 1939–45," *Canadian Historical Review*, 62, no. 4 (1981): 504–5.

80 *Vestnik*, 20 October 1943, as quoted in NAC, RG36/31, vol. 13, file 8-9-2, "Special Report for the Press Censors of Canada," 26 October 1943. See also NAC, RG2, series 18, vol. 12, file W-34-7, "Special Report for the Chief Press Censors of Canada, regarding

the 27 November Editorial of the Italian Language Publication *La Vittoria*."

81 See, for example, NAC, RG25 G1, vol. 1896, file 165-39c, part 4, "A Ukrainian Speaks," letter to the editor, *The Gazette*, 8 November 1943; NAC, RG36/31, vol. 13, file 8-9-2, "Special Report for the Chief Press Censors," 6 November 1943; and NAC, RG2, series 18, vol. 12, file W-34-7, "Special Report for the Chief Press Censors of Canada," 29 November 1943.

82 NAC, MG30 E350, vol. 1, file 29, H.W. Winkler, member of parliament, to the Hon. Gen. L.R. LaFleche, minister of national war services, 5 November 1943.

83 Ibid., LaFleche to Winkler, 12 November 1943.

84 NAC, MG26 J4, vol. 376, file 3944, N. Robertson to the Prime Minister, 1 November 1943; and University of Saskatchewan Archives (USA), George Simpson Papers, box 1, file "Citizenship Division, 1940–46," G. Ferguson to G. Simpson, 13 November 1943. See also W.R. Young, "Chauvinism and Canadianism: Canadian Ethnic Groups and the Failure of Wartime Information," in *On Guard for Thee*, 44.

85 A debate on the activities of the Nationalities Branch did take place in April 1944, when the question of appropriations for the continued operation of the Committee on Co-operation was raised on the floor of Parliament. For the text of the debate, see Canada, Parliament, *House of Commons Debates*, 1944, 2395–422. See also Prymak, *Maple Leaf and Trident*, 102.

86 NAC, RG35/7, vol. 16, file 4, England Report, appendix 4, "Nationalities Branch: Relations with the Wartime Information Board," 12 June 1944.

87 W.R. Young, "Chauvinism and Canadianism: Canadian Ethnic Groups and the Failure of Wartime Information," 45. See also Evans, *John Grierson and the National Film Board*, 228–9.

88 NAC, RG35/7, vol. 16, file 4, England Report, appendix 7, "Speech of General LaFleche to Canadian Legion," 12 June 1944.

89 NAC, RG36/31, vol. 13, file 8-9-3, minutes of meeting between Nationalities Branch, WIB, External Affairs, 12 June 1944; and NAC, RG35/7, vol. 16, file 3, R. England Report, "Advisory Committee on Co-operation in Canadian Citizenship, Part II," 12 June 1944.

90 NAC, RG36/31, vol. 13, file 8-9-3, R.A. Draper to A.D. Dunton, 13 June 1944.

91 NAC, RG35/7, vol. 16, file 3, England Report, "Advisory Committee on Co-operation in Canadian Citizenship, Part II," 12 June 1944.

92 NAC, MG30 E350, vol. 2, file "Committee on Co-operation – Correspondence, March 1944," T. Philipps to C.H. Payne, deputy minister of national war services, 15 March 1944.

93 USA, George Simpson Papers, box 1, file "Citizenship Division, 1940–46," Philipps to Simpson, 11 May 1944.

94 NAC, RG series 18, vol. 12, file W-34-7, L. Malania to the assistant under-secretary of state for external affairs, H. Wrong, 15 June 1944.

95 USNA, Records of the Office of Strategic Services, RG226, Entry 100, box 119, FNB-Int-33, "Ukrainian-American Nationalists Resigned but Pessimistic," 29 August 1944.

96 NAC, RG25 G1, vol. 1896, file 165, part 4, A.J. Halpern, British Security Co-ordination to G. de T. Glazebrook, 16 August 1944. Reproduced in Luciuk and Kordan, *Anglo-American Perspectives*, 152–3.

97 USA, George Simpson Papers, box 1, file "Ukrainian Files – 1930–57," Ukrainian Canadian Committee, "Canadian Ukrainian Refugee Fund," October 1944.

98 Department of External Affairs Records (DEA), file 2514-40c, N. Robertson to G. Pifher, Director of Voluntary and Auxiliary Services, Department of National War Services, 15 November 1944. Reproduced in Kordan and Luciuk, *A Delicate and Difficult Question*, 132–3.
    The director of auxiliary services was also told by Robertson that under no condition was he to communicate the views of the department on Ukrainian statelessness: "These are stated here only for your confidential information."

99 Ibid.

100 Ibid. A similar permit was denied Ukrainians in the United States by the president's War Relief Control Board. The Ukrainian American Relief Committee was advised to get in touch with Russian War Relief or other agencies authorised to administer relief in the Soviet Union. As for relief to Ukrainian refugees in other European countries, the board explained that it was to be "transmitted through relief committees of the respective country" and that Ukrainian Americans consequently should contact existing committees in Britain, France, Poland, or whereever Ukrainian refugees may be found. USNA, Records of the Office of Strategic Services, RG226, entry 100, box 98, UK-331–340, "Permit Denied to Ukrainian Relief Committee in Philadelphia," 6 January 1945. The Ukrainian Canadian Committee would eventually be extended a license to operate a relief agency called the Ukrainian Canadian Relief Fund.

101 Ukrainian nationalist participation in relief efforts for the Soviet Union was debated from the outset, including during the first public campaign announced in December 1942. Although the UCC declined to participate, there was agreement that the UCC's constituent organisations could do so freely if they chose. See SAB, George Simpson Papers, RGA26, box 1, file 25, "Protokoly zasidan Ekzekutyvy Komitetu Ukraintsiv Kanady" [Minutes of the Executive of the Ukrainian Canadian Committee], 15 December 1942.

For a survey of the various currents of thought in the Ukrainian-Canadian community on the question of war relief, see USNA, Records of the Office of Strategic Services, RG226, entry 100, box 119, FNB-Int-33, report no. 205, "The Ukrainians in Canada," 8 August 1944.

102 CARF, a "blue ribbon" committee, was granted a license under the War Charities Act on 23 December 1942. Although several East European aid societies, including the Ukrainian Association to Aid the Fatherland, had been organising relief since July 1941, at the beginning of 1943 CARF would take the lead in coordinating the relief effort for the USSR. On CARF, see Granatstein, "Changing Alliances: Canada and the Soviet Union, 1939–45," 81. On the relationship between the Ukrainian relief effort and CARF and, more generally, on the war work of the Ukrainian Association to Aid the Fatherland, see Peter Krawchuk, *Na novii zemli: Storinky z zhyttia, borotby i tvorchoi pratsi kanad-skykh ukraintsiv* [In the New Land: Pages from the Life, Struggle and Work of Canadian Ukrainians] (Toronto: Tovarystva Obiednanykh Ukrainskykh Kanadtsiv, 1958), 309–14; and J. Kolasky, *Prophets and Proletarians: Documents on the History of the Rise and Decline of Ukrainian Communism in Canada* (Edmonton, AB: CIUS Press, 1990), 265–7.

103 NAC, RG25, acc. no. 83/84–259, box 235, file 4603-40, "In Answer to Aid to Russia Fund," *Ukrainskyi robitnyk* [Ukrainian Toiler], 6 April 1945. See also ibid., Aid to Russia Fund to the editor, *Ukrainskyi robitnyk*, 29 March 1945.

104 Ibid., H.F. Skey, Aid to Russia Fund, to N. Robertson, under-secretary of state for external affairs, 29 March 1945, and Skey to Robertson, 25 April 1945.

105 See NAC, RG25, acc. no. 83/84–259, box 274, file 5496-40, L. Malania to H. Wrong, 24 August 1944, and N. Robertson to D. Wilgress, 31 August 1944.

106 Ibid., box 213, file 3866-F-40, W. Baldwin, chief censor of publications, Directorate of Censorship, to G. de T. Glazebrook, 28 August 1944, together with "Special Report for the Chief Press Censors of Canada," 24 August 1944.

107 Ibid., W. Baldwin to Rev. I. Shpytkovsky, editor, *Buduchnist natsii* [Nation's Future], 28 August 1944.

108 Ibid., Rev. I. Shpytkovsky to W. Baldwin, 31 August 1944, and G. de. T. Glazebrook, "Memorandum for the Legal Adviser," 9 September 1944.

109 Ibid., "Memorandum for Mr Glazebrook," 11 September 1944, and J.E. Read, assistant under-secretary of state for external affairs, to the deputy minister of justice, 20 September 1944. Section 135 of the Canadian Criminal Code reads, "Everyone is guilty of an indictable offence and

liable to one year's imprisonment who, without lawful justification, publishes any libel tending to degrade, revile or expose to hatred and contempt in the estimation of the people of any foreign state, any prince or person exercising sovereign authority over such a state."

110 Ibid., F.P. Varcoe, deputy minister of the department of justice, to the under-secretary of state, 26 September 1944; G. de T. Glazebrook to W. Baldwin, 28 September 1944; and G. de T. Glazebrook to Mr MacDougal, 13 September 1944.

111 NAC, RG25 G1, vol. 1896, file 165-39c, part 4, L. Malania to H. Wrong, 31 June 1944. See also ibid., N. Robertson, under-secretary of state for external affairs, to E.H. Coleman, under-secretary of state for Canada, 21 June 1944. The Civil Liberties Association produced a pamphlet in July entitled *The Case of the Seized Properties of the Ukrainian Labour-Farmer Temple Association: An Appeal for Justice* (Toronto: Civil Liberties Association of Toronto, 1944).

112 NAC, RG25 G1, vol. 1896, file 165-A, R.G. Riddell to N. Robertson, 19 June 1944.

113 NAC, RG2, series 18, vol. 43, file U-15-2, "Memorandum," 27 September 1944, A.D.P. Heeney, clerk of the privy council to the Hon. N. McLarty, secretary of state, 28 September 1944, and W. Haliday to J. Pickersgill, 3 October 1944.

114 Ibid., Heeney to McLarty, 24 January 1945. Three buildings in Calgary, Lethbridge, and Medicine Hat were not returned but, rather, were compensated for after long negotiations. For a full description of the final disposition of the halls and the concluded arrangements, see Krawchuk, *Na novii zemli*, 322–3; and I. Boichuk, *Borotba za lehalizatsiiu TURFDim* [The Struggle for the Legalisation of the ULFTA] (Toronto: TSVK/TURFDim, 1948).

115 See NAC, RG25, G1, vol. 1896, file 165-A, part 4, H. Wrong to the prime minister, 27 January 1945: "A movement has been started up among the anti-Soviet Ukrainians to stimulate a demand for the creation of an independent Ukrainian state. In present circumstances it is not easy to imagine a movement less likely to succeed in its purpose. I am inclined to think that none of these resolutions should be acknowledged unless the movement results in some further development which requires that notice be taken of it." King wrote in the margin of the memorandum: "I agree certainly."

116 NAC, RG2, series 18, vol. 12, file W-34-10, Wartime Information Board, "Memorandum to Members of the Cabinet," 26 February 1945.

117 See NAC, RG25 G1, vol. 1896, file 165-A, part 4, L. Malania to H. Sichel, British Security Co-ordination, 10 May 1945. Swystun's remarks were also monitored by the American intelligence service, the OSS. See USNA, RG226, entry 100, box 119, FNB-Int-33, "Ukrainian Communist-

Line Paper Reports Support for Ukrainian SSR from Ukrainian Separatist," 13 March 1945. For Swystun's position after leaving the nationalist camp, see his *Ukrainske pytannia v svitli voiennykh podii* [The Ukrainian Question from the Point of View of the War], (Winnipeg, MB: National Publishers, 1945).

118 NAC, O. Woycenko Papers, MG30 D2/2, vol. 4, file "M. Stechishin," "Dear Brother" – Michael Stechishin to Myroslav Stechishin, 23 February 1945, and "Dorohyi brate" [Dear Brother] – Michael Stechishin to Myroslav Stechishin, 5 May 1945. For a description of other prominent nationalist activists who advocated a more conciliatory attitude toward the Soviet Union, see J. Kolasky, *The Shattered Illusion: The History of Ukrainian Pro-Communist Organizations in Canada* (Toronto: PMA Books, 1979), 49, 79–80.

119 NAC, MG30 D2/2, vol. 4, file "M. Stechishin, 'Dorohyi Mykhaile'" [Dear Micheal], Myroslav Stechishin to Michael Stechishin, 24 February 1945, and "Dorohyi Mykhaile" – Myroslav Stechishin to Michael Stechishin, 27 February 1945. The argument is similarly made by Myroslav Stechishin, "Ukraina u povoiennym sviti" [Ukraine in the Postwar World] in *Na porozi novoii doby* [On the Eve of a New Era], (Winnipeg, MB: Ukrainian Self-Reliance League, 1945), 45–55.

120 Canada. Parliament. *House of Commons Debates*, 1945, 226–30; J. Kolasky, *The Shattered Illusion*, 74; and Prymak, *Maple Leaf and Trident*, 119–21.

121 NAC, RG25 F6, vol. 1022, file 139, "Memorandum to the Canadian Delegation at the United Nations Conference on International Organization from the Ukrainian Canadian Committee," 18 May 1945. The text of the UCC memorandum was virtually identical to one that was submitted to the American delegation by the Ukrainian Congress Committee of America. The groups had laboured jointly on a draft of the memorandum at a specially held preparatory meeting in Ottawa. For a copy of the Ukrainian-American memorandum, see USNA, RG226, entry 100, box 98, UK-351-360, "Memorandum of the Ukrainian Congress Committee of America re: United Nations Conference on International Organization," 14 May 1945.

122 USNA, RG226, entry 100, box 98, UK-351–360, Dewitt C. Poole to the U.S. secretary of state, 14 May 1945. Reproduced in Luciuk and Kordan, *Anglo-American Perspectives*, 159–60. See also ibid., Dewitt C. Poole, "Memorandum for the American Delegation," 4 May 1945; and USNA, State Department Records, M1286, reel 6, FBI Report, "Ukrainian American Council," 3 April 1945.

123 See Prymak, *Maple Leaf and Trident*, 124.

124 NAC, RG25 G1, vol. 1896, file 165 39C, part 4, Ukrainian Canadian Committee, "Memorandum for the Prime Minister," 23 May 1945.

125 NAC, RG25 F6, vol. 1022, file 139, D. Wilgress to N. Robertson, 25 May 1945. Reproduced in Luciuk and Kordan, *Anglo-American Perspectives*, 161.

126 NAC, MG26 J4, vol. 336, file 3650, assistant under-secretary of state, J.E. Read to the prime minister, 4 June 1945.

127 Ibid. See also NAC, RG25 G1, vol. 1896, file 165-A, part 4, R.G. Riddell to H. Wrong, 23 August 1945, and Riddell to Wrong, 8 September 1945: "Within the last few days a memorandum for the Prime Minister on Ukrainian refugees ... has been returned with the Prime Minister's approval to the suggestion it contained. The memorandum, dated June 4th, concludes with this paragraph: 'Under the circumstances it is proposed that no further action is taken in connection with representations of the Ukrainian Canadian Committee. These representations have been acknowledged briefly and non-committally.' Mr King marked this 'OK' and I wonder, therefore, if we could not file the later communication from the Ukrainian Canadian Committee of August 13th without acknowledging it. It is nothing more than a repetition of the earlier messages." Hume Wrong, the associate under-secretary of state for external affairs, penned a note in the margin of the memo simply stating "I agree."

128 USA, George Simpson Papers, box 1, file "Ukrainian Files – 1930–57," Ukrainian Canadian Committee to Prime Minister W.L. Mackenzie King, 19 December 1945. "Is this the price that has to be paid for appeasing Russia? If it is expedient to appease Russia, surely we cannot sacrifice our elementary human rights, the fundamentals of our Western civilization, for such appeasement. To sacrifice these we would destroy the fundamentals of the principles of democracy for which our boys died in the battlefields against the barbaric warfare of Hitlerism ... We cannot exchange uncertain political advantages for the very fundamentals of our way of life by sacrificing these refugees to the pressure of power politics. We are not suggesting that you interfere in the internal affairs of the Soviet Union, but since these refugees are at present in the zones occupied by the Western Allies, we feel that the implementation of this principle [of asylum] would not interfere with the internal politics of Russia, our Ally, and consequently, we would humbly suggest that something urgent should be done."

129 NAC, MG26 J4, vol. 336, file 3650, N. Robertson to the prime minister, 12 December 1945. Hilliker notes that repatriation and resettlement was an area of concern "kept under close scrutiny" by Robertson as well as Wrong "because of its domestic political importance, since various ethnic groups were pressing members of Parliament and the government for favourable treatment of their communities in Europe." J. Hilliker, *Canada's Department of External Affairs: The Early Years,*

1909–1946, vol. 1 (Montreal and Kingston: McGill-Queen's University Press, 1990), 292.

130 USA, George Simpson Papers, box 1, file "Ukrainian Files – 1930–57," G. Simpson to A. Zaharychuk, Ukrainian Canadian Committee, 17 September 1945.

131 Canadian public opinion remained sceptical about the Soviet Union and Soviet postwar intentions. See, for example, NAC, RG2, series 18, vol. 12, file W-34-10, Wartime Information Board, "Memorandum to Members of the Cabinet," 30 April 1945, and "Memorandum to Members of the Cabinet," 23 July 1945. See also Canadian Institute of Public Opinion (CIPO), "Has the Russian Government Changed? Opinion in Canada Varies Widely," 23 June 1945. The poll concluded that 44 percent of the population believed that the Soviet government had not changed in its attitudes; 29 percent indicated that a change was evident. The remainder was undecided.

132 Department of External Affairs Records (DEA), file 8196-40c, "Canadian Delegation to the Preparatory Commission of the United Nations," 22 December 1945.

133 NAC, RG25 G1, vol. 1896, file 165-A, part 4, L. Malania to H. Wrong, 5 December 1945. Reproduced in Kordan and Luciuk, *A Delicate and Difficult Question*, 135–8.

134 J.L. Granatstein, *A Man of Influence: Norman A. Robertson and Canadian Statecraft, 1929–68* (Ottawa: Deneau, 1981), 171–5.

135 NAC, RG25 G1, vol. 1896, file 165-A, part 4, L. Malania to H. Wrong, 5 December 1945.

136 Leo Malania's connection with the Gouzenko affair and the impact of the affair on his career is briefly described in Smith, *Diplomacy of Fear*, 115–16.

137 As quoted in Granatstein, "Changing Alliances: Canada and the Soviet Union, 1939–45," 85.

138 See W.R. Young, "'A Highly Intelligent and Unselfish Approach': Public Information and the Canadian West, 1939–45," *Canadian Historical Review*, 62, no. 4 (1981): 496–520; W.R. Young, "Building Citizenship; English Canada and Propaganda during the Second War," *Journal of Canadian Studies*: 121–32; and Evans, *John Grierson and the National Film Board*.

139 NAC, RG25 G1, vol. 1896, file 165, part 3, G. de T. Glazebrook, "Policy toward Foreign Groups," 2 July 1942.

140 Evans, *John Grierson and the National Film Board*, 13–14.

141 Ibid., 200–7.

142 NAC, RG25 G1, vol. 1896, file 165, part 3, D. Wilgress to the prime minister and secretary of state for external affairs, 19 May 1943.

143 Ibid., file 165, part 4, N. Robertson to the prime minister, 4 July 1944.

CHAPTER SIX

1 Martin Wight, "Western Values in International Relations," in
 H. Butterfield and M. Wight, eds., *Diplomatic Investigations: Essays
 in the Theory of International Politics* (London: Allen and Unwin,
 1969), 105–7.

2 See Hedley Bull, "The Grotian Conception of International Society," in
 Diplomatic Investigations, 51–73.

3 See Carl J. Freidrich, *Foreign Policy in the Making: The Search for a
 New Balance of Power* (New York: Norton, 1938).

4 Its effectiveness was an entirely different matter; the topic is the focus
 of E.H. Carr's *International Relations between the Two World Wars,
 1919–39* (London: Macmillan, 1947).

5 On the compatibility of order and justice, Hedley Bull writes: "It is
 true that justice, in any of its forms, is realizable only in the context of
 order; it is only if there is a pattern of social activity in which elementary or primary goals of social life are in some degree provided for,
 that advanced or secondary goals can be secured. It is true *a foritori*,
 that international society, by providing a context of order of some
 kind, however rudimentary, may be regarded as paving the way for the
 equal enjoyment of rights of various kinds." *The Anarchical Society:
 A Study of Order in World Politics* (New York: Columbia University
 Press, 1977), 86–7.

6 On the perceived role of the balance of power, the jurist John West-
 lake would write in the nineteenth century, "The international society
 to which we belong is not one for the mutual insurance of established
 governments." Lassa Oppenheim, *The Collected Papers of John West-
 lake on Public International Law* (Cambridge: Cambridge University
 Press, 1914), 124.

7 Public Records Office (PRO), Foreign Office Records, FO 181/963,
 "Record of a Meeting between the Foreign Secretary and Marshall
 Stalin," 17 December 1942. Reproduced in L.Y. Luciuk and B. Kordan,
 *Anglo-American Perspectives on the Ukrainian Question, 1938–51: A
 Documentary Collection* (Kingston, ON: Limestone Press, 1987), 123–31.

8 National Archives of Canada (NAC), RG25 G1, vol. 1896, file 165,
 part 1, W. Kossar to Dr O.D. Skelton, under-secretary of state for
 external affairs, 8 June 1939.

9 See NAC, RG2, series 18, vol. 20, file W-23, Hugh Keenlyside, "Memorandum for the Under-Secretary – Canadian War Aims," 26 November
 1942.

10 NAC, RG25 G1, vol. 1896, file 165, part 3, D. Wilgress to the secretary of state for external affairs, the Rt Hon. W.L. Mackenzie King,
 19 May 1943.

11 NAC, RG2, series 18, vol. 20, file W-23, Hugh Keenlyside, "Memorandum for the Under-Secretary – Canadian War Aims," 26 November 1942.

12 NAC, RG25 G1, vol. 1896, file 165, part 3, G. de T. Glazebrook, "Policy toward Foreign Groups," 2 July 1942. Reproduced in Luciuk and Kordan, *Anglo-American Perspectives*, 110–3.

13 Ibid., file 165, part 4, N. Robertson to the prime minister, 4 July 1944. Reproduced in B. Kordan and L.Y. Luciuk, *A Delicate and Difficult Question: Documents in the History of Ukrainians in Canada, 1899– 1962* (Kingston, ON: Limestone Press, 1986), 113–15.

14 This was also evident in the American response to Ukrainian-American appeals at San Francisco. United States National Archives (USNA), RG226, entry 100, box 98, UK-351-360, D.C. Poole, Associate Public Liaison Officer to the American Delegation, 14 May 1945.

15 NAC, RG25 G1, vol. 1896, file 165, part 4, L. Malania to H. Wrong, 5 December 1945. Reproduced in Kordan and Luciuk, *A Delicate and Difficult Question*, 135–8.

16 Inter alia, NAC, Tracy Philipps Papers, MG30 E350, vol. 2, file "Committee on Co-operation – Correspondence, September 1943," T. Philipps, "The Position," 13 September 1943, together with "The Matter Comes to a Head," 14 September 1943, and "Off the Record Notes," 15 September 1943. See also ibid., vol. 1, file 33, T. Philipps to G. Simpson, 1 October 1943.

17 Arkhiv vneshnei politiki SSSR, MID (ASSSR, MID), Fond 06 – Sekretariat Molotova, opis 5, papka 24, delo 267, S. Kudriatsev, first secretary, USSR Mission to Canada, "Zapis besedy c pomoshchnikom Gosudarstvennogo Sekretaria po Inostrannym Delam Kanady Norman Robertsonom" [Record of conversation with the under-secretary of state for Canadian external affairs, Norman Robertson], 23 October 1943.

18 Insofar as both communities were concerned with the welfare of the Ukrainian nation, it was variously suggested that the differences were more perceived than real. Even Soviet embassy officials noted that the progressive Ukrainian Canadian organisations were "nationalist" in sentiment, having placed the interests of Ukraine above the political struggle: "Ukraine, although soviet, is a priority for them. They have an unhealthy attitude with everything that concerns Ukraine and the Ukrainian nation and know little of the Soviet Union, [while] Kyiv and Kharkiv, for them, are dearer than Moscow and Leningrad. Indeed, national interest and love for Ukraine is of greater concern to them than the Soviet Union, which is secondary. Patriotism, of course, is normal and under the circumstances it would be absurd and a crime to reproach anyone for their loyalty. But when patriotism interferes with

the ability to understand political duty, then this represents a certain narrow-mindedness and immaturity. Most of the progressive [Ukrainian] organisations, here in Montreal and across Canada, inasmuch as one can judge from the comments of comrades and press statements, suggest that to a certain extent they are all nationalists, or to a lesser degree suffer from nationalist immaturity." See ibid., papka 38, delo 492, A.M. Zubov, attaché, USSR mission to Canada, "Iz dnevnyka Attache Missii SSSR Zubova, A.M." [Daily entry of A. Zubov, attaché], 19 November 1943.

Index

Aid to Russia, 129, 148, 229n117. *See also* Canadian Aid to Russia Fund

Alberta Division of Ukrainian Canadians, 79

Allied Labour News, 121

Allied-Polish relations, 19, 182

Allied war objectives: contradiction in, 5, 55–6, 91, 93–4, 95, 181, 182, 183; Philipps' views on, 51–2; prospects for Ukrainian independence, 69; status quo ante and, 54–5, 91, 178

Anglo-Canadians, 43, 50, 98, 157

Anglo-Soviet treaty, 74–5, 91

Association of Canadian Clubs, 38, 201n102

Association of Canadian Ukrainians (Ukrainian Association to Aid the Fatherland): denunciation of nationalists in Fort William, 107; denunciation of UCC, 80; moderates co-operating with, 148; relief effort, 229n117, 243n102; rivalry with UNF, 78–9; Robertson replying to, 129

Atlantic Charter: Anglo-Soviet treaty in conflict with, 74; call to abandon, 83, 94, 145, 175, 180, 181; international reaction to, 91–2; meaning and interpretation of, 67–8, 91–3, 178–9, 181, 182; UCC and, 86, 209n41

Baltics, 75, 151, 154

Beatty, Sir E., 37

Berle, A., 116, 227n81

Bland, C.H., 31. *See also* Civil Service Commission

Bogomolets, A., 81

Britain: attitudes and position on Ukrainian independence, 17, 25–6, 60, 68, 90–1; impact of political change in Eastern Europe, 152, 153, 154, 238–9n68; intelligence and diplomatic reports on Ukrainian nationalist activity, 33–4, 51, 77, 197–8n69, 217n122; relations with Poland, 19, 54, 91; relations with Soviet Union, 19, 73–4, 90, 153; status quo ante and prewar balance of power, 54–5, 91, 152, 154, 178, 219n135, 237n56

British Security Co-ordination (BSC): Canadian co-operation with, 69, 79, 144, 149–50; on Philipps, 150; report on assimilation of Ukrainians in North America, 162

Buchko, Bishop I., 35–7

Buduchnist natsii (Nation's Future), 165

Bureau of Public Information (Public Information Board): creation of foreign-languages section in, 64; superseded by WIB, 118, 138